TALES OF TRAVEL

Marquess Curzon of Kedleston

Foreword by Lady Alexandra Metcalfe

Introduction by Peter King

CENTURY
LONDON MELBOURNE AUCKLAND JOHANNESBURG

First published in 1923 by Hodder and Stoughton

This edition first published in 1988 by Century,
an imprint of Century Hutchinson Ltd,
Brookmount House, 62–65 Chandos Place, London WC2N 4NW

Century Hutchinson Australia Pty Ltd,
PO Box 496, 16–22 Church Street, Hawthorn, Melbourne,
Victoria 3122, Australia

Century Hutchinson Group New Zealand Limited,
PO Box 40–086, Glenfield, Auckland 10, New Zealand

Century Hutchinson South Africa (Pty) Ltd,
PO Box 337, Bergvlei, 2012 South Africa

British Library Cataloguing in Publication Data

Curzon, George Nathaniel Curzon
Tales of travel.
1. World. Description & travel, 1887–1920
I. Title
910.4

ISBN 0-7126-2245-4

Printed and bound in Great Britain by
Richard Clay (The Chaucer Press) Ltd, Bungay, Suffolk.

FOREWORD

It was on my return from India that I heard from the publishers about their plans to reprint this book of my father's travel series. I had been invited to Calcutta to attend the flood lighting of the Victoria Memorial which my father caused to be built eighty-five years ago to the memory of the Queen. Throughout India his name is remembered and revered for his preservation of ancient buildings. In this country he is remembered for the same reason and for his talents as a travel writer. This is the fourth book to be republished since 1984. He had a passion for travel under the most primitive, difficult and dangerous circumstances. This is proved by the frequently quoted remark, 'It gave me more pleasure to be awarded the Gold Medal of the Royal Geographical Society for exploration and research than it did to become a minister of the Crown'. I am pleased to write these few words of welcome to a new edition of one of his favourite books.

Alexandra Metcalfe

CONTENTS

INTRODUCTION TO THIS EDITION

INTRODUCTION TO THIS EDITION

We must picture two very different George Curzons as we read this book. There is the young George Nathanial who wrote most of the material in his twenties, between leaving Oxford and going out to India as Viceroy at the age of thirty-nine. The other, who prepared the youthful writings for publication in 1922–3, is now the Foreign Secretary, a post he has held since 1919, and which he soon expects to relinquish in order to take up the Premiership.

The mature politician, as he wrote the introduction to this collection of travel writings, reflects upon his youth when he found 'the chief zest of life in travel... travel with a purpose'. These purposes were first, to see the ancient things of the earth and, second, 'to form an opinion on the Eastern responsibilities and destinies of Great Britain'. There was a third purpose which the patrician Curzon did not deem fit to mention in connection with his own eminence, which was money. The young Curzon had no extensive means of his own and an allowance from his father of only £1000 a year, so that as soon as he left Oxford he turned to writing as one means of supporting himself. This continued even after he began his parliamentary career. He was elected the Conservative member for Southport in 1886 but when he went to Persia in the parliamentary recess of 1889-90 he was commissioned by *The Times* to send back articles on the political situation at £12 10s a time.

Much of the material in this book was therefore written and drafted in the course of the young Curzon's two journeys round the world and his visits to Europe and Africa over the period from 1877 to 1895. He often travelled alone and always recorded his observations in his little cardboard-covered notebooks (they can still be read in the India Office Library in London) supplemented by photographs, taken with his 'precious Kodak' which was factory-loaded before his departure with film for a hundred circular exposures. On return to London, he would use the notebooks and articles as source material for his major books—as when he returned from Persia to bury himself in a socially obscure South London suburb in order to write the classic work on the country which was published two years later.

The young Curzon's reasons for embarking on these early travels— apart from money—were the desire to achieve fame and the wish to prepare himself for a career in politics, specializing in foreign affairs. He had already achieved fame of a kind as one of the leading members of contemporary upper-class English society in the 1870s and 1880s. First had come a glittering sojourn at Eton, where he excelled in writing Latin verse, edited the *Etonian* and kept champagne and claret in his desk because 'I enjoyed the supreme cheek as an Eton boy of giving wine parties in my room'. Curzon then proceeded to Balliol where his reputation was, if possible, even more dazzling. But before he arrived at Oxford he had the misfortune to be diagnosed as suffering from an incurable curvature of the spine which meant that he was forced to wear a steel-braced corset for the remainder of his life and endure considerable pain when standing, riding or even sitting and lying. In part it was his enforced upright posture which caused his enemies— and sometimes his friends—to find him conceited, unbending and, as the famous rhyme of an Oxford contemporary put it, superior:

> My name is George Nathanial Curzon
> I am a most superior person.
> My cheek is pink, my hair is sleek
> I dine at Blenheim once a week.

Curzon did not mind being considered superior; indeed he agreed that he was, although he complained about 'that wretched doggerel'. He was tall, handsome, well-spoken, attractive to women and amusing company with his men friends.

At the same time he was accused of 'not having enough heart' which showed itself in his obvious pleasure in a wounding if witty retort. No doubt he was something of a cold fish. However, he was easily wounded himself and was totally unprepared when he was awarded a second-class degree when he and everyone else had anticipated a first. He felt sure there must have been some mistake, and when he was finally convinced it was true he whined, 'I am stamped with the brand of respectable mediocrity', something he could not abide. He would, he thought, have to 'retire somewhere and hide my face from the world'. He had been to France while still at Eton and now he took to foreign travel to try to forget the disgrace of Oxford Greats. Between December 1882 and June 1883 he visited Rome, Naples, Athens, Corfu, Cairo and the Nile, Palestine, Constantinople, Budapest, Vienna, Dresden, Prague and Berlin. He was accompanied for most of these journeys by a series of Etonian or Oxford friends and he found it impossible to erase Oxford from his memory. He must find a way of showing the examiners that they had been wrong. He returned to the university determined to win some of the famous academic prizes open to the graduate. Always a workaholic, Curzon succeeded in collecting a bag of prizes and also in gaining one of the coveted All Souls fellowships. While still a fellow, he continued to make regular visits abroad, financing them by his £200 a year stipend from All Souls and his journalistic writings which brought £200 to £300 a year. By 1886, the year he entered Parliament, he was fairly well acquainted with most of the European countries and he had saved up a few hundred pounds.

Now the opportunity was available to travel on a more extensive basis. In those days, Parliament normally rose for the summer in August and did not meet again until January or February of the following year. Curzon used the recess to travel round the world. A number of the pieces in *Tales of Travel* had their origins on this journey—for example the long one about the wrestlers of Japan. It was also during the course of this journey that Curzon arrived in India for the first time, and probably then that he made the conscious decision to write a series of books on the entire continent of Asia. The first three were published; *Russia in Central Asia* in 1889, *Persia and the Persian*

Question in 1892 and *Problems of the Far East* in 1894. The others, on the Indian Frontier, Indo-China and Afghanistan, were abandoned as his career in politics progressed. Excerpts from the material Curzon collected for the last two volumes were revived and gathered into the present book in 1923, the most famous being Curzon's delightful description of the Amir of Afghanistan.

This, then, is the broad geneology of the *Tales*. Why Curzon chose these particular essays for inclusion is explained in his introduction in which he tells us, rather to our relief, that they are intended to be 'descriptive rather than didactic'. His earlier books had been heavily laced with doses of didacticism because he never lost sight when writing them of the important rôle which the British nation had played, was playing and must in future play in the Far East. Now, turning away from the heavy stuff, he says he has found it 'a diversion, in the turmoil of public life, to put these notes into final shape'.

The essays are divided into several categories. Some are more or less pure description of places visited. Others, like the Amir, are biographical studies interspersed with personal anecdote. Throughout his life, Curzon was known for his talent as an anecdotalist, and *Tales* has one whole section devoted to 'Humours of Travel'. Each tale is in effect an anecdote which Curzon must have told and retold over the dinner table at Carlton House Terrace. 'The Top Hat at Teheran' is typical of them, poking slight fun at himself, yet not without a little name-dropping in the process. Another category of essay which, if not didactic, is at least serious, is that which reveals Curzon as explorer. The best examples of this are 'The Voice of Memmon' and 'The Singing Sands', two related studies into the mysteries of the sounds said to emanate from ancient objects or places. These show Curzon as a gifted investigator, eager to separate fact from fiction.

At the same time, we are aware of a rather too-human side to the man who clearly got considerable enjoyment from knocking scholars down a peg. This trait is also apparent in the little section on Sir Henry Lawrence and Napoleon's Billiard Table, both illustrative of Curzon as sleuth. Perhaps there is something a little ridiculous in a man who makes so much fuss over the whereabouts of Napoleon's billiard table. Finally there is a category of story which illustrates Curzon's interest in the violent and the macabre. 'The Dancing Girl of Keneh' and 'The Drums of Kairwan' show that Curzon loved a little blood and did not mind dwelling on 'the fate that has befallen so many of the rulers and statesmen with whom I was brought into contact'.

The gold thread which runs through these different coloured themes is the splendour of Curzon's style. He had a great turn of phrase and wrote with a classic elegance that is hard to match today. Take this (not from the *Tales*):

> Outside the Durbar Hall are ranged the state elephants, all mangificently caparisoned and with their heads and trunks fantastically painted in every hue of vermillion and saffron and gamboge.

Not only had Curzon a steely eye for detail, a poetic gift for atmosphere and an acute sense of the absurd, but the gods had given him the ability to write with grace on subjects as different as 'The Pig and

Whistle at Bunji' and 'By the Waters of Babylon'.

Curzon, the Foreign Minister at 64, was clearly enjoying himself as he turned over these early notebooks and articles. 'I am again the youthful rover', he exalts. The sad thing is that he wrote this in almost the last period of comparative mental ease he was able to enjoy. His peak of happiness had been reached back in 1899 when, appointed the youngest ever Viceroy, he was 'sent to heaven' accompanied by the young wife he adored and who had the added advantage of being rich enough to support his needs. By 1905 he had returned to England in disgrace, after a fruitless row with his old friend Balfour over the intrigues of the incorrigible Kitchener. The lonely Curzon remained in the political wilderness for a decade thereafter, until in 1916 he began the long journey back to power. In 1923, shortly after *Travels* was published, Bonar Law retired as Prime Minister and Curzon prepared himself to take over the supreme position. His old friend/enemy Balfour was called to Buckingham Palace to give advice. When their mutual friends from the 'Souls' asked Balfour 'And will dear George be chosen?', Balfour was able to tell them authoritatively that 'No dear George will not!' Baldwin got the job.

Curzon continued as Baldwin's Foreign Minister for a time, but within two years he was dead, some said of a broken heart. He left behind him in India a legacy which had more to do with his love of the continent's architectural history and monuments than with any more tangible record of political or economic reform. His contribution to British foreign policy from 1916 to 1924 was made under the shadow of Lloyd George and is not writ large in the history books. His influence on the formation of the Royal Air Force and other institutions of the time have been forgotten too. It is doubtful if his skill as a travel writer would, in his own estimate, have been an adequate testament for a life so dedicated to fame. There is, however, a small piece of evidence to the contrary. During the course of a boring Cabinet meeting at 10 Downing Street he once composed his own epitaph which he took home and put amongst his papers. His pencilled scrawl reads:

> In diverse offices and in many lands
> as explorer, writer, administrator
> and ruler of men
> he sought to serve his country,
> and add honour to an ancient name.

It will be noted that 'explorer' and 'writer' are placed first, and perhaps that is where in his heart of hearts the older Curzon rated the work of 'the youthful rover'.

Peter King
1988

INTRODUCTION

INTRODUCTION

Forsan et haec olim meminisse iuvabit.
VIRGIL, *Aeneid* i. 203.

I WONDER if it may be permitted to a politician to remember the days when he was only secondarily a politician, and when he found the chief zest of life in travel, not indeed in aimless and desultory travel, but in travel with that most generally unpopular of all attributes, a purpose. In my case the purpose was twofold : to see the beautiful and romantic and, above all, the ancient things of the earth—a taste which I probably share with most travellers, but which took me preferably to distant Oriental lands ; and, secondly, to see how far the study of those places and peoples would help me to form an opinion on the Eastern responsibilities and destinies of Great Britain. This was a subject in which I took from boyhood an absorbing interest, and which led me to devote many months in each year, and, after I had entered Parliament, the bulk of my Parliamentary holidays, to wanderings in all parts of Asia from the Mediterranean to the China Seas. The results of these studies were embodied long ago in books of a more or less serious character, and I have no intention to repeat any part of that story here.

But in the course of these journeys I visited many other countries and places, twice going round the world, and exploring unfrequented spots, not in Asia only, but in Europe, Africa, and America. In certain of these cases I studied rather deeply some subjects of more than ephemeral interest, I came across some remarkable persons, and I made notes of many curious scenes. I have found it a diversion, in the turmoil of public life, to put these notes into final shape, and have even thought that they might prove of interest to a larger audience.

After I had spent some years in travelling and in writing about my travels, it gave me greater pleasure to be awarded the Gold Medal of the Royal Geographical Society for exploration and research than it did to become a Minister of the Crown; and every moment that I could snatch from politics—before they finally captured and tied me down—I devoted to the pursuit of my old love.

Even now, if in rare moments I seek literary distraction, it is in the perusal of works of travel and exploration that I am certain to find it; and when foreign affairs are specially vexatious or perplexing, recreation and repose come stealing in upon me from the memories of the past. I am once again in the wilds of Asia, or on the mountain-tops, or amid the majestic monuments of bygone ages. At one moment the wonders of nature fill the picture, at another, the scarcely less remarkable masterpieces of man. The shut pages of the past unroll, and the characters written upon them a quarter of a century and more ago start again to life.

On these occasions I remember, almost with a start, that it is the middle-aged and sedentary politician who in the early nineties shot *Ovis Poli* on the Pamirs, who nearly foundered in a typhoon off the coast of Annam, and was reported as murdered in Afghanistan. I am again the youthful rover who was stoned by furious Spaniards on the quays of Valencia; who climbed to the crater of Etna in deep snow by night to witness the glory of the sunrise over Sicily and the Straits; who saw the cone of Adam's Peak throw its shadow, also at sunrise, over the folded mist wreaths that smoked above the steaming valleys of Ceylon; who stayed with Amir Abdur Rahman Khan at Kabul, and with the afterwards murdered Mehtar of Chitral; who arrested the Abbot of a Korean monastery for stealing his watch and purse, and was himself arrested as a spy in Khorasan and in Wakhan; who was wrecked off the coast of Dalmatia, and explored the source of the Oxus; who wrote travel books that, *mirabile dictu*, still find readers and have appreciated in value; and who even composed an Oxford Prize Essay in the cabin of a steamer on the Nile.

Sometimes, as I recall those days, I find myself reviving memories or telling tales that seem to belong to a past that is quite dead, not merely by reason of the change in my own environment, but also because of the revolution in the conditions of travel, or in the state of the peoples and lands which I visited. For instance, in some countries where I rode thousands of weary miles on horseback, the traveller now proceeds rapidly and comfortably by carriage or motor, or even by train. In other countries—as, for instance, Korea, which at the time of my visit in 1892 was still independent and had a Court and a King—political changes have brought about a transformation not less startling. And so it comes into my mind that there may be something in the experiences of those days that may be worthy of record before I have forgotten them, and which other people will perhaps not have the chance of repeating in exactly the same way.

The following pages contain these memories. They include nothing that has been published in any of my other books, and they have nothing to do with politics. They relate to many parts of the world, but principally to the East, which has always been to me the source of inspiration and ideas. Most of the papers are of no great length, and only a few are learned. Whether I ought to advertise or to apologise for the latter must be left to the judgment of my readers. All relate to places or incidents lying somewhat outside the ordinary run of travel. Had I written a volume of political memoirs, could I have hoped to escape controversy ? As it is, nothing that I have set down will, I trust, excite dispute. The genuine traveller quarrels with nobody—except his predecessors or rivals, a temptation which I have been careful to avoid. All countries are his washpot. All mankind is his friend.

Perhaps the most striking testimony that I could offer to the change that has passed over the scenes of my earlier journeys—and incidentally also to the chronically unstable equilibrium of the East—would be a reference to the dramatic fate that has befallen so many of the rulers and statesmen with whom I was brought in contact, and some of whom appear in these pages, in the days to which I refer. Shah Nasr-ed-Din of Persia, my audience with whom at Teheran in 1889 is mentioned later on, perished in 1896 by the weapon of an assassin. The ruler of Chitral with whom I stayed in 1894 was shot and killed by the half-brother who had sat at table with him and me only two months before. The Emperor of Annam, who presented me with a golden decoration at Hué in 1892, was deposed in 1907 and subsequently banished. The poor little King of Korea, who conversed with me in low whispers at Seoul in 1892, first saw his Queen murdered in the Palace and was afterwards himself forced to abdicate. His son, who struck me as the stupidest young man I ever met, shared the same fate. Deposition was the fate of the trembling figure of Norodom, the King of Cambodia, whom I visited at Pnompenh. The Amir of Bokhara, whom I saw in his capital in 1888, was afterwards expelled from his country and throne. Abbas Hilmi, whom Lord Cromer took me to visit at Cairo, soon after he had ascended the Khedivial throne, is also a fugitive and an exile. The life of that eminent Japanese statesman, the Marquis Ito, who was so friendly to me when I was in Japan, was cut short by the knife of an assassin. Almost alone among the Eastern potentates whose guest I was, the Amir Abdur Rahman Khan, who told me that he lived in daily fear of his life, but that his people had not the courage to kill him, died in his bed. But of his two sons with whom I used to dine at Kabul, the elder, Habibulla, was murdered in his tent, and the younger, Nasrulla, languishes in prison. His Commander-in-Chief, known as the Sipah Salar, a gigantic figure, 6 feet 3 inches in height, and of corresponding bulk, who rode at my side from Dacca to Jellalabad on my way to Kabul in 1904, died suddenly a few years later in circumstances which left little doubt that his end was not natural.

Even in Europe my diaries refer to more than one similar tragedy. As far back as 1880 I recall a visit to the picturesque castle of Herrenhausen in Bavaria, where, in a room adorned exclusively with furniture and decorations in the shape of swans, I heard the steady tramp overhead, as he passed to and fro, of the mad King of Bavaria, who ended by drowning himself in a lake. I recall very clearly, and others have related, the incidents of a dinner with King

George of Greece, who came to his death at the hand of an assassin in the streets of Salonika.

These incidents illustrate no more uncommon phenomenon than that the lives of monarchs and statesmen are subject to exceptional and fatal risks, particularly in the East. But as I recall the features and tones of those ill-fated victims, so famous or so prominent in their day, a chasm appears to open between me and the time when I saw them in the plenitude of their strength and power—and I seem to be almost living in a world of different circumstances and different men.

I have said that this volume, which, if it be found acceptable, will be followed by a successor, is intended to be descriptive rather than didactic in object, and that I hope not so much to instruct as to entertain. But a few of my subjects may be thought to make a more sober claim, or to demand a more definite apology. The portrait of the Afghan Amir, with whom I was the only Englishman to stay at Kabul in a private and unofficial capacity, is the likeness of one of the most remarkable men of his time—a man who, had he lived in an earlier age and not been crushed, as he told me, like an earthenware pot between the rival forces of England and Russia, might have founded an Empire, and swept in a tornado of blood over Asia and even beyond it. The paper entitled "The Voice of Memnon," in the investigations with regard to which I was assisted by my old Oxford tutor, J. L. Strachan

Davidson, afterwards Master of Balliol, may, I hope, be regarded as a positive contribution to historical and archaeological research. The "Singing Sands" is an essay on a subject which has always greatly interested me—namely, the mysterious moaning and muttering of the sands in desert places, as a rule far removed from ordinary ken—and which has never before been treated with the fullness which it deserves. When I began this essay I intended it merely to be a synopsis of the cases of musical or sounding sands of which I had previously heard descriptions or attempted the investigation. But, as I proceeded, the subject expanded, until I found myself producing a treatise which may possibly fill a modest place in the scientific literature of travel, while the story may still appeal to the dilettante reader by reason of its mystery and romance.

There are many other aspects of travel, apart from its incidents or experiences, which I should like to examine, but which must be deferred to a later volume. Among these is a study of the Philosophy of Travel—its character, history, purpose, methods, justification, and results; and a chapter or more on the Literature of Travel—a subject that, to the best of my knowledge, has never received attention save perhaps in the casual pages of a magazine.

Here, however, I conclude with a reflection that will certainly not offend by its seriousness. The joy of travel, while it is being pursued, lies in a good many things: in the observation of new peoples and scenes, in the making of discoveries, in the zest of sport or adventure, in the pleasures of companionship or the excitement of new acquaintance, even in the collection of often valueless objects, and the achievement of purely illusory bargains. But I think that even more does it consist in the half-intangible but still positive memories that it leaves. One can make friends with places as well as people; and an hour's, even a minute's, experience in one spot may be more precious than a sojourn of months in another. These are the intimacies that survive, and constitute a perpetual endowment. With them we can always solace the hours, whether of idleness or gloom.

Whereas the experiences of life at home, even when they are not commonplace, are apt to fade quickly, and sometimes to be completely forgotten, the incidents of travel, a quarter or even half of a century ago, stand out indelibly as though graven in steel. Each of us has his own museum of such recollections. Among mine not the least prized are these: the music of many nightingales floating across the water from the coasts of Athos; the incredible glory of Kangchenjunga as he pierces the veils of the morning at Darjiling; the crossing of a Himalayan rope-bridge, sagging in the middle, and swaying dizzily from side to side, when only a strand of twisted twigs is stretched between your feet and the ravening torrent below; the first sight of the towered walls, *minae murorum ingentes*, of Peking; the head and shoulders of an Indian tiger emerging without a suspicion of sound from the thick jungle immediately in front of the posted sportsmen; the stupendous and terraced grandeur of Angkor Wat; the snowy spire of Teneriffe glimmering at sunrise across a hundred miles of ocean; the aethereal and ineffable beauty of the Taj.

I am not going to trouble my readers by saying anything about these particular mind-pictures in this book. I merely record them in passing, as a part of my own spiritual possession, just as others will have and will cherish theirs. The things that I have preferred to set down here are experiences or memories rather less personal and fugitive, which I may be justified in inviting others, even though on paper and in print only, to share, and which, here and there, may give them a few moments of entertainment or reflection.

THE DRUMS OF KAIRWAN

THE DRUMS OF KAIRWAN

And they cried aloud, and cut themselves after their manner with knives and lancets, till the blood gushed out upon them.

1 Kings xviii. 28.

In the spring of 1885 I was in Tunis. At no time in recent history a very interesting place, it had since the French usurpation of 1881 lost what little characteristic individuality it then possessed. The Bey was a harmless puppet. His palace, which visitors flocked to see, was very much like gilt gingerbread with a good deal of the gilding rubbed off. The bazaars were inferior to those of Constantinople, Damascus, and Cairo; and the town, once so famous for its unblemished Orientalism, had blossomed into the tawdry splendour of boulevards, cafés, and four-storied hotels. I knew, however, from the map, that Kairwan was situated only about one hundred miles to the south; and Kairwan was a place that had long exercised over my mind a mystic fascination. There was something very dramatic and inspiring in the story of this secluded city, the capital of a great conqueror twelve centuries ago, the metropolis of a mighty empire, the shrine of an imposing religion, and the refuge of both religion and empire when Europe had driven them forth. Even in its long decline Kairwan had been the rallying-point and haunt of pilgrimage to the living, and the last resting-place to the dead, for the thousand tribes that profess the faith of the Prophet from the Pillars of Hercules to the Nile. For twelve hundred years inviolate—its sanctuaries undefiled by foot of Christian or of Jew—at length the holy city had yielded up its secrets to the martial ambitions of a newly fledged European republic; and the great Mosque of Okbar, and the tomb-chamber of Sidi Sahab, the companion of the Prophet, had been profaned by the sacrilegious feet of the Zouaves of France. And yet, even in her desolation, ravished and forlorn, she still retained the halo of sanctity with which centuries had adorned her brow. Though the enemy was within her gates, she was his superior by reason of a majesty which none could gainsay. Kairwan still appealed to the imagination with resistless persuasiveness of accent, and to Kairwan I determined that I must go.

Twelve hours in a French steamboat brought me at dawn on a brilliant morning to the little port of Susa, which lay in its glittering garb of whitewash—houses, walls, and roofs all drenched and crusted with the same unmitigated and blinding hue—looking like some great sea-mew preening its snowy plumage on the shore. With the assistance of a courteous Maltese gentleman, who was trading in the place, I engaged a carriage and four (saddle-horses were unknown) for the journey to Kairwan. It was not, I may remark, an equipage which would have provoked envy, though it would undeniably have excited wonder, in Hyde Park. However, it did very well for the purpose ; the animals covered the thirty-six miles in the respectable time of six hours ; and the somewhat barbaric and inelegant structure of the vehicle was, I found, only too successfully adapted to resist the excruciating inequalities of the road.

I was informed at Susa that the French, who were in military occupation both of Susa and Kairwan, had constructed a little railroad of narrow gauge between the two places, on which ran cars pulled by horses. At another time it might have been possible to obtain permission to travel by this easy route ; but I found all Susa astir with the annual visit of the French Commander-in-Chief in Africa, a certain General Boulanger, who was going up to Kairwan on the same afternoon. I judged it better, therefore, not to intrude, but to content myself with the more humble native resources which I have described.

The road on leaving Susa climbed to the summit of the hill, which is crowned by the *kasbah* or citadel, and then struck westwards over the almost level expanse. I have called it a "road," but it is only by an abuse of terms that it could be so designated, for it was merely a broad track which straggled at random across the desert, plunging over dried-up ditches and watercourses, beaten hard by the hoofs of camels and horses, and worn into agonizing ruts by the wheels of waggons. It traversed first a belt of olive orchards—many of the trunks as wizened and gnarled as the veterans of Gethsemane or the Academe—next a district growing barley and esparto grass, past the great marsh of Sidi El Hani and the tomb of the saint whose name it bears, and finally lost itself in the arid and herbless desert which is the threshold of the mighty Sahara.

For miles before reaching my destination I had seen outlined against the purple of the remote hills a white streak, from the end of which sprang up a lofty tower. In the intense and palpitating heat this line appeared to quiver above the ground, and from time to time lost all semblance of reality. But as we drew nearer it gained form and distinctness, and was soon discernible as the whitewashed and battlemented wall of a purely Oriental city. Above its crenellated summit gleamed a hundred minarets and cupolas and domes. The tall tower was the minaret of the Mosque of Okbar. I had reached the ὀμφαλὸς γῆς of the devout Mussulman of Africa.

As I approached the city walls I could see that something unusual was occurring. The mounds outside, which mark the ruins of vanished suburbs, were crowded with picturesque groups of natives, while in the plain below were gathered several hundred turbaned cavaliers in gorgeous accoutrements and streaming robes of white, some of them motionless and in serried formation, others dashing furiously to and fro, brandishing their weapons, and with the sharp points of their cruel shovel-stirrups making the beasts they bestrode execute wild curvets. These were the sheikhs and warriors of the various Bedawin tribes, who were now in nominal subjection to the French, and had been summoned from far and near to do honour to the General. On the walls of the town, daubed in huge characters upon the staring plaster, I read the words —last affront to the defenceless old fortress— BOULEVARD BOULANGER. The general was evidently the hero of the hour.

A little later he himself arrived — a smart figure, with close-cropped hair and pointed brown moustache and beard. Attended by a glittering staff, he mounted a fine horse at a short distance from the terminus of the railway, and presently reviewed the native cavalry, whom he addressed in a highly laudatory speech, the pith of which was that they were the finest soldiers in the world, next to the French — a remark which, when transmitted to their understanding through an interpreter, was received with the liveliest marks of satisfaction. A display of equestrian skill on the part of the horsemen followed, and for long the space outside the walls was a bewildering scene of dust and galloping horses and shouting men. When night fell there succeeded the unbroken calm that reigns in an Oriental city after sunset.

During the few days of my stay in Kairwan I saw the principal mosques and objects of interest. In order to effect this purpose it was necessary to be provided with a special permit from the French Commander. Prior to 1881 no Christian had ever penetrated into the interior of a Kairwanese mosque. The rare travellers who reached the town were either hastily conducted through the streets and bidden to depart—like Sir Grenville Temple in 1830, and Lord Waterford, who ten years later narrowly escaped being stoned—or were only tolerated within the walls so long as they made no attempt to intrude upon the sacred precincts. This was the case with Sir W. Gregory in 1858, M. Victor Guérin in 1861, Mr. Rae in 1876, and Lord and Lady Bective in 1881. When, however, the city capitulated without resistance to the French in October 1881, and was occupied by their troops, many persons profited by the early licence of victory to visit the hitherto inviolate shrines. Since then the permission had been wisely curtailed by the French, with whose capacity for assimilation with the natives I was throughout my visit most agreeably impressed; and my hosts, certain Maltese who supplied the French army with forage and exported *halfa* to England, informed me that leave was now by no means easy to obtain.

As they were very much afraid of losing their own contract, and dared not approach the

General on my behalf, representing him as an austere man, given to count his talents, I called myself, and was civilly presented with the requisite order. Armed with this talismanic document, I visited the great Mosque of Okbar, and passed through the carven doors into the vast and darkened *liwan*, or prayer-chamber, with its two hundred interior columns and its forest of diverging aisles—a faint adumbration of the greater glories of Cordova—and stood in the *mihrab*, or prayer-niche, the holy of holies, where the *kibleh* points the worshipper's eye and guides his thoughts to the still more sacred East. I climbed the triple tower whence every morning and evening is waved the blood-red flag that calls the faithful to prayer, and from which is seen stretched out below the panorama of the seven-sided city with its countless cupolas and towers, its intricate alleys and terraced walls, to where beyond the gates extend the scattered suburbs and now decaying cemeteries of the dead. I saw the hallowed well of *Kefayat*, or plenty, the waters of which communicate by subterranean channels with those of Zem-Zem at Mecca, as is conclusively proved by the fact that the drinking-cup of a pious pilgrim dropped into the Meccan font reappeared floating on the surface at Kairwan.

I saw too the mosque of the most recent *marabout*, or saint—Sidi Emir Abadah, who flourished only thirty years before, and who had such an influence over the then reigning Bey that he persuaded him to defray the cost of the seven-domed mosque that was to contain his remains after death, and was held in such veneration by the natives that four huge modern anchors, which repose in a courtyard outside, and which he transported with infinite difficulty across the desert from the sea-coast near Tunis, were still believed by them, in deference to the holy man's explanation, to be those which moored the Ark of Noah, after its long wanderings, to the soil of Ararat.

Lastly, I came to the particularly sacred shrine of Sidi Sahab, or Sidi El' Owaib, My Lord the Companion, a disciple of Mohammed himself, who, dying at Kairwan in the seventh century, and leaving instructions that he should be interred with three hairs from his master's beard, which he always carried in a pouch upon his breast, had been appropriately transformed by local tradition into the barber of the Prophet. This mosque, which is, if possible, of even greater sanctity than that of Okbar, I had some difficulty in entering. The custodian, an acid and sulky Moslem, was strenuous in protest and fertile in excuse. The terms of my order stated that I was to be admitted to all or any of the mosques of Kairwan. This, he declared, was not a mosque but a *zaouia* or college; such an institution being, indeed, attached to the premises. When I overruled this objection, he was swift as lightning with another. The words of the order referred, he said, to mosques *in* Kairwan; this was outside the walls. I was obliged to put it very plainly to the cunning zealot whether he would prefer to admit me, with the prospect of a *bakshish*, or compel me to return at once and report his disobedience to the Commander. Whether it was the bribe or the menace that prevailed I do not know; anyhow, I gained my object, and was conducted through courts embellished with marble pillars and sparkling Saracenic tiles to the recess where stands the sacred sepulchre, fenced round with a grating of bronze, and covered with a pall of black velvet, embroidered with Arabic inscriptions in silver, while above depend thirteen silken banners, offerings of devotion from successive Beys.

And now I come to that which was the main incident of my stay in Kairwan. One of the peculiar features of the place is the number of *zaouias*, or colleges of religious orders, which there exist. Of these fraternities, which have each a separate discipline and ritual, and number many thousand members, with corresponding branches in all parts of the Mussulman world, the most famous are those of the Zadria, Tijania, and Aissaouia; and of these three by far the most remarkable is the last. This sect of dervishes was founded by one Mahomet Ibn Aissa, a celebrated *marabout* of Mequinez, in Morocco; and his disciples, who are scattered through all the principal coast-towns of North Africa, but are especially congregated at Mequinez and Kairwan, perpetuate his teaching, and open to themselves the gates of heaven, by self-mutilation when in a state of religious ecstasy or trance. Visitors at Bona, Constantine, and Algiers have sometimes, on payment of a sufficient *bakshish*, witnessed an emasculated version of these rites, and have variously ascribed them to mercenary display or to skilful imposture. The latter has been, perhaps, the more popular interpretation, Englishmen being very reluctant to believe that any one will endure physical torture for the sake of religion, or still more, that such tortures as those described could be inflicted, not only without injury to the patients themselves, but, as alleged, to their intense delight. Aware of the number and importance of this sect at Kairwan, I was very anxious to witness one of their *zikrs*, or services, and to form my own opinion. Unluckily, it appeared that I had just missed their weekly ceremonial, which had been held on the very evening before I arrived. A happy thought of one of my Maltese friends enabled me to rectify this mischance, and to satisfy my curiosity.

In the morning as we were walking through the bazaars one of these gentlemen, who was of a humorous turn and who was interested in the success of my visit, introduced me to the native Governor of the city, a fine and portly Arab, as the son of General Boulanger. Though the General was a young-looking man, such a connection was in respect of years just within the bounds of possibility. Moreover, our arrivals in the town had coincided, and I had been seen in his company. Good or bad, the idea was greedily swallowed by the Governor; burning to testify his loyalty, he overwhelmed me with profuse courtesies, followed, as the day wore on, by frequent cups of coffee and many cigarettes.

The genial credulity of the Arab supplied the very machinery that was wanted to arrange a performance of the Aissaouia. What could be more natural than that the son of the French General should wish to see the most distinctive spectacle of Kairwan? Such a petition might even be interpreted as a semi-official compliment to the Moslem faith. My Maltese friends were delighted at the notion, and could not rest till they had paid a special visit to the sheikh or *mokaddem* of the sect, with the intimation that no less a personage than *Boulanger fils* was desirous of witnessing one of their famous celebrations. The sheikh was nothing loth, and accordingly it was arranged that on the same night at 9 P.M. I should be conducted to the sanctuary of Aissa.

When the appointed hour arrived, I presented myself at the mosque, which is situated outside the city walls, not far from the Bab-el-Djuluddin, or Tanners' Gate. Passing through an open courtyard into the main building, I was received with a dignified salaam by the sheikh, who forthwith led me to a platform or divan at the upper end of the central space. This was surmounted by a ribbed and whitewashed dome, and was separated from two side aisles by rows of marble columns with battered capitals, dating from the Empire of Rome. Between the arches of the roof small and feeble lamps—mere lighted wicks floating on dingy oil in cups of coloured glass—ostrich eggs, and gilt balls were suspended from wooden beams. From the cupola in the centre hung a dilapidated chandelier in which flickered a few miserable candles. In one of the side aisles a plastered tomb was visible behind an iron lattice. The *mise en scène* was unprepossessing and squalid.

My attention was next turned to the *dramatis personae.* Upon the floor in the centre beneath the dome sat the musicians, ten or a dozen in number, cross-legged, the chief presiding upon a stool at the head of the circle. I observed no instrument save the *darabookah,* or earthen drum, and a number of tambours, the skins of which, stretched tightly across the frames, gave forth, when struck sharply by the fingers, a hollow and resonant note. The rest of the orchestra was occupied by the chorus. So far no actors were visible. The remainder of the floor, both under the dome and in the aisles, was thickly covered with seated and motionless figures, presenting in the fitful light a weird and fantastic picture. In all there must have been over a hundred persons, all males, in the mosque.

Presently the sheikh gave the signal for commencement, and in a moment burst forth the melancholy chant of the Arab voices and the ceaseless droning of the drums. The song was not what we should call singing, but a plaintive and quavering wail, pursued in a certain cadence, now falling to a moan, now terminating in a shriek, but always pitiful, piercing, and inexpressibly sad. The tambours, which were struck like the keyboard of a piano, by the outstretched fingers of the hand, and occasionally, when a louder note was required, by the thumb, kept up a monotonous refrain in the background. From time to time, at moments of greater stress, they were brandished high in the air and beaten with all the force of fingers and thumb combined. Then the noise was imperious and deafening.

Among the singers, one grizzled and bearded veteran, with a strident and nasal intonation, surpassed his fellows. He observed the time with grotesque inflections of his body; his eyes were fixed and shone with religious zeal.

The chant proceeded, and the figures of the singers, as they became more and more excited, rocked to and fro. More people poured in at the doorway, and the building was now quite full. I began to wonder whether the musicians were also to be the performers, or when the latter would make their appearance.

Suddenly a line of four or five Arabs formed itself in front of the entrance on the far side of the orchestra, and exactly opposite the bench on which I was sitting. They joined hands, the right of each clasped in the left of his neighbour, and began a lurching, swaying motion with their bodies and feet. At first they appeared simply to be marking time, first with one foot and then with the other ; but the movement was gradually communicated to every member of their bodies ; and from the crown of the head to the soles of the feet they were presently keeping time with the music in convulsive jerks and leaps and undulations, the music itself being regulated by the untiring orchestra of the drums.

This mysterious row of bobbing figures seemed to exercise an irresistible fascination over the spectators. Every moment one or other of these left his place to join its ranks. They pushed their way into the middle, severing the chain for an instant, or joined themselves on to the ends. The older men appeared to have a right to the centre, the boys and children—for there were youngsters present not more than seven or eight years old—were on the wings. Thus the line ever lengthened; originally it consisted of three or four, presently it was ten or twelve, anon it was twenty-five or thirty, and before the self-torturings commenced there were as many as forty human figures stretching right across the building, and all rocking backwards and forwards in grim and ungraceful unison. Even the spectators who kept their places could not resist the contagion ; as they sat there, they unconsciously kept time with their heads and shoulders, and one child swung his little head this way and that with a fury that threatened to separate it from his body.

Meanwhile the music had been growing in

intensity, the orchestra sharing the excitement which they communicated. The drummers beat their tambours with redoubled force, lifting them high above their heads and occasionally, at some extreme pitch, tossing them aloft and catching them again as they fell. Sometimes in the exaltation of frenzy they started spasmodically to their feet and then sank back into their original position. But ever and without a pause continued the insistent accompaniment of the drums.

And now the oscillating line in front of the doorway for the first time found utterance. As they leaped high on one foot, alternately kicking out the other, as their heads wagged to and fro and their bodies quivered with the muscular strain, they cried aloud in praise of Allah. "La ilaha ill Allah!" (There is no God but Allah)—this was the untiring burden of their strain. And then came "Ya Allah!" (O God), and sometimes "Ya Kahhar!" (O avenging God), "Ya Hakk!" (O just God), while each burst of clamorous appeal culminated in an awful shout of "Ya Hoo!" (O Him).

The rapidity and vehemence of their gesticulations was now appalling; their heads swung backwards and forwards till their foreheads almost touched their breasts and their scalps smote against their backs. Sweat poured from their faces; they panted for breath; and the exclamations burst from their mouths in a thick and stertorous murmur. Suddenly, and without warning, the first phase of the *zikr* ceased, and the actors stood gasping, shaking, and dripping with perspiration.

After a few seconds' respite the performance recommenced, and shortly waxed more furious than ever. The worshippers seemed to be gifted with an almost superhuman strength and energy. As they flung themselves to and fro, at one moment their upturned faces gleamed with a sickly polish under the flickering lamps, at the next their turbaned heads all but brushed the floor. Their eyes started from the sockets; the muscles on their necks and the veins on their foreheads stood out like knotted cords. One old man fell out of the ranks breathless, spent, and foaming. His place was taken by another, and the tumultuous orgy went on.

Presently, as the ecstasy approached its height and the fully initiated became *melboos* or possessed, they broke from the stereotyped litany into demoniacal grinning and ferocious and bestial cries. These writhing and contorted objects were no longer rational human beings, but savage animals, caged brutes howling madly in the delirium of hunger or of pain. They growled like bears, they barked like jackals, they roared like lions, they laughed like hyaenas; and ever and anon from the seething rank rose a diabolical shriek, like the scream of a dying horse, or the yell of a tortured fiend. And steadily the while in the background resounded the implacable reverberation of the drums.

The climax was now reached; the requisite

pitch of cataleptic inebriation had been obtained, and the rites of Aissa were about to begin. From the crowd at the door a wild figure broke forth, tore off his upper clothing till he was naked to the waist, and, throwing away his fez, bared a head close-shaven save for one long and dishevelled lock that, springing from the scalp, fell over his forehead like some grisly and funereal plume. A long knife, somewhat resembling a cutlass, was handed to him by the sheikh, who had risen to his feet and who directed the phenomena that ensued. Waving it wildly above his head and protruding the forepart of his figure, the fanatic brought it down blow after blow against his bared stomach, and drew it savagely to and fro against the unprotected skin. There showed the marks of a long and livid weal, but no blood spurted from the gash. In the intervals between the strokes he ran swiftly from one side to the other of the open space, taking long stealthy strides like a panther about to spring, and seemingly so powerless over his own movements that he knocked blindly up against those who stood in his way, nearly upsetting them with the violence of the collision.

The prowess or the piety of this ardent devotee proved extraordinarily contagious. First one and then another of his brethren caught the afflatus and followed his example. In a few moments every part of the mosque was the scene of some novel and horrible rite of self-mutilation, performed by a fresh aspirant to the favour of Allah.

Some of these feats did not rise above the level of the curious but explicable performances which are sometimes seen upon English stages—*e.g.* of the men who swallow swords, and carry enormous weights suspended from their jaws; achievements which are in no sense a trick or a deception, but are to be attributed to abnormal physical powers or structure developed by long and often perilous practice. In the Aissaiouian counterpart of these displays there was nothing specially remarkable, but there were others less commonplace and more difficult of explanation.

Several long iron spits or prongs were produced and distributed; these formidable implements were about two and a half feet in length and sharply pointed, and they terminated at the handle in a circular wooden knob about the size of a large orange. There was great competition for these instruments of torture, which were used as follows. Poising one in the air, an Aissaoui would suddenly force the point into the flesh of his own shoulder in front just below the shoulder blade. Thus transfixed, and holding the weapon aloft, he strode swiftly up and down. Suddenly, at a signal, he fell on his knees, still forcing the point into his body, and keeping the wooden head uppermost. Then there started up another disciple armed with a big wooden mallet, and he, after a few preliminary taps, rising high on tiptoe with uplifted weapon would, with an ear-splitting yell, bring it down with all his force upon the wooden knob, driving the point home through the shoulder of his comrade. Blow succeeded blow, the victim wincing beneath the stroke, but uttering no sound, and fixing his eyes with a look of ineffable delight upon his torturer, till the point was driven right through the shoulder and projected at the back. Then the patient marched backwards and forwards with the air and the gait of a conquering hero. At one moment there were four of these semi-naked maniacs within a yard of my feet, transfixed and trembling, but beatified and triumphant. And amid the cries and the swelter, there never ceased for one second the sullen and menacing vociferation of the drums.

Another man seized an iron skewer, and, placing the point within his open jaws, forced it steadily through his cheek until it protruded a couple of inches on the outside. He barked savagely like a dog, and foamed at the lips.

Others, afflicted with exquisite spasms of hunger, knelt down before the chief, whimpering like children for food, and turning upon him imploring glances from their glazed and bloodshot eyes. His control over his following was supreme. Some he gratified, others he forbade. At a touch from him they were silent and relapsed into quiescence. One maddened wretch who, fancying himself some wild beast, plunged to and fro, roaring horribly and biting and tearing with his teeth at whomever he met, was advancing, as I thought, with somewhat truculent intent in my direction, when he was arrested by his superior and sent back cringing and cowed.

For those whose ravenous appetites he was content to humour the most singular repast was prepared. A plate was brought in, covered with huge jagged pieces of broken glass, as thick as a shattered soda-water bottle. With greedy chuckles and gurglings of delight one of the hungry ones dashed at it, crammed a handful into his mouth, and crunched it up as though it were some exquisite dainty, a fellow-disciple calmly stroking the exterior of his throat, with intent, I suppose, to lubricate the descent of the unwonted morsels. A little child held up a snake or sand-worm by the tail, placing the head between his teeth, and gulped it gleefully down. Several acolytes came in, carrying a big stem of the prickly pear, or *fico d' India*, whose leaves are as thick as a one-inch plank and are armed with huge projecting thorns. This was ambrosia to the starving saints; they rushed at it with passionate emulation, tearing at the solid slabs with their teeth, and gnawing and munching the coarse fibres, regardless of the thorns which pierced their tongues and cheeks as they swallowed them down.

The most singular feature of all, and the one that almost defies belief, though it is none the less true, was this—that in no case did one drop of blood emerge from scar, or gash, or wound. This fact I observed most carefully, the *mokaddem* standing at my side, and each patient in turn coming to him when his self-imposed torture had been accomplished and the cataleptic frenzy had spent its force. It was the chief who cunningly withdrew the blade from cheek or shoulder or body, rubbing over the spot what appeared to me to be the saliva of his own mouth ; then he whispered an absolution in the ear of the disciple and kissed him on the forehead, whereupon the patient, but a moment before writhing in maniacal transports, retired tranquilly and took his seat upon the floor. He seemed none the worse for his recent paroxysm, and the wound was marked only by a livid blotch or a hectic flush.

This was the scene that for more than an hour went on without pause or intermission before my eyes. The building might have been tenanted by the Harpies or Laestrygones of Homer, or by some inhuman monsters of legendary myth. Amid the dust and sweat and insufferable heat the naked bodies of the actors shone with a ghastly pallor and exhaled a sickening smell. The atmosphere reeked with heavy and intoxicating fumes. Above the despairing chant of the singers rang the frenzied yells of the possessed, the shrieks of the hammerer, and the inarticulate cries, the snarling and growling, the bellowing and miauling of the self-imagined beasts. And ever behind and through all re-echoed the perpetual and pitiless imprecation of the drums.

As I witnessed the disgusting spectacle and listened to the pandemonium of sounds, my head swam, my eyes became dim, my senses reeled, and I believe that in a few moments I must have fainted, had not one of my friends touched me on the shoulder, and, whispering that the *mokaddem* was desirous that I should leave, escorted me hurriedly to the door. As I walked back to my quarters, and long after through the still night, the beat of the tambours continued, and I heard the distant hum of voices, broken at intervals by an isolated and piercing cry. Perhaps yet further and more revolting orgies were celebrated after I had left. I had not seen, as other travellers have done, the chewing and swallowing of red-hot cinders,[1] or the harmless handling and walking upon live coals. I had been spared that which others have described as the climax of the gluttonous debauch, viz. the introduction of a live sheep, which then and there is savagely torn to pieces and devoured raw by these unnatural banqueters. But I had seen enough, and as I sank to sleep my agitated fancy pursued a thousand avenues of thought, confounding in one grim medley all the carnivorous horrors of fact and fable and fiction. Loud above the din and discord the tale of the false prophets of Carmel, awakened by the train of association, rang in my ears, till I seemed to hear intoned with remorseless repetition the words, "They cried aloud and cut themselves after their manner with knives and lancets, till the blood gushed out upon them"; and in the ever-receding distance of dreamland,

[1] For an account of this exploit, *vide* Lane's *Modern Egyptians*, cap. xxv.; and compare the description of Richardson, the famous fire-eater, in Evelyn's *Memoirs* for October 8, 1672.

faint and yet fainter, there throbbed the inexorable and unfaltering delirium of the drums.

Years afterwards, when he was in retirement, and a little while before the melancholy catastrophe that ended his life, I met General Boulanger at a private house in London. The alert and springy figure and the blonde hair of the youthful General had been replaced by the increasing bulk and the grizzled beard of the middle-aged civilian, and he wore a more paternal aspect than when I had figured for a short time as his son. But I refrained from disclosing the fact that I had ever stood to him, even in masquerade, in a filial relationship, or that I owed to him my unforgettable experience of the drums of Kairwan.

Perhaps the most comic feature of the tale remains to be told. At the time of my visit to Kairwan, I had just become a Member of Parliament in England; and the story of my innocent deception appeared in some of the English newspapers. So good an opening for electioneering propaganda was not to be lost: and the Radical newspapers of my constituency did not hesitate to point out the fraudulent and unscrupulous nature of the individual to whom the truth-loving electors of Southport had been so foolish as to entrust their representation. Now it is all forgotten; and there only lingers in my memory like a faint echo from a shadowy distance the remote and melancholy pulsation of the drums of Kairwan.

THE AMIR OF AFGHANISTAN

THE AMIR OF AFGHANISTAN

He civilised his people and himself remained a savage.
VOLTAIRE.

One still strong man in a blatant land
Who can rule and dare to lie.
TENNYSON, " Maud " (slightly adapted).

I HAVE never before narrated the circumstances in which I came to visit the Capital and Court of the famous Afghan ruler, Amir Abdur Rahman Khan. I had devoted so many years to the study of the Central Asian problem—the security of the Indian Frontier ; the policy of Russia, then in the full tide of her career of Asiatic aggression and conquest ; the part that was being played in the drama by all the countries lying on the glacis of the Indian fortress, Persia, Baluchistan, Afghanistan, Tibet, China—and I had explored so many of these regions myself, that I was beyond measure desirous to visit that one of their number which, though perhaps the most important, was also the least accessible, and to converse with the stormy and inscrutable figure who occupied the Afghan throne, and was a source of such incessant anxiety, suspicion, and even alarm to successive Governments of India as well as to the India Office in London.

I knew that the Amir was intensely mistrustful of the Calcutta Government, and I thought it not impossible that he might be willing to converse with an Englishman who had been the Minister responsible for the Government of India in the House of Commons in London, who was still, though no longer in office, a member of that House, and who had for some years written and spoken widely, though always in a friendly spirit, about the defence of the Indian frontier, and the importance of intimate relations with Afghanistan. Accordingly in the spring of 1894 I wrote a personal letter to the Amir, in which I confessed these desires, explained to him my impending programme of travel in the Himalayas and the Pamirs, and sought his permission to visit him at Kabul in the latter part of the year.

After expatiating with more than Oriental hyperbole upon all these considerations, I added a passage in which I felt a modest pride :

> Khorasan I have seen and visited ; I have been in Bokhara and Samarkand ; I have ridden to Chaman, and I have sojourned at Peshawur. But the dominions of Your Highness, which are situated in the middle of all these territories, like unto a rich stone in the middle of a ring, I have never been permitted to enter, and the person of Your Highness, which is in your own dominions like unto the sparkle in the heart of the diamond, I have not been fortunate enough to see. Many books and writings have I studied, and have talked to many men ; but I would fain converse with Your Highness who knows more about these questions than do other men, and who will perhaps be willing to throw upon my imperfect understanding the full ray of truth.

Apart, however, from the hoped-for invitation from the Amir—never before extended to any Englishman except to those in his personal employ, or to an official Mission from the Government of India, such as that of their Foreign Secretary, Sir Mortimer Durand—there were other and formidable difficulties to be overcome. The Home Government (Lord Kimberley was then Secretary of State for India) viewed my project with some anxiety; the attitude of the Government of India was veiled in a chilly obscurity, which was not dissipated until I arrived at Simla in the early autumn to plead my own case. Sir Henry Brackenbury, then Military Member, and a man of great ability and much imagination, was my one friend; the Commander-in-Chief, Sir George White, was non-committal; the Viceroy, Lord Elgin, hesitated. At a meeting of the Executive Council, however, it was decided to let me cross the frontier (on my return from the Pamirs), provided that a direct invitation from the Amir arrived in the interim; but I was told that I must go as a private individual (which was exactly what I desired), and that the Government of India would assume no responsibility for my safety.

It was while I was in camp in the Gurais Valley in Kashmir, on my way to the Gilgit Frontier, that I received a telegram from Kabul announcing the invitation of the Amir. From that moment all my anxieties were at an end, and it remained only for me to get through my

Pamir explorations in safety in order to realise my supreme ambition in the later autumn. Nearly three months later, on November 13, 1894, I rode alone across the Afghan Frontier at Torkham beyond Lundi Khana, and consigned myself to the care of the God-Granted Government, and to the hospitality of its Sovereign.

And now let me say something about the personality and career of that remarkable man, so that my readers, to whom his name is perhaps now little more than a memory, may know what sort of being it was with whom I was about to spend long days in friendly intercourse, and who was to reveal to me, with an astonishing candour, his innermost thoughts and ideas.

Born in 1844, Abdur Rahman Khan was the eldest son of Dost Mohammed, the celebrated Afghan ruler who had been alternately the foe and the protégé of the British Government. He was therefore by birth and inheritance the direct and legal heir of his grandfather, and the recognised head of the Barukzai clan. It may be a consolation to reluctant students and to naughty boys at large to know, as the Amir himself told me, that up till the age of twenty he declined to learn either to read or to write, and that at a time when most European lads have their knees under a desk he was engaged in manufacturing rifled gun-barrels and in casting guns. It was in 1864, the year following upon the death of the Dost, that he first appeared in public life, being appointed to a Governorship in Afghan Turkestan;

and after that date there were few elements of romance or adventure that his career did not contain. Here victorious in battle (for he was a born soldier), there defeated; now a king-maker in his own country, anon a fugitive from its borders; for a time the powerful Governor of the Cis-Oxian provinces, and presently an exile in the courts of Meshed, Khiva, and Bokhara; later on a pensioner of the Russians at Samarkand, and, finally, the British nominee upon the throne of a recovered Afghanistan, for nearly forty years, whether in the forefront or the background, he presented the single strong figure whose masculine individuality emerged with distinctness from the obscure and internecine and often miserable drama of Afghan politics.

It was he who placed, first his father Afzul, and afterwards his uncle Azim, on the throne; and when, Afzul having died and Azim having been defeated by a younger brother, Shere Ali, he was obliged to flee from his country into a ten years' exile, it was with the conviction, which he never abandoned, that his services would again be called for and that he would assuredly return.

For this purpose he accepted a Russian pension (the greater part of which was, he told me, systematically filched from him by peculation) and resided at Samarkand, in order that he might be near to the Afghan frontier whenever the emergency should arise. The Russians never quite recovered from their astonishment that one who had been a recipient of their hospitality and their pay should, in later years, after recovering the throne, have pursued a policy so little in accord with Russian aspirations; and for a while they consoled themselves with the reflection that this was a mere ruse, and that the true Russophil would appear later on. These expectations were sadly disappointed; for although he did not care for the British much, Abdur Rahman disliked the Russians far more, and had a very shrewd idea of the fate that a Russo-Afghan alliance would bring upon his country. Incidentally, he told me that while a refugee in Russia he secretly learned the language, and never enjoyed himself more than when he heard the Russian officers discussing their real policy in the presence of the seemingly simple-minded and unsophisticated Afghan.

In 1878 his opportunity came, when Shere Ali, inveigled by Russian promises to his doom, threw off the British alliance, and brought a British army into his country, thereby forfeiting first his throne, and, a little later, his life. Crossing the frontier, Abdur Rahman overran the whole country, and by 1880 had acquired so commanding a position that when, after the treachery of Yakub Khan and the open hostility of Ayub, the Indian Government were looking out for a suitable candidate for the throne, they had no alternative but to take the single strong man in the country, whom they forthwith installed as ruler, and then retired.

In the thirteen years that elapsed before my

visit the Amir had consolidated his rule over one of the most turbulent peoples in the world by force alike of character and of arms, and by a relentless savagery that ended by crushing all opposition out of existence, and leaving him the undisputed but dreaded master of the entire country. No previous Sovereign had ever ridden the wild Afghan steed with so cruel a bit, none had given so large a measure of unity to the kingdom; there was not in Asia or in the world a more fierce or uncompromising despot. Such was the remarkable man whose guest I was for more than a fortnight at Kabul, living in the Salam Khana or Guest House, immediately overlooking the moat of the Ark or Citadel. The Amir was residing in a neighbouring two-storied house or villa, surrounded by a high wall, and known as the Bostan Serai. In the grounds of this place he now lies buried. Our meetings and conversations took place in a large room in that building. They usually commenced at noon or 1 P.M. and lasted for some hours.

I do not propose to narrate here the long conversations, mainly of a political character, in which the Amir indulged, because, as I have before said, I do not wish this volume to become a political treatise, and because much of what he said was intended to be confidential. Later on, however, I shall narrate one of his most characteristic harangues about his impending visit to England, the invitation to which he accepted through me, since it reveals many of the most interesting traits of his shrewd but untutored intellect. In the intervals, however, of these quasi-political conversations the Amir would talk discursively about almost every topic under heaven; while, during my stay, I heard many anecdotes of his curious character and amazing career.

Perhaps before I come to these I may say a few words about his external appearance and mien. A man of big stature though not of great height, of colossal personal strength, and of corresponding stoutness of frame when in his prime, he was much altered by sickness when I saw him from the appearance presented, for instance, by the photographs taken at the Rawal Pindi Durbar in 1885. The photograph that I reproduce represents him as he was at the time of my visit in 1894. He suffered greatly from gout, and one of the favourite amusements or jests of the native compositor in the Indian Press was to convert "gout" into "government" and to say, not without truth, that the Amir was suffering from "a bad attack of government."

A large, but in no wise unwieldy figure sitting upright upon silken quilts, outspread over a low *charpoy* or bedstead, the limbs encased in close-fitting lamb's wool garments; a fur-lined pelisse hanging over the shoulders, and a spotless white silk turban wound round the conical Afghan skull-cap of cloth of silver, or of gold, and coming low down on to the forehead; a broad and massive countenance with regular features, but complexion visibly sallow from recent illness; brows that contracted somewhat as he reflected or argued; luminous black eyes that looked out very straightly and fixedly without the slightest movement or wavering, a black moustache close clipped upon the upper lip, and a carefully trimmed and dyed black beard, neither so long nor so luxuriant as of yore, framing a mouth that responded to every expression, and which, when it opened, as it not unfrequently did, to loud laughter, widened at the corners and disclosed the full line of teeth in both jaws; a voice resonant but not harsh, and an articulation of surprising emphasis and clearness; above all, a manner of unchallengeable dignity and command—this was the outward guise and bearing of my kingly host. I may add that for stating his own case in an argument or controversy the Amir would not easily find a match on the front benches in the House of Commons; whilst if he began to talk of his own experiences and to relate stories of his adventures in warfare or exile, the organised minuteness and deliberation with which each stage of the narrative proceeded in due order was only equalled by the triumphant crash of the climax, and only exceeded by the roar of laughter which the *dénouement* almost invariably provoked from the audience, and in which the author as heartily joined. Like most men trained in the Persian literary school (Persian being the language of the upper classes in Afghanistan), the Amir was a constant quoter of saws and wise sayings from that inexhaustible well of sapient philosophy, that Iranian Pope, the Sheikh Saadi.

The Amir's appearance, like that of most Orientals, was greatly enhanced by his turban. I never saw him in the sheepskin *kolah* or *kalpak* of his military uniform. On one occasion when we were talking about his visit to England he removed his turban and began to scratch his head, which was shaved quite bald. In a moment he was transformed from the formidable despot to a commonplace and elderly man. I implored him when he came to London never to remove his turban or scratch his head; and, when I told him my reason, his vanity was at once piqued, and he promised faithfully to show himself at his best.

His characteristics were in some respects even more remarkable than his features. This terribly cruel man could be affable, gracious, and considerate to a degree. This man of blood loved scents and colours and gardens and singing birds and flowers. This intensely practical being was a prey to mysticism, for he thought that he saw dreams and visions, and was convinced (although this was probably only a symptom of his vanity) that he possessed supernatural gifts. Generous to those who were useful to him, he was merciless to any whose day was past or who had lost his favour. But even in the most unpropitious circumstances his humour never deserted him. At one of his country *durbars* certain tax-gatherers were disputing with the local landowners as to the taxes to be paid. As they all insisted on speaking at once, he placed a soldier behind each of them with orders to box the ears of any man who spoke out of his turn.

On one occasion he put a man to death unjustly, *i.e.* on false evidence. Thereupon he fined himself 6000 rupees, and paid this sum to the widow, who for her part was delighted at being simultaneously relieved of her husband and started again in life.

On another occasion his humour took a more gruesome turn. It was pointed out to him by one of his courtiers that he had ordered an innocent man to be hanged. "Innocent!" cried the Amir. "Well, if he is not guilty this time, he has done something else at another. Away with him."

In this strange and almost incredible amalgam of the jester and the cynic, the statesman and the savage, I think that a passion for cruelty was one of his most inveterate instincts. The Amir often exerted himself to deny the charge or claimed that it was the only method of dealing with a race so treacherous and criminally inclined. For instance, as I rode to Kabul, I passed on the top of the Lataband Pass an iron cage swinging from a tall pole in which rattled the bleaching bones of a robber whom he had caught and shut up alive in this construction, as a warning to other disturbers of the peace of the King's highway. He revelled in these grim demonstrations of executive authority. Nevertheless, the recorded stories—as to the truth of which I satisfied myself—were sufficient to show that a love of violence and an ingrained ferocity were deeply rooted in his nature. He confided to an Englishman at Kabul that he had put to death 120,000 of his own people. After one unsuccessful rebellion he had many thousands of the guilty tribesmen blinded with quicklime, and spoke to me of the punishment without a trace of compunction. Crimes such as robbery or rape were punished with fiendish severity. Men were blown from guns, or thrown down a dark well, or beaten to death, or flayed alive, or tortured in the offending member. For instance, one of the favourite penalties for petty larceny was to amputate the hand at the wrist, the raw stump being then plunged in boiling oil. One official who had outraged a woman was stripped naked and placed in a hole dug for the purpose on the top of a high hill outside Kabul. It was in midwinter; and water was then poured upon him until he was converted into an icicle and frozen alive. As the Amir sardonically remarked, "He would never be too hot again."

A woman of his harem being found in the family way, he had her tied up in a sack and brought into the Durbar hall, where he ran her through with his own sword. Two men having been heard to talk about some forbidden subject, he ordered their upper and lower lips to be stitched together so that they should never offend again. A man came into the Durbar one day and openly accused the Amir of depravity and crime. " Tear out his tongue," said the Amir. In a moment he was seized and his tongue torn out by the roots. The poor wretch died. One day an old beggar threw himself in the way of the Amir as he was riding through the streets. The following dialogue then ensued: " What are you ? " " A beggar." " But how do you get your living ? " " By alms." " What ? Do you mean to say that you do no work ? " " None." " And you have never done any ? " " Never." " Then it is time that we were relieved of your presence." And the Amir nodded to the executioner.

His cruelty even extended to punishing acts, however innocent, which had not been authorised by himself or which seemed to trench upon his prerogative. Though I was his guest and he sincerely desired to do me honour, and did so, he could not tolerate that any of his subjects should show spontaneous courtesy to the stranger. A man who spoke to me while I was on the road to Kabul was seized and thrown into prison. A man who offered me a pomegranate as I rode into Kandahar was severely beaten and imprisoned and deprived of his property.

Nevertheless, this monarch, at once a patriot and a monster, a great man and almost a fiend, laboured hard and unceasingly for the good of his country. He sought to raise his people from the squalor and apathy and blood-shedding of their normal lives and to convert them into a nation. He welded the Afghan tribes into a unity which they had never previously enjoyed, and he paved the way for the complete independence which his successors have achieved. He and he alone was the Government of Afghanistan. There was nothing from the command of an army or the government of a province to the cut of a uniform or the fabrication of furniture that he did not personally superintend and control. He was the brain and eyes and ears of all Afghanistan. But it is questionable whether in the latter part of his life he was more detested or admired. He ceased to move abroad from fear of assassination, and six horses, saddled and laden with coin, were always kept ready for a sudden escape.

I should describe him, on the whole, in spite of his uncertain temper and insolent language, as a consistent friend of the British alliance. Though he often had differences with the Government of India, whom he loved to snub and annoy, though there were moments when the relations between them were very strained, though, when I became Viceroy, he did not spare me these conventional amenities and we were sometimes on the verge of a serious quarrel, I did not and do not doubt that on the broad issues of Imperial policy his fidelity was assured. But he acted in this respect, as in all others, from expediency alone. He knew that the British neither coveted nor desired to annex his country. As an independent Sovereign he was compelled, for the sake of appearances with his own people, to exhibit a truculence that was often offensive and at times insupportable. But at a crisis it was to British advice and British arms that he invariably turned. His name will always deserve to rank high in the annals of his own country as well as in the history of the Indian Empire.

Among the devices that he adopted in order to stimulate the patriotism and ensure the due subordination of his people and incidentally to render them more amenable to military constriction, was the issue of a map, accompanied by a Proclamation which was read out in the bazaars and mozques of all the principal towns and posted in every village.

The Proclamation was even more remarkable than the map, which indeed stands in some need of explanation. It was in the nature of a lecture, invested with all the authority of a royal *firman* or decree. I will quote a few passages from it.

I have now prepared for you a kind of map, which shows the condition of Afghanistan as compared with that of its surrounding countries. This I have done in order to enable you to study the matter attentively and to make out a path for yourselves in such a way, that good may accrue both to your country and to your religion. I am hopeful that a careful study of this map will suffice for your prosperity and happiness both in this world and the next.

In entering into the details of this map, I hereby declare that whatever has been predestined by the Almighty for each one of you, the same has been put into the heart of your King, and he is thus enabled to find suitable appointments for all. Some of you have attained to the rank of a Commander-in-Chief, while others are still in the position of a sepoy. It is, however, fitting for you all to offer thanks to God and to your King, and to be contented with your lot. You should not be envious of those who hold higher rank than yourselves, but you should rather look to those who are inferior. By doing so you will gain three benefits—first, the favour and blessing of God, for it is written that "if you express your gratitude for the blessings poured forth upon you, the same shall be increased"; secondly, the approbation and good will of your ruler; and thirdly, you will thus be enabled to hold your present position in the sure hope of obtaining advancement. For God has said, that if you offer thanks for His blessings He will increase them. The increase of blessings signifies the exaltation of rank. All blessings in this world depend upon the exaltation of position, and when a man's rank is increased he can then only be said to have obtained the blessings of this world. But if you are not contented with your present state and neglect to offer your thanks to God, and do not look to those who are inferior to you in position, but rather envy those who are above you, and ask in your hearts why such and such persons are superior to yourselves, you lay the foundation of envy and hatred, and cause many calamities to fall upon you.

Therefore, take care and listen to me, who am your King, with all your heart, and weigh well what I say, for it is of no use to make lamentations for that which has passed and gone. This advice is for all, from the

Commander-in-Chief down to the sepoy, and also for the subjects, who are inferior to all, and for those who carry guns on their shoulders. A sepoy should look upon the subjects, who are inferior to him, as members of his own society, for it is with the help of God and by the kindness of the King that he has obtained his rank. You should sympathise with the subjects, who are your own tribesmen and who are continually employed in cultivating their lands, in cutting their crops, in thrashing their corn, in gathering in the harvests and in winnowing the wheat from the chaff. They are also occupied in trade and undergo hardships and troubles by night and by day, and only enjoy a portion of the produce themselves after they have paid in the taxes which are necessary for the expenses of the State. I, who am your King, spend all this money on the army. It therefore behoves you all, whether you are men in high places or sepoys or subjects, to be grateful, because all that you pay is given back to your brothers, sons and tribesmen. By this God is pleased, religion flourishes and honour is preserved. In a like manner, the subjects should also be grateful, so that God's blessings may increase day by day, for it is written, that on him who is grateful He increases his bounties. It is therefore incumbent on you to be grateful both to God and to your King.

The real object of my teaching is that the kindness and compassion of the King towards his subjects resembles the feelings of a father towards his son ; and as it is natural that a father should be kind to his son, so it is also natural that the King should be kind to his subjects. These are also the orders of God to the King. But when the father sees the errors of his son, he admonishes and punishes him. Now this punishment is not due to ill-feeling, but rather to the excessive love which the father bears towards his son, so that he cannot even bear the sight of any wrong-doing on the part of his son ; in the same way the King has the same feelings towards his subjects as a father has towards his son. The King only wishes to spread the blessings of tranquillity and peace among his subjects and to gain a good name thereby. When a boy is young and ignorant, he hates and despises the advice of his father, but when he becomes of age and becomes endued with wisdom and intellect, he considers that there is none so kind and affectionate as his father, and it is the whole purport and desire of his life to obey the orders of his father. In the same way, I, the ruler of you Afghans, have the same desire of being kind and generous to you, even as a father is kind and generous to his son. If you are wise enough to understand and benefit by my advice, I am confident that you will see that your religion will flourish and that your country will be prosperous. May it so please God.

Considering the manner, as already described, in which Abdur Rahman Khan was in the habit of demonstrating his paternal love for his subjects, the latter, if they had one-thousandth part of the sense of humour of their sovereign, must have smiled somewhat grimly as they listened to this sermon.

One of the subjects that interested the Amir most was his claim, on behalf of himself and of his people, to a descent from the Lost Tribes of Israel. I had heard of this theory ; and I had noted the distinct resemblance of many Afghan features to the Semitic type. But when I interrogated him about it, he unhesitatingly proclaimed his acceptance of the legend. He declared that the Afghans took their name from Afghana, who was Commander-in-Chief to King Solomon ; some were descended from him, and others from Jeremiah the son of Saul.[1] On another occasion the Amir's eldest son Habibulla, whose ethnology was a little hazy, told me that the Afghans were Jews who had been conquered by Babu-Nassar (*i.e.* Nebuchadnezzar) in the time of Yezdigird, and deported to Persia, where they lived a long time. Later on they migrated to Afghanistan, where they settled in the region of the Suleiman (Solomon) Mountains, to which, in reference to their origin, they gave that name. As a matter of fact, the Hebrew descent of the Afghans has been the subject of prolonged dispute, great authorities having argued on either side. The champions of the theory point to the marked Jewish features of so many Afghans, to the great number of Jewish Christian names (*e.g.* Ibrahim = Abraham, Ayub = Job, Ismail = Ishmael, Ishak = Isaac, Yahia = John, Yakub = Jacob, Yusuf = Joseph, Isa = Jesus, Daoud = David, Suleiman = Solomon, and many others), to the fact that the Feast of the Passover is still observed by the Pathan border tribe of the Yusufzai; and to the occurrence of the name Kabul in the Old Testament (*e.g.* 1 Kings ix. 13), where Solomon, having given King Hiram twenty cities of Galilee in return for the timber and gold presented to him for the Temple, Hiram went out to see them and was very much disgusted, "calling them the land of Cabul (*i.e.* dirty or disgusting)

[1] This is the conventional account given in the best-known Pushtu history, called Tazkirat ul-Muluk, which was composed in the time of the early Duranis, and probably invented the legend.

unto this day." I believe that this reasoning is quite fallacious, the Biblical names employed by the Afghans being all in their Arabic form, *i.e.* post-Mohammedan in origin; and the Hebrew word Kabúl in the Old Testament having no connection, except in spelling, with the Afghan Kābul. The theory of a Semitic origin is now generally discredited, but there is nothing inherently improbable in the belief that some of the Afghan tribes may have entered the country from Persia (of which language they speak a patois) and may have come at an earlier date into Persia from Syria or Assyria (the land of the captivity). There I will leave the matter, to which I have only alluded here in order to record the opinions of the Amir.

And now, having given a general picture of the man, his personality and his acts, let me pass on to narrate a few of the more interesting conversations, other than on political subjects, with which he overflowed. He spoke in Persian through an interpreter; and while at times he would indulge in short and staccato phrases, at others he would pour forth a torrent of declamation that lasted for six or seven minutes without a pause.

Never was the mixture of shrewdness, vanity, and ignorance, which were so strangely blended in Abdur Rahman's character, more patently shown than in the conversation which he held with me one day in open Durbar with regard to his contemplated visit to England. He had already received an official invitation from Her Majesty's

Government, tendered through the Viceroy (Lord Elgin) to pay such a visit, and to this invitation, with calculated rudeness, he had declined for months to return a reply. I had good reason for thinking that he was postponing his answer until I arrived at Kabul, and he could hear from me personally what sort of reception he would be likely to meet with in London. From the start, accordingly, this formed a constant topic of our conversation; and I very soon realised that, while appearing to hang back, the Amir was in reality intensely anxious to come, provided, on the one hand, that he could be assured of a welcome in England compatible with his own exalted conception of the dignity and prestige of the Afghan Sovereign, and, on the other, that he could safely be absent from his country for several months of time. He would discuss these subjects with me interminably in all their bearings, being in reality much more concerned about the former than the latter. At length, towards the end of my visit, his mind was made up; the decision to pay the visit was definitely taken; the acceptance was written, in the form of a personal letter to Queen Victoria, which the Amir handed to me in open Durbar, wrapped up in a violet silk covering, embroidered with a Persian inscription. This parcel I took back to England and ultimately transmitted to Her Majesty: and unquestionably the visit would have taken place had not the Amir learned a little later on that, had he left his country, the chances were that, in consequence of the reign of terror that prevailed under his iron hand, he would never be allowed to return, and that in his absence some less fierce and dreaded occupant would be installed upon the Afghan throne.

It was in the course of one of these public conversations that the following dialogue occurred—to understand which it should be premised that the one Englishman against whom the Amir cherished an overweening, though entirely unfounded prejudice, was Lord Roberts (then Commander-in-Chief in England), whom he was never tired of accusing of having condemned and hanged, by bought and perjured evidence, many thousands of innocent Afghans upon the arrival of the British army in Kabul after the murder of Sir L. Cavagnari in 1879.[1] This monarch, who had not hesitated himself, as he boasted to me, to put out the eyes of thousands of his own subjects (after the Hazara rebellion), and who was utterly indifferent to human life, had no words of reprobation too strong for the British Commander, who had dared to punish a gross act of international treachery by the execution of the guilty parties; and he would constantly repeat that Roberts had killed thousands of innocent Afghan people and could never be forgiven. Hence the ensuing story.

[1] These charges against the findings of the Military Court at Kabul, and the consequent executions, having been taken up and repeated by the Opposition in London, the answer of Lord Roberts was read in both Houses of Parliament. His full reply, with an abstract statement of the executions, was published as a Parliamentary Paper in February 1880.

A. "When I come to England and to London and am received by the Queen, shall I tell you what I will do?"

C. "Yes, Your Highness, I shall be glad to hear."

A. "I understand that there is in London a great Hall that is known as Westminster Hall. Is not that so?"

C. "It is."

A. "There are also in London two *Mejilises* (*i.e.* Houses of Parliament). One is called the House of Lords and the other is called the House of Commons?"

C. "It is so."

A. "When I come to London, I shall be received in Westminster Hall. The Queen will be seated on her throne at the end of the Hall, and the Royal Family will be around her; and on either side of the Hall will be placed the two *Mejilises*—the House of Lords on the right, and the House of Commons on the left. Is not that the case?"

C. "It is not our usual plan; but will Your Highness proceed?"

A. "I shall enter the Hall, and the Lords will rise on the right, and the Commons will rise on the left to greet me, and I shall advance between them up the Hall to the daïs, where will be seated the Queen upon her throne. And she will rise and will say to me, 'What has Your Majesty come from Kabul to say?' And how then shall I reply?"

C. "I am sure I do not know."

A. "I shall reply: 'I will say nothing'—and the Queen will then ask me why I refuse to say anything; and I shall answer: 'Send for Roberts. I decline to speak until Roberts comes.' And then they will send for Roberts, and there will be a pause until Roberts comes, and when Roberts has come and is standing before the Queen and the two Mejilises, then will I speak."

C. "And what will Your Highness say?"

A. "I shall tell them how Roberts paid thousands of rupees to obtain false witness at Kabul and that he slew thousands of my innocent people, and I shall ask that Roberts be punished, and when Roberts has been punished, then will I speak."

It was in vain that I indicated to the Amir that things in England and in London were not done exactly in that way, and that the ceremonial of his reception would hardly be of the nature described. Nothing could convince him. This was no doubt exactly the manner in which he would have managed the business in Kabul; and London meant no more to him than a larger stage and a change of scene.

When I reflected what might have happened had the visit been paid and had the Amir been confronted with the more sober realities of British official procedure, I felt almost glad that Her Majesty's Government were spared the spectacle of the Amir's disappointment and its consequences, which might have been serious;

although the personal encounter between the two protagonists, had it ever taken place, could hardly have failed to be diverting.

The only person in England who, when I recounted the story, failed to find it at all amusing—and this perhaps quite pardonably—was Lord Roberts himself.

Knowing that I was a member of Parliament the Amir never spoke to me contemptuously, though often with a touch of sarcasm, about the House of Commons. But to others he was less reticent. On one occasion he told an Englishman in his service that he ought to go to the public *hammam* (Turkish Bath) in Kabul in order to see what in the Amir's opinion the British Parliament must be like. The Englishman duly went, and soon discovered what the Amir had in mind, for the place was full of men, and the high dome overhead reverberated with their calls for towels, soap, etc., and their usual loud-voiced conversations, until the meaning of any individual words and the words themselves were lost in the confusion of sounds, and only added to the general uproar.

Among other curious illustrations of the Amir's colossal, but childish vanity, I recall the following. He cherished the illusion, which was warmly encouraged by all the courtiers who were in the Durbar Hall, that he had a monopoly of all the talents and was the universal genius of Afghanistan, particularly in all matters of mechanics and the arts.

One day, as I was going to the Durbar, I passed through an ante-chamber in which was standing a superb Grand Piano, evidently a fresh importation from Europe, the case of which was exquisitely painted with pictorial subjects or scenes. I was told—though this was probably untrue—that the artist or designer had been no less a person than Sir E. Burne-Jones.

A. "Did you notice the Grand Piano standing in the adjoining chamber as you came in?"

C. "Yes, I did."

A. "What did you think of the painting of the case?"

C. "I thought it magnificent."

A. "I painted it myself!"

The other case was this. One day I was a little late in attending the Durbar, my watch having stopped in the morning.

A. "Why are you late to-day?"

C. "I am sorry to say that my watch stopped this morning."

A. "And yours is an English watch. Send it to me, and I will put it right without difficulty. I am a professional watch-maker myself and keep right the watches of all the people of Kabul!"

I hastily explained that my watch had resumed its full and orderly functions, and accordingly was able to save it from the hands of the illustrious amateur.

I may here anticipate somewhat by giving another example of this amusing trait. After I had returned to England I married in the summer of 1895, and sent a photograph of my wife to the Amir, who responded with a handsome present. But, as the following letter will show, he could not resist, *as an expert in phrenology*, from assuring me that I had made an excellent choice. I append the translation, which he enclosed with the original letter in Persian. The latter is reproduced on the adjoining page.

To my wise and kind friend, the Honble. G. Curzon, M.P.

After compliments and Persian titles and my sincere desire of seeing you again, also my great friendly expressions towards you, my very wise friend—I wish to inform you that I am greatly pleased and interested on reading the contents of your letters, dated March 15 and June 9. I beg to acknowledge the same and my reply is as follows: I was very much delighted to hear of your marriage, also delighted to receive Lady Curzon's photo. Thank God she is according to your own choice. I pray God will keep you (my own wise friend) successful in all the desires of this life.

I also congratulate you, my honest friend, that though you have only married one wife she is competent.

From my knowledge of Phrenology she is very wise and a well-wisher of yours and better than 1000 men.

I hope it may be God's wish, my dear friend, that you will be happy and satisfied with her always. Thanks to the Almighty you have been fortunate enough to meet with such a wife, that in the whole of England there are but a few. Faithfulness, wisdom and honesty, all these I gather from her photo and according to Phrenology. May God bless you with a goodly offspring.

And then in a final sentence leaped forth the irresistible humour of the man :

If she should at any time thrash you I am certain you will have done something to deserve it.—I am your sincere friend and well-wisher

ABDUR RAHMAN, AMIR OF AFGHANISTAN.

As a balance to this type of correspondence I append a single example of a more political letter, written to me while I was still a private person; but revealing many of the best-known features of the Amir's epistolary style. In the first part of the letter is a reference to a press report of something that I was alleged to have said about Afghanistan in England. The second part relates to the constant disputes between the Indian and Afghan Governments, arising out of the frontier warfare known as the Tirah Campaign, which occupied the greater part of 1897.

May my dear, discerning friend, His most honoured Excellency, the Honourable George Curzon, Esquire, Minister of Parliament, M.P. of the House of Commons, continue in the keeping of (God) the True Protector.

The letter of that kind friend written on December 30 A.D. 1897, corresponding to Shaban 5, A.H. 1315, reached the presence of your friend at the best of seasons. From the circumstances of your corporeal well-being joy was produced, and I rejoiced at the soundness of that dear friend's health.

As for what that kind friend wrote concerning the adverse words which have been reported to me as having been uttered by that friend, I have never had cause to complain of that kind friend's friendship, nor of his utterances concerning the State of Afghanistan; neither do I suppose any such thing. I regard you as the first of my friends, the only friend I have in the world. On this subject I have much to say, for there are many reasons for speech. When that kind friend was in Kabul, and we and you sat together in one place, and discussed our inmost thoughts about Russia and Afghanistan, and the disorder of Afghanistan, concerning the antagonism of the Russian Government, the defects of Afghanistan had still in no wise been remedied when the misconduct of a frontier contiguous to the frontier officers of the Most Glorious State of England brought about disturbance and confusion, until at length the frontier officers of that State first cast suspicion upon me for their foolish deeds and words; for they issued proclamations for a general massacre of the people of the hill-passes, and fear overtook them all, and they slew the Agents of the Most Glorious State and burned and ravaged; and several thousand men and part of the Army of the Most Glorious State died, neither did they gain anything save hostility. Alas! alas! for this nearness and proximity of Russia, and the hostility of the Afghan frontier tribes. I do not know what the end of it will be, for although I have no concern with the people of Tira and the Afridis and the peoples of Bajawar and Swat, it is now eleven months since all caravans from my dominions have been stopped, and the implements which were necessary for my engine-workshop have been detained. In proof of this I send enclosed in this packet, for your information and perusal, an Order written by the Commissioner of Peshawur for the caravan conductor (Kafila-bashi) of your friend (myself) located at Peshawur, about the detention of the oil-boxes, and I do not know what may be the reason of his (the Commissioner's) conduct. They have caused my thoughts to incline to doubt India, so that enemy and friend are passed out of my memory (*i.e.* I confuse friends and enemies). If you will again peruse the political news of India which has gone to London wherein they have said many things about (*i.e.* have cast many reflections on) my friendship, and have made (many) aspersions (you will see that) I have patiently stomached much, and by these forbearances it will be known to that kind friend that my friendship towards the Most Glorious State is very firm, for had this not been so, I too would have said something foolish ; but what shall I do, or what shall I say ? This much I will say that I remain the friend of the Most Glorious State and that loyalty thereunto abides in my heart, but the Agents of the Most Glorious State in India are endeavouring to bring about its overthrow. Please God it will not be overthrown on my part, though should the initiative (in hostility or provocation) be taken by the Indian Government, I do not know (what might happen): but, please God, (the initiative) will not be on my side, for my friendship towards the Most Glorious State is firmly established as a mountain. I hope from God that it may be the same on the other side, so that we may not become such as our enemies would desire.

Further you wrote " at this time (of writing) is the transition of the year and the renewal of the Christian date into 1898 ; therefore I send my prayers for your welfare." So also your friend (*i.e.* myself) with fullest affection, sends greetings and congratulations, (praying) that, please God, you may pass the New Year in contentment and health, and may ever remember the circumstances of your safe preservation. For the rest, good wishes. May the days of your glory and gladness be continued !

Written on Monday the 15th of the month of Ramazan the Blessed, A.H. 1315, corresponding to the 7th of February, A.D. 1898.

(Signed) AMIR ABDUR RAHMAN ZIYA'U'L-MILLATI WA'D DIN, G.C.S.I. and G.C.B.

To return to the conversations of the Amir. Perhaps the most salient feature both of his bearing and talk was his gift of polished, but mordant sarcasm, sometimes, where his own subjects were concerned, taking the form of sardonic and fearful cruelty. I will relate four illustrations of this terrifying humour which happened during or about the time when I was at Kabul. Of one of these I was a witness. It arose during a conversation about the reputation for cruelty which the Amir had been told that he acquired in England.

A. "What do they say about my system of government in England? Please tell me the exact truth."

C. "They say that Your Highness is a very powerful but a very severe ruler, and that you have repressed with great harshness all hostile movements among your turbulent and rebellious subjects."

A. "But they say more than that. They say that I am a cruel and bloody barbarian, and that I do not know how to govern my people or to give peace and order to my country."

C. "They may criticise Your Highness's methods. I do not presume to offer an opinion as to the results."

A. (a little while later). "Is there a paper in England called the *Standard*?"

C. "Yes."

A. "Is it a good paper? Does it speak the truth?"

C. "Broadly speaking I believe that it does."

A. "Is there a city in your country called Birmingham? Is it a large city? How many inhabitants has it? And is it well governed?"

C. " Yes, it is a very large city and it has over three-quarters of a million of people, and I believe that it prides itself on its municipal administration.

A. " Is there also another city called Manchester and is it like Birmingham ?

C. " It is also a very large city with a very great population and is reported to be well governed."

A. (producing a small piece of newspaper from a fold in his robe). " Here is an extract from the *Standard*, which you say is a good paper and a truthful paper, and which says that in Manchester, which is a great and well governed city, last year there were —— murders and in Birmingham —— murders ; and that many of the murderers were not captured and executed. Is that true ? "

C. " If the *Standard* is quoting official statistics, I have no doubt that it is true."

A. (turning to his courtiers standing in a crowd at the other end of the room). " What is the population of my country ? "

Courtiers. " Your Majesty rules over eight millions of people."[1]

A. " Ah, and how many murders were committed in the whole of Afghanistan last year ? "

Courtiers. " Under Your Majesty's just and benevolent rule, where law and order are perfectly maintained, only six murders were committed in the entire country, and the guilty were caught and condemned to immediate execution."

A. (turning to me). " And this is the country

[1] I believe the real number was nearer 5,000,000.

and these are the people whom I am accused in England of not knowing how to rule, and am taunted with being barbarous and bloody and cruel. Birmingham only has one-tenth of my population and Manchester only one-fifteenth, and they are well-governed cities, and yet —— murders are committed there in the course of a year, and, as the *Standard*, which is a truthful paper, goes on to say, in a great many cases the murderers were neither caught nor executed."

I own that I found it a little difficult to pursue, with dialectical advantage, this strain of conversation. On the other hand, the paucity of crimes of violence in Afghanistan, if it was true (as may well have been the case), was undoubtedly due, neither to respect for law nor to excellence of administration, but to the reign of terror that prevailed and to the horrible tortures inflicted upon persons suspected of murder.

One day there came running into a Durbar being held by the Amir, streaming with sweat, and in the last stage of exhaustion, a Herati Afghan, who claimed to have run all the way from Herat without stopping, in order to tell the Amir that the Russians had crossed the frontier and were advancing into Afghanistan, and he appealed for a reward from his grateful Sovereign.

A. (who did not believe the story for one moment). "Did you see the Russians with your own eyes? And how many were they, and how many guns had they with them, and by what road are they marching ? "

H. " Your Majesty, I saw them with my own eyes, and there were 20,000 men, and they had many guns with them, and they are advancing rapidly upon the Herat—Kabul road ; and they will soon be here, and I ran ahead of them without stopping, for days, in order that I might warn Your Majesty of the danger which is so near."

A. (to his courtiers). "This faithful man had the good fortune to be the first to see the Russian army cross the frontier near to Herat, and he has run all the way here in order to warn us of the danger. How can we sufficiently reward him ? I will tell you. He also shall have the good fortune to be the first to see the Russians arrive, and we will put him in a place where he will have a better chance than any other man. Take him to the highest tree in this place, and tie him to the highest bough of the tree, and let him remain there until the Russians come—and then he shall descend from the tree and bring us the news, and he shall obtain his reward."

And so the faithful Afghan was taken and tied up in the tree ; and there he remained strung up aloft until he perished, as a warning to all other faithful Afghans whose fidelity was pursued at an unwarrantable sacrifice of the truth.

My next story is more genial in its development, though no less sinister in its consequence.

One day there was being counted out in the Durbar Hall before the Amir a great pile of gold

(Bokharan *tillas*, bangles, and other coins), prior to being sent to the mint to be coined. The Afghan ministers were seated on the ground counting the *tillas*, and the Amir was looking on.

As the counting proceeded, a *harem* girl, who was dressed in man's clothes in order to act as a spy, and who was standing in the background, observed that one of the principal Afghan ministers (whom we will call Suleiman Khan) was abstracting some of the gold *tillas*, and had already secreted eighteen in his worsted sock while pretending to scratch his leg. She accordingly wrote a note which she passed to one of the court attendants, who whispered in the ear of the Amir.

The Amir took no notice, and the counting continued, until all the gold had been counted or weighed. Then, following a familiar practice, he apparently forgot all about the tribute, and commenced a line of discursive reflection on an entirely different topic.

A. "A great many people say that the Afghans are not a white-skinned people, and they say, for instance, that their skins are not so white as those of the Russians or the English. Tell me, is this true?"

Courtiers (unanimously). "Your Majesty, there could not be a greater lie. No people have whiter skins than the Afghans, and we are convinced that no Afghan has so white a skin as Your Majesty."

A. (much gratified). "That is true, and to

prove to you that it is the truth, I will show you my own leg!"

Thereupon the Amir—who at one of my audiences did exactly the same thing to demonstrate to me the same proposition, though in a more agreeable context—proceeded to pull his white cotton pantaloons up the calf of his leg, and to expose the colour of his skin, which (I am bound to say) was extraordinarily white, considering that his complexion was somewhat sallow, and that he had a thick growth of black or, at least, dyed hair.

A. (to his courtiers). "There, as you see, is the calf of my leg, and you can note how white is the skin."

Courtiers. "Your Majesty, we never saw so white a leg, and the legs of all Russians and Englishmen are brown in comparison."

A. "That is true. But let me see if my people and my courtiers are as white skinned as myself, or if they are less so. (Then, turning to the throng) Haji Mohammed, let us see your leg! Ali Akbar, let us see yours! (The two legs, exhibiting various degrees of yellowish pigmentation, were then satisfactorily exposed.) Suleiman Khan, let us see your leg!"

S. K. "Oh, Your Majesty, I beg you to excuse me. I have been suffering for some time from a severe ague in the lower part of my legs and I dare not pull down my sock."

A. "It will never do for my servant not to follow the example of his Sovereign, even if his skin, as may be expected, is much less white. Pull down your right sock, Suleiman Khan ! "

S. K. " I implore Your Majesty to be merciful. I am suffering the most acute agony from my ague. I must return at once to my house and have medical treatment. I entreat Your Majesty to have pity upon your faithful servant."

A. " Pull down your sock, Suleiman Khan."

Thereupon the guilty sock had to be pulled down, and the fatal gold Bokharan *tillas* rolled one by one on to the floor.

The Amir, speechless with rage, threw himself back on the divan and for some time did not utter. Then he shouted, " Take him away to the prison, strip him of all his wealth, and let him be no more seen."

(It was told to me at Kabul, though I cannot vouch for it, that this and no less was the fate of the unhappy Suleiman Khan.)

Another incident happened soon after I left Kabul, the victim of which was an officer whom I had seen daily during my visits to the Palace. This was a dapper little figure, the Commandant of the Amir's Bodyguard, who was always in attendance, in a beautiful uniform, in the Durbar Hall. He had, when a boy, been one of the Amir's favourite *batchas* or dancing-boys (an amusement much favoured in Afghanistan), and when his master attained to power, he had been promoted stage by stage until he had reached his present eminence.

This man was believed, or found, to be guilty

of some act of disloyalty or treachery to his Sovereign, and the latter heard of it before the culprit discovered that he had been detected. The scene happened in full Durbar, when one day the Amir told the story of the culprit's guilt, while he stood before him in his brilliant uniform, and thus announced the punishment :

" A *batcha* you began and a *batcha* you shall end. Go back to your house and take off your uniform and put on your petticoats (the dancing-boys in Afghanistan dance in petticoats), and come back and dance here before the Durbar."

The wretched man, a General, and forty years of age, had to do as he was bidden, and to come and dance in the garb of a girl before the assembled Court of Kabul. Can anything more refined in its cruelty be imagined ?

I could tell many more anecdotes, some of them even more grim, of this remarkable man. One of his strangest traits was his unbounded and unconcealed contempt for his own people. Now and then he would burst out in a torrent of denunciation in open Durbar. He would say, " The Afghans are cowards and traitors. For years they have been trying to kill me, but they cannot succeed. Either they have not the courage to shoot or they cannot shoot straight." And then he would turn to the assembled courtiers and shout out : " Is this not true ? Are you not a craven and a miserable people ? " And with one accord, with bowed heads, they would reply : " Your Majesty, we are ! "

One day he was enlarging upon this theme, and he told me two anecdotes in illustration of it. He said that when a few years before he had succeeded in defeating the rebellion of his cousin Ishak Khan, largely owing to the fact that some of the rebel regiments had deserted their leader on the battle-field (he seemed quite pleased at this, as though it showed that he himself had not won by the superior value or courage of his own troops), he had held a review at Mazar-i-Sharif in Northern Afghanistan. His loyal regiments marched past before him, and they included the battalions that had deserted from the enemy. The Amir himself was seated on a chair on a little mound, and the troops were defiling, four abreast immediately below him. As they approached, he noticed that one of his cousin's soldiers held four cartridges between his extended fingers, and, as he drew near, the man suddenly put up his rifle and fired point blank at the Amir from the distance of a few paces.

"And did he hit me?" the Amir shouted. "Not a bit. Just at that moment I leaned aside to speak to one of my Generals and the bullet passed under my armpit and went through the leg of a slave who was standing behind me! Was not that good?" And then he burst into a roar of laughter at this admirable joke, and at the gross ineptitude of the Afghan soldier, who could not kill him even at the distance of a few feet.

Another of his stories illustrating the alleged timidity and cowardice of his people was as follows. He said that when he went to India to see Lord Dufferin, he was accorded a great military review at Rawal Pindi, and that after the review, which was held in pouring rain, he dismounted and entered the Durbar or reception tent prepared for him. There was a big table standing in the tent, and upon it was a miniature cannon. At sight of this object his terrified staff called out to him to hide, because the gun would infallibly go off and kill him.

"What did I say to them?" (he added to me). "I said 'Cowards and fools! You think that this is a real cannon. It is only a machine to cut off the end of a cigar.'"

Great as was his contempt for his people, he did not mean to run any risks or to give them any opportunity of getting rid of him before his time. On one occasion he was suffering severely from toothache, and decided to have the offending tooth taken out. The surgeon prepared chloroform, whereupon the Amir asked how long he would have to remain insensible. "About twenty minutes," said the doctor. "Twenty minutes!" replied the Amir. "I cannot afford to be out of the world for twenty seconds. Take it out without chloroform!"

The Amir was very proud of his gift of ironical retort, and he furnished me with two illustrations of it, which evidently caused him the greatest satisfaction. He told me that on one occasion a Russian officer on the North-west Frontier, somewhere near Maimena or Andkui, had written him a letter to say that he proposed to exercise a force of 500 men, both cavalry and infantry, near the frontier, and he hoped that the Amir would not be alarmed, or regard this as a hostile proceeding. "Certainly not," replied the Amir, "he had no objection at all, the more so as he proposed to exercise a force of 5000 Afghan troops opposite the same spot." No more was heard of the Russian proposal.

The second occasion occurred in the course of one of our conversations. I had produced one day an extract from an English newspaper which spoke of a new British gun that could throw a projectile for a distance of 15 miles. The Amir showed neither curiosity nor surprise. But a little later he turned to the Commandant of his Artillery, who was in the Durbar room, and asked him in a casual way what was the range of the new gun which he, the Amir, had just made and sent to Herat. "Fifty miles," replied the Commandant, without turning a hair.

The Amir enjoyed very much talking about personal and domestic details, and sometimes would tell me stories about the private lives of his courtiers, who had to stand by looking rather sheepish while they heard the secrets of the *harem* revealed to a stranger in their presence. One day I was suffering from toothache and had a swollen face. This gave him an excuse for a dissertation on dentistry of which, as of every science, he claimed to be a master. Four things, he said, were bad for the teeth—meat, sweets, cold water, and wine. He had suffered very much from bad teeth himself, particularly when he was in Samarkand, and since the age of forty he had worn entirely false teeth. These had been put in by a dentist from Simla, and from time to time he would take out the plate while speaking. In Samarkand, however, he could put no trust in the Russian physicians, because thirty-two of his own followers fell ill and went to the Russian hospital, where every one of them died. Accordingly he studied medicine, including dentistry, himself, and ever afterwards treated both himself and his followers.

He was also much interested in the marriage laws and customs of different countries. Monogamy, as practised in England and Europe, he held to be a most pernicious system. Firstly, there being, as a rule, more women than men in European countries, monogamy meant that a large number of them remained unmarried, which was a cruel and unnatural fate. Secondly, if a man was only allowed by law to take one wife the country swarmed with "children of God," *i.e.* illegitimate offspring. In fact, the British Colonies, Australia, Canada, etc., were maintained as places to which to send these progeny, for whom there was no room at home. However, it was all due to our damp climate. Reared in perpetual water and mud, the English people were like rice, while the Eastern peoples, living on a dry soil, resembled wheat.

Englishmen accordingly were not strong and

could not possibly manage four wives, like the Moslems. As to the late period of many English marriages (instancing my own), that was due to the fact that there were so many beautiful women in England, that a man was never satisfied, and always thought that by waiting he would get something better still.

I might, from the well-charged contents of my note-book, carefully made up every night during my stay in Afghanistan, tell many more tales of my unusual and astonishing host. Perhaps some day I may narrate some of my dealings with him, when, instead of being a visitor at his capital, I became the head of the Government of India and was called upon to correspond with him in an official capacity. He was a very difficult person to handle and a very formidable opponent to cross.

In my numerous interviews I flatter myself that I succeeded in winning the Amir's confidence, and he certainly spoke very kindly of me in his Autobiography, published by his Secretary, who acted as interpreter at our meetings. Upon me he left a profound, even if a somewhat chequered impression. Before I left Kabul he had made and presented to me with his own hand a gold star, inlaid with rubies and diamonds, and engraved with a Persian inscription. It is reproduced on the outer cover of this book.

Seven years later, *i.e.* in October 1901, Amir Abdur Rahman Khan died at the comparatively early age of fifty-seven, though he was commonly believed to be much older. On that occasion the following Proclamation, with which I close my chapter, was issued by his son, Habibulla, who succeeded him :

> The blessed corpse of the august and potent king, according to his will, was carried to the Royal Taralistan with great pomp and honour, and he was interred in the ground, and placed in a place where is the real and ultimate abode of man. That august and potent monarch, that King of pleasing and praiseworthy manners, expired and sank in the depth of the kindness of God. May his abode be in Heaven !

In summing up his character, I do not think that I can find a better description than the final verdict which was passed by the Roman biographer upon the Emperor Hadrian, the studied antitheses of which have a peculiar appropriateness in the case of the Afghan Amir: "*Severus laetus, comis gravis, lascivus cunctator, tenax liberalis, simulator simplex, saevus clemens, et semper in omnibus varius.*"[1]

[1] Spartianus, *De Vita Hadriani*, 14. 11.

THE VOICE OF MEMNON

THE VOICE OF MEMNON

As morn from Memnon drew
Rivers of melody.
TENNYSON, " The Palace of Art."

LONG before the *dahabeah* enters upon the great sweep of river that skirts the pylons of Karnak, the traveller has strained his eye to discover whatever traces may be visible of the once mighty city, the metropolis of an empire, and the mausoleum of its kings—Egyptian Thebes. How much or how little will be remaining of the hundred temple-towers, the shrines and statues and obelisks without number, the avenues of sphinxes, the princely palaces and fortresses, the sculptured courts and colonnades ? On the eastern bank the ruins of Karnak stand up in solid and monumental grandeur ; but on the western the eye wanders over the level expanse that stretches to the foot of the hills, wherein lie the rifled secrets of the Tombs of the Kings, without at first encountering more than a few confused heaps or mounds, scarcely distinguishable from the sand which surrounds them. Presently, however, our gaze is arrested by two dark objects, situated at a greater distance from the river than the ruins already observed, and differing from them both in appearance and elevation. They seem to rise up like twin martellos or watch-towers from the desert, and to stand apart in melancholy solitude. The spectacle is strange and puzzling, and for a moment our imagination is at a loss for a key. Suddenly it flashes upon us that the two mysterious objects which have excited our astonishment are none other than the famed Colossi of Thebes—the Vocal Memnon and his mute companion.

A walk of a little over a mile from the river bank brings us to the base of the statues. As we approach them through the allotments of clover and maize, they loom up higher and higher, until, as we stand at their feet, their stupendous shapes almost exclude the sky. Placed on the very fringe of the cultivated soil, where the furthermost Nile deposit is cut short by the first wave of sand, they stand between the dead and the living, and seem like two grim sentinels stationed to guard the entrance to the desert behind. At other times, when the inundations are abroad and the surrounding country is turned into a sea, they tower with an even greater solemnity above the waters. The Nile stretches in an unbroken level from its own channel till it washes their pedestals and laves their massive feet. How vividly do we realise the prophet's description of "populous No, that was situate among the rivers, that had the waters round about it, whose rampart was the sea, and her wall was from the sea."[1] It is under these conditions and at sunset that the pair should be seen. Then, as the glowing disc sinks behind the hills that enclose the Valley of the Tombs of the Kings and the dwindling radiance of the heavens is repeated in the mirror of the flood, they brood like huge black spectres over the darkening scene. Keats must have heard of this moment when he wrote in " Hyperion ":

> . . . . a vast shade
> In midst of his own brightness, like the bulk
> Of Memnon's image at the set of sun
> To one who travels from the dusking East.

Blacker and huger each moment the figures become, their monstrous shadows thrown forward upon the lake, till at length even the afterglow has faded, and, still as death themselves, they fitly preside over the deadly stillness of the southern night.

A closer inspection enhances rather than detracts from the majesty of the images. They are planted 54 feet apart, and face towards the south-south-east. Each represents a colossal male figure seated upon a throne, which is itself supported by a pedestal. Though the faces of both have been hacked out of all human resemblance, yet the shapeless blocks of stone seem endowed with an indefinable sentience, as if, though bereft even of the similitude of human

[1] Nahum iii. 8.

features, their sight could pierce the endless vistas of space and time. The arms are attached to the sides and recline upon the stalwart thighs; the hands, with fingers outstretched and turned slightly inwards, are placidly disposed upon the knees; the legs, like two mighty columns, rest against the throne and lift up the lap of the Colossus to the sky. The whole attitude is that of a giant who has sat himself down to take his repose after the fatigues and turmoil of successful war. The height of the figures is 51 feet without, and 64 feet with, the pedestal; but of the latter, 6 feet are now buried beneath the accumulations left by the Nile. Before these had been formed, and when the pedestals were bare to their foundations, when, further, each head was framed in the full spreading wig of the Egyptian Pharaohs, and when the faces and bodies were intact, the impression produced must have been such as could be felt rather than described. Between the legs of each statue are small figures of the wife and mother of the King; a figure of his daughter stands by his knee. On the two sides of the two thrones are deeply incised pictures of the Nile gods of Upper and Lower Egypt, who are plaiting together the stems of the papyrus and the lotus, the emblems of the two provinces.

Every one knows that these statues are effigies of the same King—Amunoph, or Amenhotep, or Amenophis III., one of the most famous Sovereigns and conquerors of the Eighteenth Dynasty, who reigned at Thebes about 1500 B.C., and was the husband of Queen Thiy and father of the heretic King Amenophis IV., or Akhnaton, one of whose daughters married the recently discovered Tutankhamen. The cartouches on the backs of both figures contain the King's name. Known, too, is the name of the architect—the same as that of the royal master who delighted to do him honour—Amenhotep, son of Hapu, whose own statue, richly adorned with inscriptions, is in the Boulak collection at Cairo. Thereon we read :

> For my lord the King was created the monument of sandstone. Thus did I according to that which seemed best in my own eyes, causing to be made two images of a noble hard stone in his likeness in this his great building, which is like unto heaven. . . . After this manner made I perfect the King's images, wonderful for their breadth, lofty in their height, the stature whereof made the gate-tower to look small. Forty cubits was their measure.[1] In the glorious sandstone mountain wrought I them, on this side and on that, on the east side and on the west. Furthermore, I caused to be built eight ships, whereon they were carried up and set in his lofty building. It will last as long as the heaven endureth.

From this interesting record we gather that

[1] Taking the cubit to be the ordinary cubit of 18¼ inches, this corresponds fairly well with the actual height given above. Others, reckoning by the royal cubit of 20⅔ inches, have made the original height 69 feet, and accounted for the difference by supposing that the heads were once surmounted with the *pshent* or duplicate crown of Upper and Lower Egypt, so frequent a feature in colossal representations of the Pharaohs. It is probable, however, that these figures were without the *pshent*, both because no trace of it is observable upon the head of the southern or unrepaired Colossus, and because there were found in the immediate vicinity, and are now to be seen in the British Museum, two statues in black granite of the same Amunoph—precise facsimiles on a smaller scale of the Colossi—both of which are wigged but uncrowned.

the material of the Colossi was derived from quarries lower down the Nile, probably from those in the hills of Toora above Cairo, that they were towed or floated up the river on great barges, and were then erected before the outermost pylons of the magnificent temple which Amunoph III., in addition to his works at Luxor and Karnak, was building as a memorial of himself in the western quarter of Thebes. The famous sculpture of the Colossus on a Sledge in the grotto of Ed-Dayr (so happily adapted by the late Sir E. Poynter, P.R.A., to the subject of one of his best known pictures) will give us some idea of the arduous passage of these mighty blocks, estimated as weighing 1200 tons apiece, from the river bank to their final resting-place before the pylons of the royal temple. The latter, which has perished utterly, has itself been described as "probably the greatest work of art ever wrought in Egypt."

The most superficial observation discloses several points of difference between the pair. The southernmost Colossus is a monolith, and has evidently suffered less from the hand of the destroyer than its companion, though its face and breast are mutilated beyond all recognition. The more northern statue resembles the other from the ground up to its waist, being composed of the same dark breccia or composite stone; but its upper parts consist of five tiers of a lighter sandstone, roughly hewn, and built up one on the top of the other, in rude semblance of arms and chest and head. The thrones and pedestals of both are adorned with deeply incised figures and hieroglyphics; but the feet of the northernmost are covered with a network of inscriptions in Greek and Latin, extending over the instep and reaching half-way up the leg. This latter is the celebrated Vocal Memnon. Its history and interpretation are the problems which I am about to discuss.

The first question to settle is: When did the mutilation of the one and the shattering of the other (thus necessitating its repair with a different material) take place, and to what agencies are they to be ascribed? Writers have commonly devoted their entire attention to the vicissitudes of the Memnon, without turning a thought to the damage inflicted on the Amunoph. But the two cases must be considered together, and may be found to throw a reciprocal light upon each other; for though a catastrophe arising from natural causes might have overtaken the one while sparing the other, yet the hand of a human destroyer would not be likely to have purposely exercised a similar discrimination.

Of the authorities on the subject to whom weight must be attached, Strabo, who visited Thebes about 20 B.C., and found the northernmost statue in ruins, the upper half having been hurled to the ground, says that the people of the district attributed the downfall to an earthquake.[1] Pausanias, on the other hand, travelling

[1] Strabo, *Geog.* xvii. 816.

in Egypt 150 years later, mentions a local report that the statue, clearly not yet repaired, was one which Cambyses had shivered[1]—a belief which is countenanced by several of the inscriptions upon its feet.[2] The researches of the French writer, M. Letronne, whose industry poured a flood of light upon the entire subject,[3] showed that an earthquake did take place in Egypt in 27 B.C., shortly before Strabo's visit, and that it wrought terrible havoc among the edifices of Thebes. It has accordingly been accepted—and the conclusion is one which it is impossible to resist—that the destruction of the Memnon occurred at that time and from those causes. Hence has ensued the rejection of the idea that Cambyses had any hand in the work of demolition, which has been set down as the indolent fabrication of a later age.

But here the experience of the fellow Colossus may well be invoked. In its case the mutilation is obvious, but only partial, and is such as could not conceivably have been effected by a convulsion of nature or by the mere lapse of time. May we not therefore reconcile the two explanations, and believe (1) that Cambyses, the great iconoclast, the assassin of the sacred bull, the defiler of temples and tombs, spent his frantic but feeble rage upon these as upon other images,

[1] Pausanias, *Attica*, i. 42-3.

[2] *Corpus Inscriptionum Graecarum* (ed. Boeckh), 4730, 4741, 4745, 4749, 4756.

[3] *Œuvres Choisies de A. J. Letronne*, édites par E. Fagnan, vol. ii., Paris, 1881.

hacking at their features and fronts, and perhaps, by so doing, weakening the stability of the Memnon; but (2) that the latter owed the ruin of its upper half to the earthquake of 27 B.C.? In this way we account for both phenomena, viz. the intentional mutilation of the Amunoph and the undesigned overthrow of the Memnon.

But how, it may be asked, did it come about that the name Memnon was ever applied to the northern statue? The utmost ingenuity has been expended upon the solution of this problem. Each school has been struck by the remarkable confirmation afforded of its own pet hypothesis. Those who explain all mythology by the simple key of the Solar Myth—an intrepid and romantic band—have fastened with avidity upon the evidence of sun-worship at Thebes and other places where the name of Memnon is found, and have seen in the reputed image of the son of Eos an effigy of the sun-god himself. Others have supposed that the speaking statue was called Memnon from the prophetic qualities attributed in Oriental mythology to the head of that hero. The foolish suggestion has even been made that the name was given because the sounds heard resembled the syllables *mem-non*. A more defensible theory is that Memnon, whom most classical writers connect with Ethiopia, is a figure that might not unnaturally be found in the Egyptian pantheon; and to this idea the title Memnonium, commonly given to the western quarter of Thebes and to the temples of Abydus, lower down the river, has been supposed to lend support.

In reality, however, Memnon had probably nothing to do with Egypt at all. From a comparison of the various authorities by whom the legend is mentioned, Memnon, if he ever existed, must have been an Asiatic prince, who came from Susa, and led a force of Asiatic Ethiopians to the relief of Troy, where he was slain, according to most accounts, by Achilles. How, then, are we to account for the presence of the name in more than one place in Egypt, and for the popular tradition which associated him with that country ?

No evidence exists that any such connection was suspected till the later period of the Greek settlement in Egypt, when it appears in the Greek papyri of Thebes, and in the pages of Strabo and Diodorus Siculus. There can be little doubt, therefore, that it owed its origin to the omnivorous credulity of the Greek immigrants. Eager to find, wherever they went, a confirmation of the Homeric legend, they fell easy victims to the fictitious identification of famous names. Sir Gardner Wilkinson has pointed out that Miamun was a title of Rameses II., whose great palace-temple at Thebes, now usually called the Rameseum, is probably the Memnonium of Strabo, and whose other temple at Abydus is called Memnonium by the same writer. The name *Mennu* appears also in the Egyptian vocabulary applied to the memorial temples erected by the kings in the Necropolis of Thebes. Miamun or

Mennu might easily be converted into Memnon, and we should thus account for the name both at Thebes and Abydus. It would be transferred with equal plausibility to the statue of Amunoph, and with even greater force if the latter had already developed its vocal powers. For not only would Amenophis find an obvious Hellenic equivalent in Memnon, but the image speaking at sunrise would irresistibly suggest the lamented hero plaintively addressing his mother, the Dawn.

We may therefore conjecture that the title of Memnon had in this case no more abstruse origin than an accidental similarity of names, greedily snatched at by Hellenic pilgrims and enhanced by the supposed corroboration of a popular mythology supplied by the vocal portent. That the delusion was not shared by the natives is expressly stated by Pausanias, who says that the Thebans would not admit that the statue was of Memnon, but ascribed it (as we have seen, with perfect justice) to one of their own countrymen, Phamenoph. Two Greek inscriptions upon the left leg repeat the same conviction.[1]

And now as to the vocal powers so mysteriously acquired by the northern Colossus, which made it one of the wonders of the ancient world. Already we have seen that this statue, having probably suffered injury at the hands of Cambyses, was almost certainly overthrown, the lower part alone being left standing, by an earthquake in 27 B.C. There is no mention of any sounds

[1] *Corp. Insc. Graec.* 4727, 4731.

before the latter year.[1] It is a significant fact that Strabo, the first recorded visitor after the earthquake, is also the first who relates the phenomenon. He says that a noise as of a slight blow was believed to issue at sunrise from the upright portion of the figure. He heard it himself, but, he adds, was unable to say whether it proceeded from the Colossus or from the pedestal, or from the people standing round, though he was in the last degree unwilling to believe that such a sound could possibly emanate from the stone.

From this time forward, a consistent series of witnesses testify to the continuance of the miracle. Tacitus tells us that Germanicus, who visited Egypt in A.D. 19 on his way to Syria, inspected the ruins of Egypt, and bestowed particular attention upon the speaking image,[2] though his enthusiastic language may be held to reflect the popular beliefs of his own day rather than of those whose history he was writing. Certain it is, however, that from the reign of Nero onwards the Memnon acquired a wider renown. Then for the first time we find the favoured pilgrim recording his gratitude after the most approved modern fashion, in a Greek or Latin inscription, sometimes metrical, sometimes the reverse, upon the legs of the statue. These compositions are

[1] Except in inscriptions of the second century A.D. (*Corp. Insc. Graec.* 4730, 4741), which embody the legendary beliefs of the day. Writers of a much later date reproduce the same fancy, viz. that prior to the sacrilege of Cambyses Memnon had uttered articulate sounds.

[2] *Annales*, ii. 61.

of varying merit according to the taste or ability of their authors. One of the best is a Greek stanza carved upon the front of the pedestal by one Asclepiodotus, imperial procurator, and a man of culture, which may be literally rendered thus:

> O sea-born Thetis, know that when
> His mother's torch is lit
> Memnon awakes and cries aloud,
> Fired by the warmth of it.
> Beneath the brow of Libyan heights,
> Where Nilus cuts in twain
> The city of the glorious gates,
> He wakes to life again.
> Yet thine Achilles, who in fight
> Ne'er slaked his savage joy,
> On the Thessalian plains is mute,
> Is mute on those of Troy.[1]

Juvenal, who is believed to have been in Egypt in the reign of Domitian, is the next visitor of importance. His words—

> Dimidio magicae resonant ubi Memnone chordae,[2]

leave no doubt that the figure when seen by him was still in the same truncated condition. Lucian, who was, and Pliny, who was not, an eyewitness,[3] both mention the phenomenon. But the zenith of celebrity appears to have been reached in the time of Hadrian. That indefatigable sightseer, with his wife Sabina and a large suite, several times visited and heard Memnon; and so great an impetus was given to the expedition by the

[1] *Corp. Insc. Graec.* 4747. [2] Juvenal, *Sat.* xv. 5.
[3] Pliny, *Nat. Hist.* xxxvi. 58.

imperial patronage, that we find nearly thirty inscriptions dating from this reign. Pausanias, also a visitor about this time and an auditor of the miracle, confirms the description of Juvenal, and adds the interesting detail that the noise resembled the snapping of a harp-string. Inscriptions of a later date prove that the sound from the shattered base continued to be heard till the reign of Septimius Severus. The year 196 marks the last recorded instance.[1] From that date till the present time the hero has remained speechless, and

> Memnon's lyre has lost the chord
> That breathed the mystic tone.

One fact has been made abundantly clear by this narrative, viz. that the " rivers of melody " which, in Lord Tennyson's somewhat hyperbolic phrase, " morn from Memnon drew," flowed only while the upper half of Memnon did not exist. We may therefore give the *congé* at once to all the pretty stories of Aurora kissing her son upon the lips and the latter uttering an articulate reply, which have captivated the not too critical fancy of the poets or of prose writers claiming a more than poetical licence. The only two authors of anything like contemporary date who give currency to the fiction are Lucian and Philostratus. The former puts the conceit into the mouth of a professional liar in one of his Dialogues [2] with the

[1] *Corpus Inscriptionum Latinarum* (ed. Mommsen), 51.
[2] Lucian, *Philopseudes*, c. 33 ; cf. *Toxaris seu Amicitia*, c. 27.

manifest object of discrediting the ridiculous tale. Philostratus, relating the travels of Apollonius of Tyana in the first century A.D., quotes the account of a certain Damis, who accompanied the pagan mystic to Thebes. Damis describes the statue as that of a young and beardless man,[1] whose eyes sparkled, and whose lips spoke as they faced the rising sun, and who appeared to bend forward in an attitude of salutation.[2] As the evidence summarised above proves that Memnon was at the time of Apollonius's visit only a sundered and headless block of stone, the philosopher is not to be congratulated upon these practical testimonials to the veracity of his Boswell.

From the fact that the last attested instance of Memnon having spoken was in the reign of Septimius Severus, it may be inferred that something must then have happened to suspend the continuance of the sound. We know from his biographer[3] that the Emperor himself visited the statue—the last of the Caesars who did so—though, as no inscription is found containing his name, it is almost certain that he was unsuccessful. These circumstances supplied M. Letronne with the very clue which was lacking to explain the restoration described in an earlier paragraph of this article. His reasoning may be held to

[1] Both Colossi were almost certainly bearded; *vide* the statues of Amunoph III. in the British Museum.

[2] Philostratus, *De Vita Apollonei Tyanei*, lib. vi. c. 3, 4; cf. *Heroica*, c. 4, and *Imagines*, lib. i. c. 7.

[3] Spartianus, c. 17.

have established that the five tiers of sandstone were added by Severus in the desire to propitiate the mute divinity and to reawaken his full powers of utterance. The futility of these pious intentions, and the coincidence of the repair of Memnon with the commencement of his long silence, will have an important bearing upon the discussion that will presently follow.

The later history of Memnon may be dismissed almost in a sentence. From the beginning of the third century A.D. a cloud of impenetrable darkness settles down upon his fame and fortunes, and no suspicion was entertained that the vocal image still existed at Thebes till it was re-identified between 1737 and 1739 by Pococke, who copied some of the inscriptions and published in his travels a description and drawing of the statue. Norden, the Danish traveller, had visited the spot in December 1737; but from the report which he sent to the Royal Society in London, in 1741, it does not appear even to have crossed his mind that the northern Colossus was that of Memnon, though he copied a few of the inscriptions and made a drawing of the lower half of the figure. From that time onwards the investigation proceeded with ever-increasing interest, notwithstanding that the natives, till prompted by foreign tourists, persisted in describing the images as those of a male and female, whom they called Shaama and Taama, thus unconsciously, even in their ignorance, preserving the original and authentic name.

There remain two points of considerable interest before I pass to the explanation of the so-called miracle. These are, the nature of the sound and the conditions under which it was heard. I have shown that it was described by Strabo as the kind of noise resulting from a slight blow, and by Pausanias as resembling the snapping of a harp-string. The former idea is reproduced in one of the inscriptions,[1] where it is spoken of as a high-pitched note, and is compared to the sound produced by striking brass; the latter is confirmed by the language of Juvenal (*magicae chordae*) and by the word *crepare* employed by Pliny. We may conclude that it was a clear, somewhat metallic, sound, varying in pitch and intensity—sometimes a shrill, sharp, twanging note, at others a fainter and more ringing vibration.

Of the eighty-seven legible, or partially legible, Greek and Latin inscriptions upon the legs which have been collected by the indefatigable assiduity of a succession of scholars, thirty-three contain a reference to the hour or time of day at which the phenomenon was heard. On eighteen occasions it is mentioned as having happened at the first hour, or sunrise, on eight between the first and second hours, on six at the second hour, on two between the second and third hours, on three at the third hour. Two alone date the miracle before sunrise. Nine of the writers, including the Empress Sabina, testify to having heard it

[1] *Corp. Insc. Graec.* 4725.

twice (sometimes, but rarely, on the same morning); four of them, including Hadrian, three times; two of them four times; and one, a soldier of the Third Legion, no less than twelve times. Two, of whom Sabina is one, relate that they failed on their first visit, but were more fortunate on the second. Another was not successful till the third time of asking. Septimius Severus, as we have seen, never heard it at all. Of those inscriptions, for the most part in Latin, which specify the month, twelve refer to February and eleven to March. These were by far the most propitious months, perhaps because they may have been then, as now, the favourite season for ascending the Nile. These figures, which are not without a distinct bearing upon the issue, tend to show that the voice of Memnon was most commonly heard at sunrise, as soon indeed as the rays fell upon the statue (cf. Strabo, Tacitus, Pliny, Pausanias and Lucian), but on some occasions not till a later period of the morning. The sound was far from uniform in its occurrence, as the small number of inscriptions, out of the thousands of persons who must have visited Memnon, would alone suffice to show; but those who repeated the experiment might expect in the long run to be rewarded for their perseverance.

We are now in possession of all the facts available to assist us in the elucidation of the prodigy. Two alone of the many hypotheses that have been put forward are worth considering, or present any features of probability. A multitude of wild conjectures, based on imagination, but claiming a pseudo-scientific or mechanical interest, crumble away as soon as they are touched by the merciless finger of fact. There remain the rival theories that the voice of Memnon was a fraud practised by the Egyptian priesthood, and that it was a natural phenomenon to be explained by physical causes.

The former theory was very popular a century ago, and found eager exponents among French writers and *savants*, who, during and after the Napoleonic expedition, took an absorbing interest in the monuments of Egypt. One of these, M. Langlès, wrote a special dissertation on the subject. Another, M. Salverte, the author of a work on occult science, even knew how the sound was produced. Between the lips or somewhere in the figure of the statue was a lens or mirror on which the rays of the morning sun, being condensed, were applied to the expansion of metallic levers, which set in motion a series of hammers, which in their turn struck the granite!

The theory of sacerdotal fraud found, however, its most powerful and plausible exponent in the English antiquarian Sir Gardner Wilkinson, in a paper read before the Royal Society of Literature in London, on December 18, 1833, in his *Topography of Thebes* (1835), in his *Modern Egypt and Thebes* (1843) and in the earlier editions of Murray's *Handbook to Egypt*; and was then repeated by a long sequence of writers. So eminent an authority may claim to state his own case, and accordingly the following passage is reproduced from the third of the above works (vol. ii. 158-164), which may be taken to represent the matured opinions of the author:

> The priests, who no doubt contrived the sound of the statue, were artful enough to allow the supposed deity to fail occasionally in his accustomed habit; and some were consequently disappointed on their first visit, and obliged to return another morning to satisfy their curiosity. . . . In the lap of the statue is a stone, which, on being struck, emits a metallic sound, that might still be made use of to deceive a visitor who was predisposed to believe its powers; and from its position, and the squared place cut in the block behind—as if to admit a person who might thus lie concealed from the most scrutinous observer in the plain below—it seems to have been used after the restoration of the statue; another similar recess exists beneath the present site of this stone, which might have been intended for the same purpose when the statue was in its mutilated state.

Wilkinson then related that in the year 1824, when he first tested the musical stone, the nature of the sound did not appear to tally with the account given by ancient authors; but that in 1830, having noticed the phrase "as of smitten brass" in one of the inscriptions, he again ascended, struck the block with a small hammer, and received from a knot of peasants whom he had posted below the gratifying response, "*Ente betídrob e'nahás*," "You are striking brass." This "convinced him that the sound was the same that deceived the Romans, and led Strabo to observe that it appeared to him as the effect of a slight blow." And, he triumphantly concluded, " that it was a deception there can be little doubt. The fact of the Emperor Hadrian hearing it thrice looks very suspicious, and a natural phenomenon would not have been so complimentary to the Emperor when it sounded only once for ordinary mortals."

It will be observed that Wilkinson, in the above passage, started with the assumption, which he clearly expected to carry conviction to every mind, that the priests were at the bottom of the pretended miracle, and then proceeded to fit into it, first, the recorded conditions under which the phenomenon occurred, and, secondly, his own local experiments and observations. As regards the assumption, though somewhat defiantly stated, it is one with which *per se* I am not disposed to quarrel. No one acquainted with history is likely to be overburdened with confidence in the integrity of the Egyptian hierophants or to feel any peculiar temptation to take up the cudgels on their behalf. We may admit that these holy persons would have been quite capable of practising the deception had it been feasible or had it in the remotest degree served their purpose. Talking trees and speaking stones are not unknown features in sacerdotal annals. The duplicity of the priests is a natural phenomenon more familiar to the public mind than many of the best-attested phenomena of Nature herself. It is not, however, on these grounds that Wilkinson won credence for his theory and succeeded in foisting it upon the popular acceptance; it was because he supplied, or appeared to supply, evidence of a confirmatory character from his personal inspection of the statue. This testimony has never been examined, and therefore, in the opinion of the majority, has never been shaken; whilst by those who have taken the opposite side in the argument it has been tacitly ignored. Indeed, I incline to the opinion that of all those who have written about the Memnon Wilkinson is the only one who really made the ascent. If, however, his account of its existing condition, and the inferences which he is thereby led to draw, can be shown to be incorrect, any adventitious importance accruing to the theory of imposture from the evidence of the figure will disappear, and the case will have to be judged upon the facts and phenomena recorded at an earlier stage of this discussion.

Having stated that there is a sonorous lump of stone in the lap of the image, Wilkinson proceeded to assert that there is a squared place cut in the block behind it, which might—and in his opinion, no doubt, did—conceal a hidden juggler "after the restoration of the statue." As it is well established that Memnon never spoke after his restoration—*i.e.* after the superimposed ranges of sandstone, in one of which this hollow space is said to exist, were added to the broken base—it is immaterial to the question whether such a cavity exists or not. At the most it would indicate, if true, that deception may have been attempted—and, if so, unsuccessfully attempted—after the repair—a supposition in itself damaging to the hypothesis of original fraud, inasmuch as it suggests an endeavour to reproduce by artifice what had previously arisen from other causes. Wilkinson was evidently aware of this initial flaw in his contention. Accordingly, he proceeded to remedy it by stating that there is another recess, equally favourable to the designs of an impostor, situated not behind, but beneath, the sonorous stone, and in the base, from which tradition, without a responsible dissentient voice, declares that the sound emanated. He was thus *ad utrumque paratus.* If a suspicious cavity is wanted in the broken Memnon, it is there : if in the repaired Memnon, it is there also. Memnon, in fact, cannot escape with untarnished reputation; he can never have spoken without, like the Trojan horse, harbouring a secret of treachery in his interior.

Unfortunately for Wilkinson, his statements in both cases are invalidated by an examination of the Colossus, and have only been accepted by those who have never put themselves to the trouble of climbing on to the lap of the giant. A ladder—the resource of Lilliput in a similar emergency—and a footrule are all that is required. An investigation conducted with the aid of these appliances removed all doubt from my mind and revealed the following as the actual condition of the Memnon.

The original block is split downwards from the waist or starting-point of the Roman masonry by a great lateral fissure, converging towards the bottom, and obviously due to natural causes, among which we can refer it to none other than the famous earthquake of 27 B.C. It extends from side to side of the base, and is visible from below, whence it was noticed by Pococke. This great natural cleft is the earlier artificial recess of Wilkinson. Towards the top, where the new tiers begin, the crack widens to a width' which varies from 17 to 31 inches, at the front of it being the lap of the old statue, and at the back the bottommost range of the later addition. Here, in the jaws of the rent, a block of sandstone—17½ inches long from right to left, by 22½ inches broad from front to back, and 10 inches deep, and of corresponding colour and material to the Roman superstructure—is caught and suspended. Its sonorous qualities when struck do not differ from those of any other stone in a similar position, and are apparently due to its detached and pendent situation. In any case, we can hardly accept as a final court of appeal the organs, however sensitive, of the Theban fellahin. Behind and above this stone is a gap in the masonry of the restoration, from which it has either fallen or been pulled out, the block immediately above the gap having sunk down into it to a depth of several inches, and in so doing having broken away from the Roman cement still clinging to the under surface of the block next again above.

If the block immediately above the gap were hoisted up to its original level, and the fallen stone extricated from its present resting-place, it would fit into the space which it once occupied and the gap would disappear. This fallen stone is the musical stone,[1] and this gap is the second artificial recess of Wilkinson!

We are now in a position to estimate the verification of the latter at its proper value. For, summing up, we see that neither before nor after the restoration was any recess artificially hewn in the figure, nor any sonorous stone intentionally deposited in the lap of Memnon. The lower cavity was the result of a natural convulsion; the upper cavity has been produced, we know not when, by the very causes—probably the mischievousness or destructiveness of the Arabs—which also detached the so-called musical stone from its surroundings, and dropped it into the mouth of the crack below. Accordingly, the case in these respects entirely collapses.

So much for the direct evidence supplied by the statue, which, instead of positively countenancing the theory of fraud, negatively contradicts it. The indirect evidence derived from the recorded facts is more conclusive still, and on the

[1] The indecision of Wilkinson himself is shown by the fact that whereas the sounding stone in his later works is this block, in his letter to the Royal Society (*Transactions*, vol. ii. pp. 451-6) it is identified with the stone in the breast, immediately above the gap. We may conjecture that the superior sonorous qualities of the suspended stone ousted the earlier claimant from its proud position.

very points where Wilkinson claimed its support is in reality fatal to his contention. He argued that the inconstancy of the phenomenon, its scant respect for ordinary mortals, and its partiality to the Emperor Hadrian were proofs of a deep and calculating deception. But he conveniently forgot that if Memnon spoke three times for the Emperor, he declined to utter at all upon the first visit of the Empress, who, as we hear from an inscription composed by one of her ladies-in-waiting, was inflamed with anger at the affront;[1] that he also sounded thrice for three other persons, none of them of imperial rank;[2] that two visitors, a simple citizen of Caesarea Philippi, in Galilee, and an unknown Roman were four times honoured;[3] and that whilst his most lavish favours were conferred upon an untitled soldier of the Third Legion, twelve times successful,[4] his crowning rebuff was reserved for another Emperor—Septimius Severus. There is nothing, indeed, to show that persons of high rank were more fortunate than their inferiors in the social scale, though it is only natural that the successes of the rich and cultured should have been commemorated rather than those of the mass, who in many cases can have had neither the interest nor the taste to command an inscription. The irregularity of the portent will be seen to have a very different meaning. Had

[1] *Corp. Insc. Graec.* 4729.
[2] *Ibid.* 4721-2; *Corp. Insc. Latin.* 45, 54.
[3] *Corp. Insc. Graec.* 4750; *Corp. Insc. Latin.* 40.
[4] *Ibid.* 34.

the priests been responsible, we may be sure that Memnon would have spoken with far greater consistency and with a much superior discrimination.

In addition to the points already mentioned there are a number of others, ignored by Wilkinson, but collectively forming a body of circumstantial evidence, the significance of which cannot be overlooked. If the priests manufactured the sound, how are we to account for the recorded variations in its quality and pitch? Why should the impact of a hammer or similar instrument upon a lump of stone sound on one occasion like a snapping harp-string, on another like ringing brass? Why, again, should the voice on some days have been heard at sunrise, and on others not till two or even three hours later in the morning? Such a delay might be inconvenient to the visitors, and would be extremely disagreeable to the incarcerated musician. Are we to believe that for two hundred and twenty years a succession of athletic priests climbed up without ladder or visible appliance under cover of the night, and climbed down on the ensuing day, in both cases defying and defeating all observation? Memnon could not, like the famous chess-playing automaton forty years ago at the Crystal Palace, be occasionally withdrawn from view while the operator effected his ingress or egress. He sat in staring isolation upon the open plain, whence he could be seen for miles, where sceptical spirits must have kept watch through many a night and day, and where we are justified in declaring that such a design would have been quite incapable of execution. Finally, how comes it that for one thousand five hundred years after the erection of the Colossi, and long after the Greeks under the Ptolemaic Dynasty had entered Egypt, not a breath was whispered of the marvel; whilst two hundred and twenty years later, after an interval, as we are required to believe, but as was never even insinuated at the time, of highly successful charlatanry, the jugglers suddenly lost their cunning, and the miracle ceased at the very moment when such a witness to paganism would have been of inestimable value as a set-off to the growing popularity of the Christian faith? Did the Egyptian priesthood enter upon an orbit of deceit twenty years B.C., and complete it two hundred years A.D., being, as it were, in apogee in the reign of Hadrian? Above all, can we possibly mistake the import of the fact that the period during which Memnon spoke was precisely co-extensive with the period during which he remained shattered and unrepaired—a condition which presented no further, but, on the contrary, considerably less, advantages to the artifice than when he was whole?

This also must be borne in mind, that, supposing all such difficulties removed, the sacerdotal caste had not the slightest interest in practising the fraud. Memnon was not a national or local divinity; he had no temple, and was not worshipped save by superstitious tourists at

Thebes; there is not a shred of evidence to show that in the native mind any religious or devotional idea whatever was connected either with the statue or with the phenomenon; among the multitude of inscriptions upon the legs there is not a single one in Egyptian characters, demotic or hieroglyphic. On the contrary, we have seen that the Thebans persevered, in spite of the obstinate credulity of the Greek or Roman pilgrims, in offering a correct interpretation of the image; whilst one inscription on the left leg contains the remarkable and conclusive statement that the name Amenoth and the title of an Egyptian king were given to it by the priests themselves.[1]

I hold, then, that the case against the priests is quashed by the most overwhelming testimony, and that the theory of deception can no longer be sustained. And, therefore, I am driven to the other alternative; for, if the sound did not proceed from human, manifestly it must have been due to natural, causes. So little, however, is it necessary to accept this solution as a *pis aller* that it will be found to be the only one with which all the data hitherto mentioned accord, and which at once explains and reconciles the seemingly conflicting phenomena of the case. When we remember that the mysterious sound was not heard till the figure was broken in twain, nor after the fracture had been repaired; that it was heard either at or soon after sunrise, and

[1] *Corp. Insc. Graec.* 4731.

at no other time of the day;[1] and that it presented no particular uniformity of occurrence or principle of manifestation—the conclusion irresistibly suggests itself that it was due to some peculiar relation between the warmth of the rising sun and the great block of cracked and sundered stone. If the action of solar heat can be shown without improbability to have produced the noise described, the various difficulties that have been raised one and all disappear. The phenomenon cannot possibly have been regular in its occurrence or uniform in its moment of action, because on different days of the year the sun will have risen in a different quarter of the heavens, and with varying power—sometimes striking with vehement rays directly upon the statue, at others requiring to pierce through an envelope of mist or vapour before its genial warmth could reach that riven heart of stone. This was why Memnon replied to-day in a musical whisper, as though faintly acknowledging the salute, to-morrow with a sharper intonation, as though smitten with sudden pain; why he proved no respecter of persons, and drew no distinction between the humble legionary and the crowned Caesar; why to some of his worshippers he spoke

[1] There are two inscriptions (*Corp. Insc. Graec.* 4722, 4725) in which its occurrence is apparently dated before sunrise; but the vagueness of the terms employed—in one case πρὶν πρώτης ὥρας, in the other πρὶν αὐγὰς ἀελίω—leaves us in doubt as to the precise hour intended. The "first hour" might signify either sunrise or the space of an hour following; the second phrase is still more ambiguous. The discrepancy, therefore, is one which cannot be pressed, and which, if proven, might be explained as the result either of exaggeration or of illusion.

with such gracious iteration, to others was so inexorably or incontinently dumb. The power that was in him was communicated from without, and could not be exercised save at the instance of another. Though his lyre was ready strung, the only fingers that could awake its music were the rays of Phoebus Apollo.

Such is the line of reasoning that appeals to those who hold, with me, that the explanation of the mystery is to be sought in natural causes, and who believe that the sound was in some way or other due to the expansion in the stone of which the base was composed, brought about by the sudden rise in temperature at dawn. The transition from comparative chilliness to sensible warmth is often very rapid in those climes, the sun on clear mornings diffusing a penetrating glow almost the moment he has topped the horizon, and speedily exhausting the dews or vapours of the night. In these circumstances, a physical change of a somewhat marked description in the substances affected is not surprising, and much more when, as in this case, the particular substance affected was a siliceous conglomerate peculiarly lacking in homogeneity of composition, and with its natural coherence still further impaired by numerous accidental cracks and fissures. Such an object would be extremely susceptible of thermometric variations, and might be compared to a stringed instrument, the chords of which were over-tautly stretched.

Nor is this hypothesis left to stand alone, for

it is supported by other well-attested instances in which sounds of musical quality have been known to emanate from stones or rocks at sunrise. One of the most frequently quoted is the phenomenon reported by Baron von Humboldt as occurring on the banks of the Orinoco, where tones as of an organ are heard to proceed at that hour from some granite rocks permeated with deep and narrow crevices. Humboldt did not, as is frequently alleged, hear the music himself, but he described it as being testified to by reliable witnesses, including the European missionaries, who called the sounding stones *loxas de musica.* He himself attributed the sound to currents of heated air escaping through the crevices. The sonorous properties of certain sand-slopes or hills in different parts of the world, especially in Asia, are to be referred to quite different causes, and though quoted by Sir D. Brewster and others, when speaking of Memnon, cannot be accepted as presenting any analogy. But the members of the French Scientific Commission sent by Napoleon I. in the wake of his marauding column up the Nile (who, having anticipated Wilkinson in his wholesale scepticism about the Memnon, may be claimed as unbiassed witnesses) left on record that on two occasions—once in the granite quarries of Syene, and again in one of the temples of Karnak—they heard at sunrise the same strange cracking sound, reminding them of the simile employed by Pausanias, viz. of a snapping chord. Sir A. Smith and a party even heard, or thought they heard, the sound proceeding from the pedestal of Memnon himself.[1] Dr. Brugsch also testified to having heard a similar note in 1851 among the ruins of Karnak. These parallel cases are valuable, both as proofs that the vocal Memnon was not a unique portent, and as buttresses to the theory of natural causation.

Whilst, however, the miracle has been generally attributed by this school of scientific exegesis to the action of the sun's rays upon the chilled stone, different and inconsistent explanations of the precise physical origin of the sound have been advanced by various writers. Some, like Humboldt, have believed it to be due to the passage of quick currents of air set in motion by the sudden change of temperature through the crevices of the shattered monolith. But in that case one is tempted to ask why the same result should not have been produced by other and still more favourable atmospheric conditions, such, for instance, as the prevalence of a high wind. Others have imagined that under the influence of the sudden heat small fragments of the stone, which was without doubt extremely elastic in nature, splintered and broke off with a ringing noise. But, were that so, the phenomenon should have been visible as well as audible, and there can be no reason why it should not be repeated to this hour. Others, again, and these are the majority, laying stress upon the hetero-

[1] *Revue Encyclopédique*, 1821, vol. ix. p. 592.

geneous ingredients of the stone, have supposed a slight superficial rupture between its component particles, resulting in a sharp vibration. If, however, the integral quality of the stone were alone concerned, the southern statue, which was hewn from the same quarries, ought to have been no less amenable to caloric influence, and should have divided with Memnon the prerogative of speech.

In my opinion, the phenomenon can only be satisfactorily explained by bearing in mind and correlating two separate factors of the case—viz. (1) the composition of the stone, already described, and (2) the abnormal condition of the statue during the period of vocality, consequent upon the damage wrought by the earthquake. By this convulsion Memnon was not only severed in twain, but shaken to his foundations, deflected from his original level, and scarred by innumerable seams and rents, one of which, as has been shown, almost bisected his still surviving half. To account for the production of the sound, we must believe that in one or other of these cracks there occurred, under the waxing heat of the solar rays, a sudden displacement of some movable portion of the figure, an instantaneous shifting or rubbing of one face of stone upon another—in short, a disturbance of physical continuity sufficiently violent in its operation to communicate a sonorous shock to the atmospheric medium, through which it reached the ear of the listener outside. The phenomenon would then be analogous to the commonplace incident of the cracking of an iron bar in a grate under the growing heat of a powerful fire, or to the spasmodic ringing of a newly ignited stove. Among those who accept the natural explanation, there are some who, as I have hinted, have attributed the music to the whistling of the wind through the fissures caused by the earthquake. I see no reason, however, for thinking that the wind played any part in the phenomenon. The dawn in the East is commonly a very tranquil scene.

Whether I have supplied the true interpretation or not—and the opportunity of scientific proof can unfortunately never be obtained [1]—in this direction lies, as it seems to me, the only possibility of successfully prosecuting the inquiry. Human agency, I claim at least to have shown, was utterly unconcerned in the manifestation; and if Nature, the great Thaumaturgus, has in the Vocal Memnon propounded an enigma of which it is beyond the scope of existing knowledge to supply more than a hypothetically correct solution—if she whispered to those two centuries of a bygone world a secret to which no Prometheus has yet revealed the key—let us be content to recognise in the mystery an additional tribute to the manifold dispensations of her genius.

And here, well satisfied if in the above remarks

[1] Unless, indeed, the upper half were again dismantled and the statue restored to its mutilated condition—an experiment which might be recommended could we be certain that the base had not been tampered with, and its vocal capacities irremediably destroyed by the repairs of Septimius Severus.

I have removed any prevalent misapprehensions or diffused a more accurate knowledge about this interesting statue, I take leave of the colossal pair still seated on the Theban plain in sublime unconsciousness of the varying sentiments which they have excited in the breasts of so many successive generations. There they sit, the two giant brethren, scorched by the suns of more than three thousand summers, ringed by unnumbered yearly embraces of the wanton stream. By their side Stonehenge is a plaything, the work of pigmies. They are first even among the prodigies of Egypt; more solemn than the Pyramids, more sad than the Sphinx, more amazing than the pillared avenues of Karnak, more tremendous than the rock-idols of Aboo-Simbel. There they sit, patient and pathetic, their grim obliterated faces staring out into vacancy, their ponderous limbs sunk in a perpetual repose, indifferent alike to man and to Nature, careless of the sacrilege that has been perpetrated upon the mortal remains of the royal house whose glories they portrayed, steadfast while empires have crumbled and dynasties declined, serene amid all the tides of war and rapine and conquest that have ebbed and flowed from Alexandria to Assouan. There they sit and doubtless will sit till the end of all things—*sedent aeternumque sedebunt*—a wonder and a witness to men.

THE FALLS OF THE ZAMBESI

THE FALLS OF THE ZAMBESI

> The fall of waters ! rapid as the light
> The flashing mass foams shaking the abyss ;
> The Hell of Waters ! where they howl and hiss
> And boil in endless torture.
>
> BYRON, *Childe Harold*, Canto IV. St. 69.

WHEN I was President of the Royal Geographical Society I collected and presented to the Society, where they were hung in one of the rooms, a series of large - scale photographs of the great waterfalls of the world. I do not suggest that great waterfalls are more wonderful or more inspiring than great mountains,—for indeed it is ridiculous to compare the two,—but they are much more rare, and they combine in a peculiar degree the qualities of beauty and power. In the first place, the known great waterfalls of the world (I exclude cataracts and rapids) can be counted on the fingers of the two hands, whereas the famous mountain spectacles may be numbered by thousands. Secondly, even if we cannot go to the Himalayas, a few hours' journey will show us scenes of exquisite mountain glory on the European continent. On the other hand, the great waterfalls are not to be found in Europe at all. To visit them we have to travel thousands of miles ; and the majority of their number are so remote that till within the last quarter of a century they were still unknown to the white man, and even now have not been seen by more than a few score of Europeans. And finally there is something in the setting and the movement of the falls,—the smooth slide of the great river over the lip of the abyss; the crash of the waters as they plunge into the chasm or are shivered on the rocks below; the smoke-spray now rising in mighty columns into the sky, now drifting, interlaced with rainbows, in the breeze; the framework of vegetation, tropical, it may be, in its superb luxuriance; and lastly the course of the current, as collecting itself after the leap it tears its way, often through gorges of indescribable grandeur,—there is something in all this that presents a variety of effect, both sensational and aesthetic, with which even the greatest of mountains, immovable and unchanging in its bulk, austere in its snowy purity, terrible in its majesty, and remote with its unscaled precipices and its untrodden peaks, cannot vie. Another element of difference is that while the mountains have no voice but that of the storm, the great waterfall never ceases to thunder even under the brightest of skies, and fills the spectator with awe as well as admiration.

Fortune has never enabled me to visit the magnificent Falls of Kaietuk (commonly called Kaieteur) in British Guiana, where the River Potaro, a confluent of the Essequibo, hurls itself into a basin 740 feet below; nor the Iguasu Falls of the Parana River in the Argentine, rushing through an archipelago of islands and plunging into a gorge of surpassing beauty; nor the Tequendama Falls, nearly 450 feet high, near Bogota in Colombia; nor the Grand Falls of Labrador—all of the above in the American Continent; nor again the Orange River Falls in South Africa, the ugliest waterfall, situated in the most repellent surroundings, in the world. As these are so little known I add a chapter about them and about some others which may be of interest to those who desire to study and to visit these wonders of Nature.

But I have seen Niagara, of which I will say nothing, except that man is hard at work despoiling and defaming this masterpiece of Nature; the two falls of the Yellowstone; the various waterfalls of the Yosemite, of which something will be said in my second volume; the wonder-spot of Gersoppa in South India; and the Victoria Falls of the Zambesi, which, as perhaps the most astonishing of all, I propose here to describe.

Known to the natives as Mosioatunya or the Smoke Sounding, they were first discovered by Livingstone in 1855. Now that the country, in British hands, has been opened up by the railway, they are accessible to any one who, being in South Africa, can spare the time for the long journey from Cape Town or Natal to the river. Of such a scene a photograph is more eloquent than any description; nor am I clear that any word-picture of any great waterfall that I have ever read has given me an adequate idea of the reality. If, then, I reproduce what I wrote about the Victoria Falls, directly I had seen them, it is not so much that I hope to succeed where others have failed, as that, having penned the following words in the train that took me away from the Zambesi, they may possess the slight merit of a vivid and unblurred impression.

In all countries where there is a dry and a wet season a waterfall will differ greatly at different seasons of the year. Gersoppa is nearly dry before the end of the cold weather; but after the rains the volume of water discharged into the chasm, which is nearly 900 feet in sheer depth, is so great that the fall itself is rendered invisible by the spray. The same holds true of the Victoria Falls. They are at their lowest before the rains, which begin in December; and visitors in the dry season—*i.e.* between September and December—console themselves for the relatively meagre wisps and driblets of water which in many parts of the fall are all that come over the edge, by the better opportunities that they enjoy of examining the walls of the great chasm which the resistless river has been eating through unnumbered ages into the heart of the black basalt. At that season a man can wade across many parts of the river at no great distance from the top of the fall, for the water is seldom more than two feet to three feet in depth, and often much less. Large sections of the black cliff are entirely exposed, and it is possible to walk out from Cataract Island or from Livingstone Island, which are both on the top of the falls, and to stand on the very brink of the naked edge. The Devil's Cataract, adjoining the left bank, and the Rainbow Fall, in the centre, are then the only considerable mass of water; and, as appears from the photographs that are taken at that period, even the Rainbow Fall, which was of surpassing grandeur when I saw it, and presented an uninterrupted sheet of water, is split up into separate cascades. On the other hand, when the sun is shining, which it is more apt to do in the dry weather, the effect of the rainbows, tilted against the fall at innumerable angles, and following the spectator with their scintillating hoops as he moves, is finer and more constant.

It is in April and May, when, though the rain has ceased at the falls, the swollen water from the uplands far in the interior reaches them, that they are at their highest, and then the river pours in a flood like that of Niagara over the lip, and plunges in an unbroken sheet into the shrouded abyss below. This must be a glorious spectacle. But such is the density and fury of the spray-storm rising into the air like the smoke of some vast cauldron, that the spectator within 100 yards of the cataract can see nothing at all, and gets little beyond a drenching for his pains.

Perhaps a visitor at the "mean" epoch—*i.e.* when the rains have been sufficient to fill the river and produce a great mass of water, but not so overwhelming as to blot out the view—is the most fortunate. Anyhow these differences of season and their effects are enough to account for the widely different verdicts that have been passed upon the Victoria Falls by those who have described them. They are also responsible for the complete inadequacy of any photographic representation to do justice to the majestic grandeur of the scene. It is clear that, when the river is in flood and the falls are concealed behind an impenetrable screen of spray, no camera can be used with effect. This explains why the majority of illustrations in books, which were naturally taken under favourable conditions of sky and sun, are so inadequate. At low water the photographer, or, for the matter of that, the sightseer, should be warned off.

One of the glories of Niagara is the great sweep of water, deep and swift and irresistible, in the bed of the river above the cataract. The Zambesi presents a very different spectacle. Although at a short distance above the falls it expands into a broad lake, where regattas can be held and sailing is a safe and agreeable pastime, as it approaches the hidden chasm it becomes parcelled up into innumerable channels and rapids running through boulders and between grassy tufts and islets, and is in many parts fordable in dry weather. A canoe can then take the sightseer with perfect safety to any of the larger islands, and will probably run aground on the way. The two islands most commonly visited, because they are on the lip of the fall, are Cataract Island and Livingstone Island ; on the latter, the tree upon which the great missionary-traveller cut his initials still exists (although no trace of the inscription survives) and is not by any means dying, as the guide-books say. From either of these islands some of the most awe-inspiring views of the falls can be obtained.

This breaking-up of the river above the falls, giving it the appearance of pushing its way through a rock-strewn trough or shallow depression in the surrounding jungle, rather than of carrying islands upon a broad and liquid bosom, is perhaps disappointing to the stranger, and renders it surprising that so relatively moderate a volume of water—though more than a mile in width—can produce so amazing a spectacle when it falls. It also explains why the crest of the cataract, instead of being, as at Niagara, a glittering sweep of green, curving like some monstrous billow to the fall, is broken into separate foaming channels, which sometimes swerve asunder as they leap the edge, and are churned in rocky saucers at the very summit of the cataract, before they take the final plunge.

But, the edge once passed, the Victoria Falls appeared to me, when I saw them in the month of January, to excel in grandeur any spectacle of the same kind in the world. For they possess two incomparable features. In the first place, the cliff-wall down which they are hurled is sheer from top to bottom, 350 feet to 400 feet of perpendicular descent, uninterrupted save where in some places gigantic masses of basalt, split off or eroded by the same process as has formed the chasm itself, lie at the base and shatter the descending columns into a tempest of foam. Conceive a black wall, as high as Shakespeare's Cliff at Dover, nearly as high as the Cross of St. Paul's, and more than a mile in length, and over the top of this tremendous precipice a continuous cataract of water toppling down from the sky, save in the three places where larger islands, carrying their growth of jungle right to the edge of the abyss, have protected a section of the cliff, and interposed a gleaming surface of ebon rock between the snowy fleeces of the falls on either side.

The second feature is more remarkable still. The majority of falls can only be seen at an angle from the banks of the river below, or from a considerable distance, should the river make a bend, or from some convenient artificial standpoint, like the Suspension Bridge at Niagara. But here, at the Zambesi, Nature herself has supplied the most wonderful platform which it is possible to conceive, with belvederes or outlook towers built out at convenient points for the spectator to take his view. The formation of the gorge is responsible for this astounding feature. Although the river discharges itself in an almost straight line (unlike the great curve of the Horseshoe Fall at Niagara) into the chasm below, there is only one outlet from this chasm, and that is about three-quarters of the way across from the right or southern bank, where the entire water that has come over the fall forces its way through a single aperture only 100 yards wide into the whirlpool known as the Boiling Pot, and commences its zigzag descent through the 45 miles of cañon towards the sea.

The consequence is that except at this spot the entire volume of water as it falls is pent up in the chasm, which is seldom more than 150 yards in width, and has to flow from left to right in order to make its way out by the solitary gap. And here comes Nature's unique gift. From left to right or from right to left we can walk along the near side of the chasm from end to end, save at the point of exit, and gaze at the falls immediately opposite, as though we were standing in some showman's panorama and were looking across an intervening hollow, devised to assist the illusion, at the painted canvas beyond. Only here is no artificial picture, but the living masterpiece of a more than human showman; tangible, because the scud of the spray-storm lashes us in the face; throbbing with movement, because the heaven above and the earth beneath appear to be equally in travail; audible, because in our ears is the rattle of eternal thunder.

The main portion of the bank which provides this great natural stage or platform—stretching from the southern end of the falls, where is the Devil's Cataract, to the gap through which the entire river charges into the Boiling Pot—is the well-known Rain Forest. The name is appropriate as well as picturesque, for the spray from the falls, rising in a stupendous column from the chasm below, falls in an incessant rain-shower on this tongue of land—three parts tree-jungle and one part grass; a rain so overpowering that it drips in torrents from every branch and leaf, rustles in the coarse grass, lies in pools on the ground, and in a very few minutes soaks the sightseer to the skin.

Along this strip of land, which constitutes the eastern boundary wall of the chasm, and is exactly on a level with the lip of the falls, a pathway has been made through the sodden grass and the dripping trees; and from this pathway, at the distance of every 50 to 100 yards, smaller tracks strike out to the vantage points at the edge of the chasm, which I have likened to belvederes. At any one of these bastions a man can walk to the very brink; immediately opposite him, and so close that he can almost pitch a stone into it, is the descending wall of foam; and from the pit below there leaps up in volleys like small-shot, and with a fury that blinds and stuns, the eternal spray-storm. Sometimes it completely obscures the cataract, only a few hundred feet at the most away, and renders it almost impossible for a man to stand upright. Then, as it drifts with the wind, through the seams are visible the yellow and white crests as they flash along the opposing summit, and the descending squadrons as they pitch into the booming depths below.

There are many points of view from which we can study the mile-long race of water thundering like a cavalry charge to its doom, and then perishing in the clatter of its terrific downfall. We can cross the gorge by the filigree span of the railway bridge—an ornament rather than a desecration to the scene—and inspect the farthermost fall close to the northern bank; we can clamber along the thin serrated ridge of rock known as the Knife Edge, which connects the farther bank with a big rocky buttress, clothed from base to summit with forest trees, which here projects like a huge pyramid into the stream, and forms one pillar of the gateway through which the river rushes into the Boiling Pot 400 feet below; or, crossing again to the near bank, we can enter the Rain Forest and scramble out on to the aerial promontory known as Danger Point, where, crouching on a hummock of slippery stones, within a foot of the edge, we can look straight opposite at what is called the Rainbow Fall. At the season at which I saw it this was by far the most imposing spectacle. The spray-storm surges upwards from the bottom of the chasm with a concussion like the firing of machine guns and with a force that takes away the breath. But as the mist-wreaths waver and divide, through the rifts are seen the parallel and interminable files of the cataract, careering to the edge and leaping it in a hurricane of foam. Here it is that the thunder echoes most loudly from the gloomy caverns of the abyss: here the stinging buffets of the whirlwind lash the face with the most pitiless fury; and here the smoke-clouds, spouting like portentous geyser-jets into the air, scatter aloft, and, dissolving, wreathe the chasm with a perpetual crown.

The next most imposing view is from Cataract Island. One can stand here on the upper lip of the fall and look down the whole length of the prodigious trench or fissure into which it plunges. The bottom is only dimly visible through the watery whirlwind, but now and again amid the swirl can be seen the sullen and foam-flecked surface of the river in the pool. From the jagged rocks at the bottom the foam spurts upwards with a rush like a thousand maroons, and the detonation claps from crag to crag as though concealed forces were firing volleys at each other from emplacements in the confronting cliffs. The phenomenon of the rising spray-storm is best studied from this point. For we can see, as the water splinters on the rocks or plunges into the pool at the bottom, how in ordinary circumstances it would explode outwards and spend its force in the open. Here, however, before it can do this the spray is beaten back by the opposite cliff, and is caught as it falls by the blasts of displaced air, and whirled aloft in a hurricane of sleet. As this shoots upward it impinges on the sides and summit of the cliff, and streams down in innumerable minor cascades, destined to meet with the same fate again and again, as they are snatched up in the eddies of the revolving tempest and are swept once more into the air. No waterfall in the world can show any spectacle—though it is sound as well as sight—to compare with this.

At one place on the farther or northern bank we can descend by a rocky path to the bottom of the gorge, and, passing through the exquisite jungle known as the Palm Grove, where the fronds of the overhanging trees drip with an everlasting shower, can reach the level of the river, at the point where it forms the backwash of the Boiling Pot. This is not to be compared with the rapids or with the vast circular basin known as the Whirlpool at Niagara, for the torrent, as I saw it, showed no great violence, and the space is confined. A swimmer might have trouble in the eddies of the backwash, but there is no reason why he should be drowned. In fact, the Zambesi rapids are not at any point in the cañon to be compared with those of Niagara, which battered the life out of Matthew Webb, and through which idiotic couples, tied up in padded mattresses inside a cask, have sometimes won an inglorious way to lucre and an undeserved respite from the grave.

The zigzags of the Zambesi Cañon—again a result of the astounding geological formation—are an unparalleled feature, and it is possible, at more than one spot, to stand on a ridge where on one side the river hundreds of feet below is rushing madly to the right, and on the other is coursing equally furiously to the left. But neither in the volume of water, in the mountainous billows thrown up by the rapids, nor in the breadth and tumult of the current can the Zambesi below the cataract be compared with Niagara.

In scenery, the surroundings of the Victoria Falls greatly surpass their American rival. For every pinnacle and rocky buttress is clothed from top to bottom, at least in the rainy season, with a clustering forest-growth; and the contrast of the white storm of the cataract and the gloomy swirl of the torrent with the brilliant green of the verdure amid which it pursues its course, is a fascination that never palls. But here again, though we are in the tropics, the vegetation, with rare exceptions, has none of the exuberance which those who know Asia associate with the term; and the surroundings of the Indian waterfalls immensely exceed in natural beauty anything that the Zambesi can show.

Thus we arrive at the conclusion that, while in secondary features the Zambesi Fall may yield to some of its competitors in other climes, in all those attributes which concern the fall itself, and are of primary value, it is pre-eminent, and may deservedly be called the greatest river-wonder in the world. Never can there fade from the mind of one who has seen it the vision of those towers of descending foam, the shouting face of the cataract, the thunder of the watery phalanxes as they charge and reel and are shattered in the bottom of the abyss, or the spray-spumes whizzing upwards like a battery of rockets into the air. As the train plunges slowly into the forest and takes us back into the everyday world, the mist-clouds steaming like smoke through the trees and forming a dense white canopy 1000 feet in height in the sky, and the low thunder, whose reverberations still fill the air, conclude a unique experience and crown an imperishable memory.

THE GREAT WATERFALLS OF THE WORLD

THE GREAT WATERFALLS OF THE WORLD

> The sounding cataract
> Haunted me like a passion: the tall rock,
> The mountain, and the deep and gloomy wood.
>
> WORDSWORTH, "Tintern Abbey."

IN the preceding chapter I have incidentally mentioned some of the great waterfalls of the world, other than those of the Zambesi, which I there described. I append a few words here about their features and dimensions, and may add that I know of no place where the same information, which is the result of a good deal of research, can be found collected.

NORTH AMERICA

Niagara, of which I refrain from adding one more to the countless descriptions by much more gifted pens, was the first of the Great Falls that was known to the white man. It was first reported by Samuel Champlain in 1613, and first seen by Father Hennepin in 1677. But so dazed was he by the sight, or so prone to exaggeration, that in the first edition of his book (1683) he made the height 500 feet, and in the second edition

(1697) 600 feet. The actual dimensions are: Canadian Fall, 158 feet, American Fall, 162-169 feet.

The *Grand Falls of Labrador*, which are on the Grand or Hamilton River, were discovered in 1839 by John McLean. A mile above the falls the river is 400 yards wide; but it then contracts as it passes through a series of rapids until at the escarpment it is only 50 yards in width. The sheer fall is 316 feet in depth, and the roar is heard at a distance of 20 miles. Immediately below the falls the river turns sharply to the south-east and rushes through a cañon 25 miles long, the cliffs of which are 400 feet high. The Indian name for the falls is Pat-ses-Che-wan, *i.e.* "The narrow place where the water falls." These falls, which are of great splendour, have, owing to the difficulty of access, been seen by but few Europeans.

The Yosemite Falls.—It is not necessary to do more than allude here to these famous Californian Falls (a description of which will be found in my second volume), since they are so well known and have been visited by so many thousands of persons. Their surroundings, in which every grace of beauty is combined with every element of grandeur, make them perhaps the most exquisite of all the world waterfalls, although in volume and awe-inspiring quality they are not to be compared with the great river falls that I have elsewhere described. They were only discovered by white men as recently as 1850. The triple Yosemite Fall consists of three cascades, respectively 1600, 634, and 400 feet high, or a total of 2634 feet. The Vernal Falls are 400 feet. The Nevada Fall is 640 feet. The beautiful Bridal Veil, so often photographed against its background of ebon rock, is 900 feet. These falls, however, being fed by no great volume of water, except after heavy rain, are as a rule more beautiful than imposing, their height and volume being both dwarfed by their stupendous setting.

I have not included in this list the Falls of the *Yellowstone River* in the Yellowstone Park, which I have also seen, because they are much less remarkable than the gorge in which they are set, and are barely entitled to be included among the great waterfalls of the world.

South America

In this Continent, with its mighty rivers, its amazing scenery, and its still only half-revealed secrets, are to be found unquestionably the most remarkable series of waterfalls in the world. The majority of them are quite unknown in Europe, and are only slowly finding their way into geographical writings. Were they more accessible they would attract admiring pilgrims from all parts of the globe.

Kaietuk (commonly known as Kaieteur).—This, which is perhaps the most symmetrical and perfect of all the single falls, is to be found in

British territory. It is on the Potaro River, a confluent of the Essequibo in British Guiana. It was quite unknown until discovered in 1870 by C. Barrington Brown, Government Surveyor in that colony.[1] The name in the Indian dialect signifies Old Man Rock (*tuk*=rock), the story being that a venerable Indian, who had become a nuisance to his neighbours, was put into a bark-canoe and shot over the fall, which his spirit was supposed henceforward to haunt.

The river Potaro, flowing through tropical vegetation, is from 350 to 400 feet in width, and 20 feet in depth in flood times, when it reaches the top of the chasm. Running at the rate of four miles an hour it precipitates itself in a sheer descent of 740 feet between rocky cliffs into the vast cauldron below; 500 cubic feet of water have been computed to plunge every minute into the depths. Behind the falls is an immense cavern in the cliff, into which myriads of black swallows continuously flash through the spray. The falls are believed once to have been much higher, the rock being of a soft and friable description. Correspondingly the gulf below is being gradually deepened. Some day regular expeditions will be organised from George Town to see this marvel, which, in the features before referred to, is, in my opinion, unique.

Roraima and Kukenam.—Far inland on the borders of the same British colony, where the

[1] *Canoe and Camp Life in British Guiana*, pp. 203-5, 212-23. London, 1876.

frontiers of British Guiana, Brazil, and Venezuela meet, are the two mountain wonders of Roraima and Kukenam. Side by side, separated only by a deep and wooded gorge, these two great natural fortresses rear their mighty bastions to a sheer height of from 1500 to 2000 feet from the forests and savannahs of the lower slopes, while their level summits are commonly enshrouded in rolling mists. In shape not unlike Cape Mountain, but more than double the height—since Kukenam is 7856 feet, and Roraima 8625 feet high—and each from 10 to 12 miles in length, they are by far the most remarkable natural fortresses in the world. It is the water collected in pools and lakes on the rocky and boulder-strewn summits which, after rain, spills over the edge and drops for a sheer 1500 feet into the forest below, producing the waterfalls and cascades, with which the names of Roraima and Kukenam are linked. They are visible when in spate for an immense distance, hanging like snowy fleeces against the background of rose-red rock over which they plunge. When Tennyson, in finding a site for his Palace of Art, wrote :

> A huge crag-platform, smooth as burnished brass
> I chose. The ranged ramparts bright
> From level meadow-bases of deep grass
> Suddenly scaled the light.
>
> From those four jets four currents in one swell
> Across the mountain streamed below
> In misty folds, that floating as they fell
> Lit up a torrent-bow,

it might well have been of Kukenam and Roraima that he sang.

Over three hundred years ago Sir Walter Raleigh must have heard both of Roraima and of its waterfalls, when he wrote :

> I was informed of the mountain of Christall, to which in trueth for the length of the way, and the evil season of the yeare, I was not able to march nor abide any longer upon the journey ; we saw it a farre off, and it appeared like a white Churche towre of an exceeding height. There falleth over it a mightie river which toucheth no part of the side of the mountaine, but rusheth over the top of it, and falleth to the grounde with a terrible noyse and clamor, as if 1000 great belles were knockt one against another. I think there is not in the world so strange an overfall, nor so wonderfull to beholde ; Berreo told me it hath diamondes and other precious stones on it, and that they shined very farre off ; but what it hath, I knowe not, neither durst he nor any of his men ascende to the toppe of the saide mountaine, those people adjoyning being his enemies, and the way to it is so impassible.[1]

Sir Robert Schomburgk saw Roraima as far back as 1838 and 1842, but did not come close to either mountain. C. Barrington Brown, the surveyor, whom I have already mentioned, when exploring on the Upper Mazaruni River in 1870, saw from a distance of 38 miles an enormous waterfall leaping from the north-east face of Roraima, and described it as the highest waterfall in the world. This was the fall seen by J. W.

[1] *Discovery of Guiana* (Hakluyt Society), 1848, p. 101.

Boddam-Whetham in 1878, and thus described by him:

> Towards the northern end of the mountain, a magnificent cascade, whose lip seemed to be below the summit, sprang in a broad silvery arch right down into the green depths, barely touching the rocky wall in its descent.[1]

Both of these travellers, and others after them, who visited the spot, declared Roraima to be unscalable, and serious writers speculated upon the unknown fauna—survivals of a prehistoric era—that might be found on the summit. Upon this foundation Conan Doyle built one of his most imaginative stories.[2] It was reserved for Sir Everard im Thurn, who was determined to penetrate the mystery, in company with H. I. Perkins, to discover a sloping ledge by which it is possible alternately to creep and climb up the south-west wall of Roraima; and along this ledge subsequent explorers, including one lady,[3] have mounted to the plateau at the top.

I can recall no more exciting moment in the history of travel than when, on the morning of December 18, 1884, im Thurn, having scaled the crag-wall, peered over the broken edge, and looked, for the first time, so far as is known in the history of man, upon the summit of Roraima. A wilderness of uncouth boulders and pinnacles and jumbled cliffs met his eye—interspersed with

[1] *Roraima and British Guiana*, p. 228. London, 1879.

[2] *The Lost World*. London, 1912.

[3] Mrs. Cecil Clementi, *Through British Guiana to the Summit of Roraima*. London, 1920.

water-holes and pools and tarns, the feeding-ground of the far-seen cascades. Two of these falls he especially noticed, that on the southern face of Roraima, over 1000 feet high, which feeds the Kamaiun River, and that on the opposite face of Kukenam, 1300 feet in height, which is the source of the Kukenam River.

I have dwelt at some length on the Falls of Roraima and Kukenam, partly because of their strange and fantastic surroundings, partly because, although not permanent river falls in the ordinary sense of the term, the catchment area being far too small, they are yet, when in flow, in all probability the highest uninterrupted falls in the world, and, owing to the rains and mists which continually envelop the summit of the two mountains like a cap, are almost invariably in action. I would sooner myself see Roraima and Kukenam, with these white banners hung against their crimson ramparts, than almost any natural spectacle in the world.

The *Guayra Falls*, on the Parana in Brazil, are not really a waterfall, but are an amazing series of cataracts, the finest in the South American Continent.

The *Tequendama Falls*, on the Bogota or Funza River in Ecuador, only 17 miles from the capital city of Bogota, are situated in lovely scenery, an amphitheatre of forest-clad hills sloping to the edge of a rock-walled gorge. Above the escarpment the river contracts to a width of 20-30 yards, and the sheer fall is 443 feet (Humboldt miscalculated it at 574 feet). Owing to the small volume of water in the river this fall is to be classed with Gersoppa in South India rather than with its greater rivals.

The *Iguasu Falls*, on the Argentine-Brazilian border, are on the Curutiba River, an eastern affluent of the great Parana River, and in their contour and dimensions somewhat resemble Niagara, being 50 feet higher and 1250 feet broader than the latter. The scenery and vegetation are, however, far more beautiful. The river is nearly two miles wide at some distance above the falls, but contracts to a total width of 1365 yards before it takes the plunge, which is 170 feet in depth. The fall is divided by rocky pinnacles and islands into three sections, the Brazilian Fall, 2000 feet wide, in shape resembling a horse-shoe (like the Canadian Fall of Niagara), the Insular Fall, and the Argentine Fall, which is a double fall of 189 feet, and is 1200 feet in width. Much of the river, as it falls, spills on to lower ledges of rock, throwing up immense clouds of spray and producing a reverberation which is heard for miles. A column, as it were of white smoke, floats eternally above the war of waters ; and the *mise en scène* is equal, if not superior to, that of any other great fall. Below the falls the river is pent between narrow cliffs of rock which are not more than 400 feet apart. The whole is framed in the most luxuriant tropical vegetation.

Laja River Falls in Chile.—This river is the main branch of the Rio Bobbio, which debouches into the Pacific near Concepcion. The falls, like those of Niagara, are twofold, being separated by a rocky and wooded island which descends to the level of the pool. But they are of inferior altitude, being only 106 feet high.

Africa

The *Great Falls of Aughrabies*, on the Orange River, situated 80 miles from the town of Upington, were discovered by George Thompson in 1824. These are the most unapproachable and the least beautiful of all the great falls of the world, being situated in a country destitute of all vegetation or indeed of any sign of life. The Orange River, which is a mile wide some distance above the main fall, is then split up into a number of channels by boulder-strewn granitic islands and masses of rock, until it is barely 60 feet wide at the lip of the main fall, which plunges for a sheer 400 feet into a sullen abyss. Thence for many miles it races through a gloomy and inaccessible cañon, the walls of which are nearly 500 feet high, emerging later on near the border of what was formerly German South-West Africa. Meanwhile many other cascades drop laterally into the gorge, which presents a spectacle of gigantic buttresses, sheer precipices, and appalling desolation. When the river is in flood the torrent overlaps the chute and becomes a raging cataract, sweeping everything before it. In this condition it is unapproachable, and has never been seen by any white man. Though far from remote it is for the above reasons the least known, and perhaps the least visited of all the great falls of the world.

India

Gersoppa or Gairseppa Falls (also known as Jog).—These are situated on the river Sharavati, which divides the Bombay Presidency from the Native State of Mysore, and are 35 miles distant by road from the small seaport of Honavar, itself 350 miles south of Bombay. During the monsoon, *i.e.* in June, July, and August, when the river is in flood, the falls are so swathed in mist as to be invisible, and nothing is heard but the thunder booming up from the abyss. In winter, however, which was the season of my visit (November 1900), the channel above the falls is not more than 80 yards in width, and can be crossed by light bridges thrown from island to island. The great beauty of the falls, which are four in number, the Raja or main fall on the right bank, the Roarer, the Rocket (so-called because it spurts in a series of jets), and La Dame Blanche (a white sheet of foam), consists in the depth of the fall, which is 830 feet sheer, the two first-named falls meeting in the course of their descent, and in the exquisite framing of the tropical forest. Owing to the configuration of the ground the Gersoppa Falls can also be seen to greater advantage than almost any other fall of corresponding height, and are being increasingly visited, mainly, owing to superior facilities of communication, from the Mysore side. The pool at the bottom of the falls, hollowed out by the force of the water, is 132 feet deep. I never remember a more beautiful sight than that of the falls from a terrace seat near the Mysore Rest House. Would I might sit there once again.

Falls of the Cauvery.—I also saw the Falls of the Cauvery at Sivasamudram (on the boundary between Madras and Mysore), which are discharged over a cliff 250 feet high, in a series of separate cascades of great size and volume. The two main falls are called respectively, in the native language, the Sky Spray and the Heavy Spray, and they vary at different seasons of the year from a roaring cataract to a vertical plunge. The water power thus generated has been harnessed for the service of man ; and a little way down the stream on the left bank is the great station which transmits the power to the goldfields of Kolar, 90 miles distant, and to the cities of Bangalore and Mysore.

New Zealand

Few persons have seen the *Sutherland Falls*, on the south-west coast of the Southern Island—so-called from their discoverer, a prospector of that name, who came upon them in the year 1879. The Falls, which are fed by the Arthur River, are situated 16 miles from the head of Melford Sound, one of the great fiords that pierce the coast of the island. They are three in number, resembling in this respect the principal Yosemite Fall, the height of the three sections, which plunge over the edge of a vertical cliff into hollow basins or pools, being respectively 815, 751, and 338 feet, or a total of 1904 feet. They are seen to the greatest advantage in summer, when the snows are melting, and, as time passes, will be more and more recognised as one of the wonders of the southern hemisphere.

My catalogue, thus completed, may turn out not to be exhaustive, since from time to time rumours are heard, usually in the still unexplored parts of South America, of great waterfalls known only to the natives and unseen by the white man. In due time every one of them will be discovered, and some later generation will more accurately tabulate their characteristics and virtues.

"LEST WE FORGET"

"LEST WE FORGET"

There is nothing new except what is forgotten.

ANON.

I

THE DEATH-BED OF SIR HENRY LAWRENCE

ONE of the most remarkable phenomena in life is the carelessness with which people observe, or rather fail to observe, that which is daily and even hourly under their eyes, either paying no attention to it because it is so familiar, or failing to inquire from sheer lack of interest or curiosity. Of the millions of persons who pass in the year through Trafalgar Square, how many could tell you the number or identity of the bronze heroes who adorn or disfigure its open spaces? Not even the fact that he is riding without stirrups probably induces more than one passer-by in ten thousand to inquire who is the Royal horseman on a pedestal in the top left-hand corner. How many people who daily drive or ride past the nude Achilles in Hyde Park take the trouble to inquire how he came there or what he represents? Take an even stronger case. There are London streets which some of us traverse every day of our lives for years. If we were suddenly challenged to name either the order in which the shops occur for a distance of 100 yards on the side of the street which we affect, or still more the names, is there one in a hundred of us who could survive the ordeal? Familiarity breeds not merely contempt, but in the case of ordinary objects, or objects which we encounter every day, complete forgetfulness if we have ever known, complete indifference if we have not.

In the course of my travels I have come across two cases of this indifference or forgetfulness, in circumstances where the very reverse might have been expected by every law of probability, so astonishing that it would have been impossible to believe them had they not actually occurred. In both cases I was the accidental means of detecting the lapse; and I owed the discovery to the habit which I have pursued in every one of my travels, and which I believe to be the secret of accurate observation—namely, of acquainting oneself, so far as possible, with the facts of a case or the features of a scene before coming in contact with it. In this way you know what to expect that you will find. But you are also in a position to note what is wanting either in the narratives of your predecessors or in the situation itself.

In December 1899 I paid my first official visit, as Viceroy of India, to Lucknow, and among my earliest proceedings was an inspection of the crumbling ruins and consecrated grounds of the Residency. They bear but slight resemblance now to the aspect they wore at the date of the famous siege; for time and loving care have passed the tender fingers of oblivion over the scars, and have converted a heap of debris into an exquisite garden, from which emerge a few battered walls and skeletons of buildings, embowered amid the luxuriant verdure.

But the interest lies in them rather than in the pleasaunce, and any Englishman, at all familiar with the history of the Mutiny or the incidents of the siege, wanders eagerly from ruined building to building, or where they exist, from one shattered apartment to another, seeking to identify the actual scenes of so much suffering and so much glory.

So familiar was I from previous reading with the incidents of the siege that I had no difficulty in moving from site to site and identifying the localities, in so far as they survive. After inspecting the Residency, I was conducted into an adjoining and semi-ruined building. On the battered wall inside a great open verandah I saw a white marble tablet fixed, which contained this inscription:

Here Sir H. Lawrence died 4th July 1857

"With all respect," I said at once, "here Sir Henry Lawrence did not die." "But how," was the natural retort, "can that be? This inscription has been on the wall for fifty years—

ever since the Residency was consecrated as a national memorial at the end of the Mutiny. Thousands of persons who fought in the Mutiny have passed through the building since. Hundreds who were in the Residency at the time of the siege, and at the moment of Sir Henry's death, have visited the verandah. All of them have seen that tablet on the wall. Not one has ever questioned its accuracy. Can it have been reserved for you in the year 1899 to correct an error that must have existed for half a century and to show that every one has hitherto been wrong?" "Yes," I said, "indeed it has, and I will ask leave to take the party to the inner room in which Sir Henry Lawrence actually did die."

I then passed through the verandah to the inner room or drawing-room of Sir Joseph Fayrer's house (the building in question), and remarked that that was the spot where Sir Henry Lawrence had breathed his last. There was still general incredulity as to my statement; whereupon, remembering that Sir Joseph Fayrer, who had tended Lawrence in his last hours, was still living at the age of seventy-four in England, I suggested that a plan of the house and its apartments should be sent to him, without any mention of the dispute that had arisen, and that he should be asked to mark upon it the room and the spot where the hero's spirit had fled.

After a time came back the plan with Fayrer's mark on the apartment and upon the place which I had indicated. The mendacious tablet was in due course removed and transferred to the correct site, where it may be seen in the accompanying photograph.

In the following year came out Sir Joseph Fayrer's book:[1] and in it were printed, not merely the details of Lawrence's last hours, but a copy of Lieut. Moorsom's plan of the Residency buildings, made in 1857 (p. 130), and a plan (whether stimulated by my inquiry or not I do not know) of Dr. Fayrer's own house (p. 132).

From these it will be seen that the injured man, mortally wounded by a shell on July 2, 1857, while lying on a couch in an upper room in the Residency, had been carried over and laid down on a bed in the open verandah of Dr. Fayrer's house, whence after a time, owing to the severity of the fire, he was moved into the inner room or drawing-room where at 8 A.M. on the morning of July 4 he expired.

Apart from the interest of historical accuracy, I do not know that any vital importance attaches to the question whether even a great man and a hero breathed his last in this or that exact spot. But I have never ceased to be amazed at the heedlessness which for fifty years had permitted a stream of visitors, some of them eye-witnesses of the tragedy, and many of them

[1] *Recollections of my Life*, London, 1900. An earlier letter from Dr. Fayrer to Colonel Wilson, dated December 23, 1864, giving the particulars of Sir H. Lawrence's last hours when they were still fresh in the Doctor's memory, is printed in the *Life of Sir H. Lawrence*, by Sir H. Edwardes and H. Merivale, vol. ii. 373-7, London, 1872.

intimately acquainted with every detail and incident of the siege, to pass by, without detecting or correcting the error.

II

The Billiard Table of Napoleon

My second experience was at St. Helena in 1908. During a compulsory stay of a fortnight at Grand Canary and the subsequent long sea voyage to St. Helena, I had made a careful study of every available work about the Emperor's residence in that island (having indeed provided myself with a miniature library for the purpose), and when I arrived at Longwood, the scene of his five years' exile and ultimate death, I was as familiar with the identity and history of every room in the building, as though I had lived in it myself.

My knowledge was soon put to an unexpected test. As I entered the house I found the French Consul, who, as representative of the French Government, was living at New Longwood (the property having been handed over by the British Government to Napoleon III. in 1858), about to conduct a party of French visitors round the building. In the entrance room, upon the walls of which hung a board inscribed "Salle d'Attente," he was expatiating upon the uses to which this apartment had been put in the time of the Emperor. "This," he said, "was the Reception

Room where His Majesty received his guests." "Excuse me," said I, "this was, at any rate in the first few years of the Emperor's residence, the Billiard Room: it was always known and described as such; in it stood the billiard table on which he used to knock about the balls either with a mace or with his hands, but which, after he became tired of the game, he had removed." The Consul had never heard of the table or of the Emperor's amusement upon it; but observing that I seemed to have a greater acquaintance with the contents of the house than himself, he very courteously asked me to take the company round, which I proceeded to do, explaining with sufficient fullness the purpose to which each apartment had been put, and the furniture which it had contained. Thus I acted as guide in a house which I had never previously seen. The Consul, with much good humour, offered to vacate his post permanently in my favour.

The Billiard Room of Napoleon, which was originally built on to the house by Admiral Sir George Cockburn in 1815, when he reconstructed Longwood for the accommodation of the Emperor, is the largest room in the building, being 26 feet 6 inches long, 17 feet 6 inches broad, and 12 feet 4 inches high—and having as many as five windows. It is built of wood, and the inner walls are painted a dark green, through which in some cases could be seen the names that had been cut by earlier visitors. Here a billiard table had been placed by Sir Hudson

Lowe in July 1816 for the delectation of the illustrious inmate; and here in the early days he used to play with his staff, and to knock the balls about with the young lady from the Briars (daughter of the English purveyor of Longwood), Miss Elizabeth Balcombe, afterwards Mrs. Abell, whom the Emperor used to call Mlle. Betsee and the French writers to describe as Miss Betzi. In the later editions of her vivacious work,[1] which were ampler than the first,[2] Mrs. Abell thus recalled the experiences of her youth:

> Billiards was a game much played by Napoleon and his suite. I had the honour of being instructed in its mysteries by him; but when tired of my lesson, my amusement consisted in aiming the balls at his fingers, and I was never more pleased than when I succeeded in making him cry out.

And again:

> I caught sight of the Emperor in his favourite billiard room and, not being able to insist on having a game with him, I bounded off, leaving my father in dismay at the consequences likely to ensue. Instead of my anticipated game, I was requested to read a book by Dr. Warden, Surgeon of the *Northumberland*, that had just come out.

Later on, when Napoleon used this room for working, he would spread his maps and plans upon the billiard table. Finally he asked to have it removed altogether; and from that date to the time of my visit it had disappeared from

[1] *Recollections of the Emperor Napoleon*, by Mrs. Abell, London, 1873, pp. 176-7.

[2] *Ibid.*

view, no book about the furniture and equipment of the exile (of which there are many) having succeeded in tracing it.

Later on I went to lunch with the Governor at Plantation House, so famous as the residence of Sir Hudson Lowe. It is a very pleasant and solidly built structure of the English middle-sized country-house type, erected in the early nineteenth century, and containing some good-sized rooms. I asked to see any furniture that might have belonged to Napoleon, and learned that the only pieces were a big English-made mahogany book-case from Old Longwood, a mirror, and a third piece from New Longwood, which the Emperor had of course neither ever seen or used.

In an unused room, however, at the back of the house my eye fell upon an English billiard table of a rather remarkable type. It had six legs instead of eight, and its dimensions were 11 feet 4 inches by 6 feet 1 inch, and there was an inlaid pattern of ivory and some coloured wood round the edge. I asked if there was any history attached to it and was informed that there was none.

" That," I said at once, " must be the billiard table of Napoleon. How can it be any other? Would the British Government ever have provided so ornamental a table for one of its own servants? When Napoleon turned out the table from the entrance room at Longwood what became of it? Manifestly it reverted to the possession of the Government. What then would

Sir Hudson Lowe do with it? The obvious course was to move it to his own house, where it has remained ever since, being too big and too heavy to part with and too interesting to sell."

This chain of reasoning seemed to have a good deal to be said in its favour, until my attention was called to the disconcerting fact that there was a very fresh-looking ivory tablet on the side of the table, containing the well-known name of "Thurston & Co., London." Refusing to be convinced, I suggested that an explanation should be sought from that firm of their connection with what I still persisted in regarding as this historic piece of furniture.

A few months later my humble essay in inductive logic was justified; for I heard from the Governor that in 1898 the table had been thoroughly repaired, when Messrs. Thurston had supplied new cushions and pockets and had affixed their ivory mark. Further inquiry elicited that the table was no other than Napoleon's, an old inhabitant of the island, still living, having been told so by Mr. Stephen Pritchard, who was a young man in St. Helena during Napoleon's exile. The tradition, however, seems to have died out at a comparatively early date, as the table fell into a state of disrepair. Indeed, one Governor was proved to have used it at first as a carpenter's bench, and later as a screen across a door leading into the back-yard!

On a closer examination the bed of the table was found to be a marvellous piece of joinery, consisting of small pieces of inch-thick oak dovetailed together like a parquet floor (I suppose that in those days slate was either difficult to procure or was unknown). The marking board (by Fernyhough of 36 Silver Street, Gordon Square, London) still hangs in the room and is certainly the original board belonging to the table, the scoring only showing up to 21, which was the old game when people played with the mace or butt.

Such was one of the minor discoveries which my visit to St. Helena enabled me to make—perhaps I may tell elsewhere about the others. But I still remain lost in wonder at the *nepenthe* which for three-quarters of a century had drugged the successive occupants of Plantation House and their innumerable visitors into complete oblivion of so interesting a prize.

THE PALAESTRA OF JAPAN

THE PALAESTRA OF JAPAN

> Ostenditque humeros latos, alternaque iactat
> Bracchia protendens, et verberat ictibus auras.
>
> VIRGIL, *Aeneid*, v. 376.

AMONG the most fair and fanciful of cities is Kioto, the ancient seat of the Empire and capital of Japan. For a thousand years it was the cage whose gilded bars immured the unseen but sacred person of the Mikado. Within the blind walls of the palace-enclosure the Royal *fainéant* dawdled away a linnet-like existence. Outside, the bulk of his people torpidly acquiesced in the rule, however fallible, of a son of the gods. Under the guise of an Imperial theocracy, Japan was in reality a playground for the military adventurer, and Kioto the focus of Court intrigue. A heavy curtain of mystery, the joint weaving of the palace and the priesthood, enveloped the sacred pile, and hermetically concealed it from alien eyes. It was only in the latter part of the last decade that the folds were torn asunder, and that Kioto became accessible to foreigners. The Mikado and his Court were moved to Tokio; the Castle was dismantled; the temple doors were thrown open, and the traveller was at liberty to ransack shrines and secret places and sanctuaries with inquisitive impunity.

The town is exquisitely situated in a cup between mountain ranges, quaintly outlined, and clothed with an astonishing wealth of trees. From the eastern range, where the visitor is probably lodged, he will get a wonderful outlook, both at sunrise and at nightfall. In the early dawn the entire city is drowned in a sea of white vapour, from which only the huge hooded roofs of the temples emerge, black and solemn, like the inverted hulls of gigantic ships. Suddenly, across the mist booms the sonorous stroke of some vast temple-bell, and rolls away in melancholy vibrations. At night the dusky mass of houses, stretching for miles, twinkles with the light of a thousand lanterns that glimmer from the lintels and dance along the streets. A swarm of fire-flies would seem to be flitting in the aisles of some dim and sombre forest, from whose recesses float upwards the indescribable hum of congregated humanity, street cries and laughter, the sound of voices, and the tinkling of guitars.

At festival time, and when the *matsuris*, or religious holidays, are celebrated, Kioto is especially worthy of a visit. The whole town turns out merry-making; the temple precincts are blocked from morn till night by gaily-dressed crowds; the tea-houses overflow with customers; the singing girls extract rich harvest; and copper pieces rain into the tills of itinerant purveyors of entertainment and theatrical shows. One street in particular is ablaze with a succession of gaudily-decorated booths, containing acrobats, jugglers, story-tellers, peep-shows, pantomimes, and plays. These are crowded from daybreak to sunset, and a forest of clogs and sandals, suspended on the outer wall, testifies to the thronged condition of the pit within. In the dried-up bed of the river which intersects the town, and which at different periods presents the opposite appearance of a gutter and a torrent, will probably be erected a gigantic booth, surrounded with gaudy bannerets flying from lofty poles. A stream of passengers pouring into the entrance shows that some exhibition of interest and popularity is being enacted within. It was in the wake of such a crowd, and on such an occasion, that, at Kioto, I first made acquaintance with the *palaestra* of Japan.

We do not require the authority of the bas-reliefs of Thebes and Nineveh, or even of the 32nd chapter of Genesis, to learn that wrestling must have been one of the earliest methods of conflict in vogue among ancient peoples. The light of nature must have very soon suggested this mode of encounter between human beings. Weapons may not always have been forthcoming. A duel of blows, *i.e.* a boxing match, would involve the victory of the more practised. Whenever two combatants were engaged in a personal struggle, it would be the spontaneous instinct of the one who was placed at a disadvantage, either of implements or of skill, to close with his adversary, and submit to the practical test of bodily agility or strength. In this way would he be most likely to equalise the handicap of fists, or club, or sword. But here, again, there would be an inequality of conditions in favour of the stronger muscles and more seasoned strength, to redress which the study and science of wrestling would come into being. Hence it is not surprising to find that, among the peoples of whose remote history records are preserved, wrestling seems to have been early reduced to a system and practised as an art.

We are perhaps best acquainted with the types of wrestling in use among the ancient Greeks, and among our own countrymen in the extreme north and west of England; familiar to us, in the one case, from the illustrations on vases and sculptures, in the other from the yearly exhibitions of the craft that are given in London. African travellers have also written curious accounts of the art as practised among negro tribes. To all these systems Japanese wrestling offers certain points of resemblance, but to none more closely (though with notable points of divergence) than to the ancient Homeric fashion, as described in the famous contest between Ajax and Ulysses in the twenty-third book of the *Iliad.* The early manner of Greek wrestling was as widely distinct from the later, from the trial of skill described by Plutarch as τεχνικώτατον καὶ πανουργότατον τῶν ἀθλημάτων,[1] as was a cross-

[1] Plutarch, *Symposium*, ii. 4.

bow from a Martini-Henry rifle; and among the many evidences of primitive habit and ancient date supplied by the Homeric poems, the story of the wrestling match might be quoted as a not insignificant item. The art was manifestly as yet in its infancy; there was an ingenuous laxity of rule; the performance was a rough-and-tumble one at the best; and if Ajax and Ulysses had depended for fame on their feats in the *palaestra*, the reputation of neither would have long survived. In Japan, a country combining a feverish proficiency in many of the habits of advanced civilisation with uncompromising relics of feudal crystallisation, we observe a similar innocence of science, and adhesion to archaic tradition, in the ways of the wrestling ring.

On the day that I speak of, at Kioto, the contest announced was between the combined representatives of that city and the neighbouring town of Osaka, and the champions of the modern capital, Tokio. The latter, in spite of the double recruiting ground of their adversaries, achieved an easy victory—a result which was received with extreme despondency by the local partisans, but was fortunately unattended by the scenes of violence that occurred on a famous occasion of a very similar character in our own history, when, on Lammas Day, 1223, the wrestlers of London having paid a visit to those of Westminster, and gained a victory at their expense, the bailiff of Westminster and his myrmidons, whose patriotism was incensed at the local discomfiture, picked a quarrel with the triumphant Londoners, and drove them back with slaughter into the precincts of the city. No such savage reprisals followed the collapse of the heroes of Kioto and Osaka on this occasion. Only a reproachful silence overhung the piqued and disgusted crowd.

I must here explain that I am not now writing about *Jiu-Jitsu,* the more familiar form of Japanese exercise or wrestling, which is taught as the art of self-defence, but about *Sumo*, the ancient, traditional, popular, semi-scientific, semi-religious wrestling of Japan; *Sumo* with its professional schools in that country, its forty-eight chief devices (each with eight variations), its guild of carefully-trained, intensively fed, obese practitioners, its ritual, half-serious and half-comic, its still unshaken hold, corresponding to the vogue of football in England, upon the populace in Japan. Twelve years ago, long after my Kioto experiences, a troupe of forty of the more eminent professors of this art came to England and gave a series of performances at the Japan-British Exhibition at Shepherd's Bush. I saw them there as I had seen their compatriots twenty years earlier in Japan: and the existence and methods of this school struck me on both occasions as one of the most curious survivals in that country, where the traditional and the up-to-date are so strangely interwoven.

In 1863 Sir Rutherford Alcock wrote:

Wrestling is to the Japanese what the ring is to us and something specially national. Every prince has a whole group of wrestlers, and their pride is to have the biggest, heaviest, and fattest; so that they generally look as bloated, overfed, and disgusting as prize oxen for the butcher at Christmas. I am at a loss to understand how such men of flesh and fat can put on any great strength—they grapple very fiercely but seldom seem to throw each other.

Since those days Japanese wrestling has experienced much the same transition as overtook its counterpart, once practised by kings and nobles in England (Henry VIII. was quite a good wrestler, and a century and a half later Monmouth courted popularity by occasionally indulging in a bout in rustic sports) when in the growing disrepute of Feudalism, it passed from the mansions of the great to the village green and the fairs and festivals of the people. Similarly in Japan, when the old order was broken up by the Revolution, and the castles, retinues, and princely maintenance of the nobility became a thing of the past, wrestling lost its hold upon the titled classes and became the sport of the crowd. But even so, it retains a quasi-hieratic prestige, because of its connection with the celebrated Ekoin Temple at Tokio, the strict etiquette and observances of the guild, and the popularity attaching to its principal practitioners, who are regarded in Japan with almost as much reverence as a great bull-fighter at Seville or Madrid.

To an outsider, unversed in the esoteric rules of the art, the performance is apt to appear more comic than serious—and I found the greatest difficulty in believing, either in Japan or London, that the scene which I witnessed had a scientific or a symbolic importance. But I will endeavour to be fair by giving the latter wherever I can.

The scene of action at Kioto was the booth in the dried-up river bed to which I referred. It was built and roofed with wattled bamboos, between whose interstices the air entered and made a pleasing temperature. The interior accommodated several hundred persons, mainly squatted on the ground, though a small, raised platform, divided into compartments, ran round the wall, for the accommodation of wealthier or more luxurious patrons. Every eye was directed at a raised structure in the centre, rectangular in shape, and about 18 feet square, constructed of bags of sand, packed one upon the other to a height of about 3 feet above the floor. At the four corners of this parallelogram were tall poles reaching to the roof, with gaudily-coloured flags, inscribed with native characters, depending between them at the top. This dais is said to have been a four-columned temple in its origin and still to retain a symbolic significance. In its centre a circle, about 12 feet in diameter, was marked out by a plaited belt of straw, worked into the soil, and was strewn with smooth yellow sand. This was the arena in which the combatants were about to engage, and out of which one of the two must hurl or thrust or throw his adversary before he could claim the victory.

A third person was also admitted on to the

raised artificial platform. This was the umpire, a grotesque sworded figure, clad in a reproduction of the old court costume of Japan, with projecting skirts, and a stiff excrescence standing out like wings on either side of his back, and flapping as he moved. Carrying in his hand, as an emblem of his office, a species of lacquered fan, which at critical moments he fluttered furiously, he took his stand just outside the magic circle, recited to the audience in a prolonged shriek the names of the combatants, placed them in position, and then went off into an unintelligible gabble of sound, growing louder and louder, and quicker and quicker, till the moment the wrestlers had closed, when his ejaculations culminated in a succession of screams, while he danced about the platform like a maniac, to get a fair view of the contest, to decide the points, and to adjudicate upon fair play.

And now as to the combatants themselves, the Milos of Tokio and Osaka, the pets of the national *palaestra.* Though for days I had seen their photographs being hawked about the streets, I must confess I was staggered when I set eyes upon the living originals. As their names were called out, from opposite sides there advanced on to the arena a pair of huge and burly figures, veritable Goliaths of Gath, marvels of flesh whatever they might be of muscle, tall in stature, big of girth, and elephantine in proportions—a wholly different type of animal from the average Japanese, who is a squat little fellow, nimble as a monkey, and less than 5 feet in height. Some of the wrestlers were men of medium height, but the majority were of extravagant size and dimensions, and appeared to belong to a distinct species, the peculiar attributes of which had been transmitted by a careful manipulation of the stock from one generation to another. They wore their hair in the old Japanese fashion, now rapidly falling into desuetude, with a stiffly-greased top-knot brought forward and laid horizontally upon the crown. Their features were not conspicuous for refinement, and wore an expression of intolerable swagger. Their bodies were plentifully embellished with small circular patches of sticking-plaster, concealing artificial burns—a prescription very popular in the Japanese pharmacopœia as a counter-irritant to any pain or malady that may happen to be in existence—or with the cicatrices which similar patches had once covered, and rows of which extended symmetrically down their brawny backs. Like the Homeric wrestlers, they were naked save for a *περίζωμα* or girdle—in this case a broad tasselled belt of dark blue silk, passing between the legs and round the loins, and fitting so tightly to the figure that the antagonist could with difficulty squeeze his fingers in to get a grip.

The rival competitors having stepped on to the arena, I naturally anticipated that they would soon fall to. Such expectations were based on a most mistaken estimate of the elasticity of the Japanese code, in which preliminaries, if importance be measured by time, transcend at least tenfold the trial of strength itself. These preliminaries may be divided into two parts: self-advertisement on the part of each individual champion, and co-operate bravado by the pair before the real bout begins. Either wrestler first advances with great solemnity to the edge of the platform, and faces the crowd. Lifting his right leg high in the air, and extending it as far as possible from the body, he brings it down on the ground with a vigorous stamp, at the same time that he also brings down his right hand with a resounding smack upon his right thigh. Then up goes the left leg, and along with it the left hand, and down come both with a thud at a similar angle on the left side; which done, and having strained and tested his sinews by this remarkable manœuvre, the wrestler straightens himself and gazes proudly around at the gaping audience. Then he lounges to a corner of the platform, sips a mouthful of water from a small wooden pail, and squirts it through his lips over his arm and chest and legs. Next, a paper napkin is handed to him by an attendant, with which he carefully wipes his face and body. Finally, from a little wooden box affixed to the corner-pole, he takes a pinch of salt between his fingers, and tosses it into the air for luck. This act I was told had also a moral significance, as indicating a complete absence of ill-will between the combatants, while the pundits further ascribe to it some unexplained sacrificial value.

These precautions satisfactorily completed, the champion probably goes through the stretching and stamping performance once again, until at last he is ready to play his part in the serio-comedy that then ensues.

Both athletes now take up their positions on opposite sides of the ring, and, squatting down upon their haunches, *vis-à-vis*, stretch out their arms and gently rub together the palms of their hands, which they then open outwards with a gesture of magnificent civility. Having satisfied this formality, which appears to correspond to the handshake of two English pugilists, they retire once more to their respective corners and repeat the performance with water, paper napkin, and salt. Some seven or eight minutes must have been consumed in these formalities, and patience is well-nigh exhausted, when at length they proceed into the middle of the ring, and again squat down like two monstrous baboons, exactly opposite each other, and with their foreheads all but touching.

The judge now plants himself on one side, brandishes his fan, and commences the series of mystic ejaculations before alluded to. While his jabber waxes fiercer and fiercer, they are seen to rise slightly from the crouching attitude, and to face each other with alert eyes and out-stretched arms, ready to grip or to rush in. But not yet is the visitor sure of his money's worth; for even at this advanced juncture one or other of the antagonists will casually loaf out of the ring, stroll back to his corner, and resume the water and salt masquerade—a gratification for which he finds all the readier excuse if, as frequently happens, one of the two parties has seized an unfair advantage in grappling, and the umpire has called "False start." A similar plea, too, may justify the interpolation of a fresh scene in the comedy, such as the rubbing of a little sand under the armpits, or a seizing of the corner-pole with both hands, and straining against it with full strength. When I asked any of my neighbours what they thought of this by-play, they grinned and said, "It is Japanese fashion"; with which simple effort of ratiocination their minds appeared to be quite content.

At length, however—after all these struttings and stridings, these rinsings and rubbings, and feints and fiascoes—our Daniel Lamberts are once more in the ring. What happens when they are at length engaged?

Now, wrestling may be described as consisting of three varieties: that in which the object is to defeat the adversary by any means whatever, without much consideration for fair or foul; that which, while enjoying a generous latitude, is yet subjected to certain recognised prohibitions and disqualifications; and that, every phase and move of which is regulated, partly by written laws, partly by unwritten etiquette. Of the last named, the system in vogue in Cumberland and Westmorland—which is the most scientific in existence—is the best illustration; the Devon and Cornish system is a fair type of the second; while of the first or most primitive we find samples in times and countries as remote as among the Greeks of Homer, in certain parts of Lancashire at the present day, and in the *palaestra* of Japan.

The object of the Japanese wrestler is to force his opponent to touch the ground with any part of his body other than his feet, or to eject him altogether from the magic circle, designated by the margin of plaited straw. It does not seem to matter much how he does this, whether by dint of superior weight, or strength, or agility, or by means of pushing, or tugging, or lifting, or throwing. He may hit his antagonist with his fist or even seize him by the hair. Sometimes the struggle is the work of a few seconds; sometimes it is prolonged for minutes. As a rule, the men seem most averse to grappling; or if by chance they have succeeded in closing, instead of aiming at a firm and fair grip, they will encircle each other's shoulders or body with one hand, while with the other they make frantic efforts to grab hold of the tight waistband of the adversary, in order to secure a more reliable purchase. Thus their energy is consumed in the double effort to wriggle out of reach themselves, and yet to catch hold of their antagonist. Sometimes the more powerful man, like Ajax, in the 23rd Book of the *Iliad*, will lift his opponent clean off the ground. Sometimes, too, the latter, like Ulysses, will reverse the advantage by the exercise of cunning. Sometimes, like the two Homeric heroes, they sprawl side by side. Occasionally the contest degenerates into a butting and thrusting match, as though between a pair of gigantic rams. But very rarely is any real danger incurred, or damage done, and a spectator might attend the Japanese ring for a lifetime and never witness such a scene as is described in the *Lady of the Lake*, where Scott demonstrates the prowess of Lord James Douglas in the wrestling match by thus describing the condition of his vanquished opponents :

> For life is Hugh of Larbert lame,
> Scarce better John of Alloa's fame,
> Whom senseless home his comrades bare.

The distinguishing feature of the Japanese contest seemed to be that nothing was unfair ; any movement was permissible ; no part of the body was forbidden. One result of this is very much to shorten the struggle. As a rule, it was over in a very few moments, or at most in a few minutes—a ridiculous contrast to the exorbitant time consumed in preliminaries. One of the two combatants was thrust or pitched or rolled or tumbled out of the ring. He picked himself up and retired on the one side ; the victor stepped down on the other ; the audience applauded and another pair came on.

The performance at Kioto, which, after a repetition of much the same incidents scores of times in succession, became somewhat monotonous, was relieved by two episodes of a more exaggerated, though unconscious, absurdity than anything by which they had been preceded. In an interval between two stages of the competition there advanced on to the platform, one after the other, two prodigiously fat boys. I say boys, though, had I not been told that their ages were only sixteen and seventeen, I should never have guessed that these mountains of flesh, with cheeks like footballs, bellies like hogsheads, and legs like an elephant's, were anything but mature and overfed men. They wore the same scanty costume as the wrestlers, with the addition of a long and gorgeously embroidered satin apron, which depended from below their paunches to the ground. One of the pair, I was told, was the son of a distinguished wrestler; and if he might be taken to represent a smaller edition of his parent, he certainly spoke volumes for the probable proportions of the sire. I expected that these two youthful prodigies would at least give some exhibition of agility or brute strength. But not a bit. They were far too tender to wrestle, and were merely intended for parade. Each in turn went through the solemn dumb show before described. They extended and brought down with a stamp their puffy legs; they smacked their hands upon their corpulent thighs; they spread out their clumsy arms and protruded their rotund paunches; they gazed around with an air of ineffable complacency; and then they strutted off the ring with as much composure as they had marched on.

The other episode was a wrestling match between the grown-up counterparts of these Gargantuan boys ; in other words, between two monsters whose appearance suggested that of fattened bulls at a Christmas show. They were clearly the idols of the ring, and were received with immense plaudits. Great flaps of superfluous fat hung about the body of the larger, and his stomach stood out like an inflated balloon. His rival was scarcely his inferior in size or ugliness. No part of the formula was omitted by these Titans. They raised and planted their unwieldy legs ; they spanked their massive thighs ; they squatted and drank water, and sprinkled salt, and rubbed their shining skins with the paper napkins. Finally, like two hippopotami, they collided. There was a sort of convulsive thrusting and heaving ; a quaking and yielding of vast surfaces of flesh ; a sound of crumbling and collapse ; and then, all in a moment, the fatter of the two fat men, whose science was not on a par with his suet, rolled off the platform like a beer-barrel, and tumbled down with a crash into the crowd.

In the second bout he was bent upon revenge. His tactics were simple but efficacious. When his opponent rushed in to grapple, he stood still like a mountain, and the smaller man, crushed by sheer *avoirdupois*, rebounded off him, and subsided in a heap upon the floor.

I afterwards inquired how it was that this strange and abnormal type of manhood was produced, and I learned that it was by the practice of eugenics *in excelsis*. The wrestlers are selected in boyhood from the progeny of parents of unusual size: they are dieted and treated from the earliest years; as they grow up and enter the ring they are attended by a special bodyguard of masseurs, trainers, barbers, clothiers and cooks; they are encouraged to consume an incredible amount of strength-producing food; and they constitute a separate guild, graded, numbered, and registered according to their capacity. How a selected body of Japanese champions would fare against our North Country or West Country wrestlers I cannot conjecture. For sheer weight no Englishman could compete with these fleshy prodigies. But I expect that he would give them a good deal of active exercise to which they are unaccustomed: and I should be prepared to wager a reasonable sum as to which would first find himself "on the mat."

PAGES FROM A DIARY

I

THE DANCING GIRL OF KENEH

Take her up tenderly,
Lift her with care ;
Fashioned so slenderly,
Young and so fair.

T. Hood, " The Bridge of Sighs."

THE dance was over. We had looked on at the contortions and wrigglings, the undulations and oscillations of the bodies of the girls as they performed on the deck of the boat. So violent had been their movements that the coins which hung on their gauzy dresses rattled and rang. The usual accompaniment had been furnished by the castanets of the dancers, the two-stringed cocoa-nut fiddle of the seated musicians, and the thrumming of the *darabookah*, or native drum. One of the girls, more agile than her companions, had lain down on the carpet and rolled over and over with a champagne bottle on her head containing a lighted candle stuck in its neck.

The company, departing for their native village of Keneh, famed for its school of dancers, had to cross a narrow plank between the steamer and the steep bank of the Nile. Suddenly a cry was raised that one of them, either jostled as she stepped ashore, or slipping on the plank, had fallen overboard. Looking over the side of the boat and listening to the confused noise in the bows, I saw something black float by on the surface of the water a few feet away. Little as I guessed at the moment, this was the head and hair of the drowning girl, who had gone without a struggle or a sound to her doom.

Quickly lowering a boat, we pulled down stream and lifted out the body 150 yards farther down.

On the muddy bank, lit only by the flicker of a solitary lantern and the remote glitter of the stars, lay the poor child's body, the head thrown back, the brown bosom bare, the bedraggled finery clinging round the limbs that half an hour before had tripped and twisted and turned. For three-quarters of an hour we endeavoured in vain to restore respiration amid the piercing cries of the other members of the troupe. It was of no use. One more unfortunate had gone to her death, and the Nile—a very fatal current into which to fall—had claimed another victim. I collected £10 on board and sent it to the *Mudir* of Keneh for distribution to the girl's relatives. But so handsome was the price, or so tempting the bribe, that when we came down stream again a deputation from Keneh awaited us to implore the favour of another performance.

II

THE ARAB RUNAWAY AT NEJEF

Asshur shall not save us ; we will not ride upon horses.
Hosea xiv. 3.

THE holy shrine of Nejef, one of the two most sacred places of the Shiah faith, situated in the Arabian desert, was my destination. There I was to be the guest of a learned *Mujtahed* or Mussulman Doctor of the Law, bearing the appropriate and high-sounding title of the Bahru' l' Ulum, or Sea of Science; and he had commissioned his brother, a demure and courtly Seyid, to greet me and bring me to the city. It was very cold in the early morning. In the distance on the left the tower of Birs Nimrud peered above a blue sea of vapour which enveloped the lower part of the great *tepe* or mound of burnt bricks from which it springs. Immense flocks of wild geese rose with loud clamour from the surrounding marshes and flew in a perfect cuneiform formation, behind their squadron leader, at a great height in the sky.

Not a sign of human life or habitation broke the stark monotony of the desert. But as the sun climbed above the horizon, a spark of fire, dwindling and then glowing again, scintillated on the sky-line, where the rays of the mounting orb splintered on the golden dome of Nejef.

The Seyid and I were riding side by side, and I was receiving instruction from him in the history and mysteries of the sacred places, when there approached us a gaily caparisoned cavalcade, in the midst of which curvetted and caracoled a magnificent white Arab steed. On his back were a velvet saddle-cloth, and a high-peaked Arab saddle, studded with silver; and the heavy shovel-stirrups, hanging loose at his side, jangled to and fro as he leaped and pranced. The two parties met; and thereupon I learned that this splendid animal, the private property of the Seyid, and the prize inmate of his stable, had been sent out by my host, in order that on his back I might make a becoming entry into the sacred city.

To me, however (I am not ashamed to confess), the prospect of exchanging my good horse and English saddle for the doubtful amenities of the Arab equipment and the exuberant frolics of this impassioned steed, made no appeal; and I felt a shrewd suspicion that my entry into the site of such holy memories, if honourable, would also be rapid. I recalled the unhappy experience of the Cardinal Balue in the pages of *Quentin Durward*, and I was resolved to escape a similar fate. With extreme civility, therefore, I pressed upon the Seyid the consideration that the laws of courtesy did not permit me to deprive him of his own horse, and that I should regard it as the highest honour to ride at his side into the town. I urged him therefore to exchange the animal that he was riding for this more showy mount. Although he displayed almost as much reluctance as I had done to make the exchange, he presently consented, and proceeded to dismount.

No sooner, however, had he placed one foot in the huge shovel-stirrup, hardly had the other leg swung in the air over the pointed crupper than, like an arrow from the bow, the proud Arab was off into the desert. No Derby winner ever covered the course at Epsom in more approved style or at a more headlong speed. I can see the steed and his rider now, the white mane and long tail of the horse stretched taut, the brown *aba* or cloak of the Seyid bellying and streaming (like the purple coat of the Cardinal) in the wind, his snow-white turban swaying over the head of the runaway, the thud of the hoofs growing fainter and fainter on the hard gravel of the desert, as horse and rider disappeared into the void. In almost less time than it has taken to write these sentences, they were a speck on the horizon, and finally vanished altogether from view. Nor, until I entered the gates of the city, did the holy man reappear, flushed and pouring with perspiration, but mounted on another and less fiery steed.

On the next morning, after seeing the sights of the place, we rode out through the high walls of the town on our way to the mosque of Kufa, five miles distant. The Seyid still did me the honour of accompanying me ; but this time I observed that he was mounted on a fine white female donkey, behind which trotted a young foal. When I asked him why he did not ride his own beautiful horse, he replied that he would mount it a little outside the city. Later on he said that the exchange would be effected at Kufa. But Kufa came and was passed, Kifl came, Birs Nimrud came, and before sundown we had reached Babylon. But still the secure and patient ass bore the form of the prudent Seyid of Nejef, and the not less prudent Englishman on his Baghdadi horse and his English saddle rode contentedly at his side.

III

THE ROBBER OF KHAGAN

> A territory
> Wherein were bandit earls, and caitiff knights,
> Assassins, and all flyers from the hand
> Of justice, and whatever loathes a law.
> TENNYSON, " Geraint and Enid " (*Idylls of the King*).

WHEN I came back again into India from the Pamirs in October 1894, after leaving Chilas, I crossed by the Babusar Pass (13,400 feet) into the Khagan Valley and descended by that route at Abbottabad, where I was to stay with my friend, that eminent soldier and charming man, Sir William Lockhart. Four years later he was to be my first Commander-in-Chief in India, though his tenure of that high office was lamentably brief, being terminated by his death in Calcutta in March 1900.

Lockhart had told me that the Khagan Valley, which, though inside the borders of British India, was left pretty much to itself, had an evil reputation for its bad characters, who escaped easily across the border into the Alsatia of Kohistan. He had accordingly insisted on sending out a detachment of Gurkhas who were to help me over the pass, which was likely to be deep in snow, and to guard me during my transit through Khagan.

These sturdy little fellows, though brave as lions in warfare, and belonging to a race of natural mountaineers, were strangely upset by the ordeal of crossing the pass in deep snow, and had themselves to receive, instead of rendering, assistance. One of them turned sick and burst out crying, and I had to lift and hold him on to a pony. The difficulty of the pass, however, once surmounted, we then rode for two days down the exquisite valley of Khagan through lovely woods of pine and cedar, crossing repeatedly, by cantilever bridges of rude timbers, the rushing Kunhar river that foamed and roared below. I was escorted by the head of the friendly family of Seyids, who are the principal land-owners and (under the British Raj) the practical rulers of the valley, and by his brothers and cousins.

The farther we descended the more beautiful was the scenery, which became Swiss in its tone and beauty. Tall plumy pines clothed the sides of the ravine to the water's edge, and even sprang in the bed of the stream. This sometimes widened into crystal-clear pools, anon roared hilariously in rapids and cascades. I rode over ground littered with pine-needles and cones. The villages or hamlets consisted of log-huts built on the steep slope of the hill, so that the back of the house sprang straight from the hill-side, or at most was raised above it by two horizontal rows of logs, while the façade was sometimes two storeys in elevation, with verandahs. The side walls were built of big logs and stones, but the front, as a rule, consisted of upright timbers. Outside the villages were great stacks of grass and other herbs.

Nearing Khagan the timber and scenery acquired a more English character. Chestnuts and sycamores, yellow with the autumn, abounded. Many of the trees were pollarded, and bundles of dry leaves on sticks were trussed up in the forks for winter use. From every village emerged numbers of tall, spider-waisted, big-turbaned, handsome Seyids, every one apparently a brother or a cousin of the chief. Each as he came up stretched out his right hand, in the palm of which were two rupees, to be politely touched and returned. The dress of the men was very different from that with which I had so long been familiar among the dark communities of the Hindu Kush. The Khaganis wore a big turban, white, or of a dark blue tartan, with long ends hanging down behind. An overcoat reached nearly to the knee, and was tightly drawn in by a waist-band at the waist. Below this were loose *puttee* or cotton knickerbockers ; white *puttees* were bound round the legs with black fastenings, and on the feet were leather shoes turned up at the point. All manner of leather straps and belts were distributed about the person. The men's faces were very yellow in colour, and the majority wore a beard and moustache which was shaven bare over the middle of the lip. The beard of my host, Ahmed Ali Shah, was stained a brilliant red, and his manners were those of a Renaissance courtier. The hair was worn long, and turned up at the ends upon the back of the neck. The entire appearance of the Khagan Seyids suggested in fact some human vanity and no small taste.

On the second night we camped on a grassy slope just outside the principal village of Khagan. My own little Kabul tent was placed on the left side of the miniature terrace, and just above it was pitched the large tent of the Gurkha escort, four of whom were to be on duty by day and the remainder by night.

Tired out by my long day's ride, I ate my simple dinner in the little tent, and after writing my diary, went to bed between ten and eleven. The bed consisted of a leather roll stretched on rings between the two *yakdans* or leather trunks, which are the most serviceable form of travelling baggage in those regions. Slung on mule-back in the daytime, they serve both as packing-cases, seat, and bedstead in the tent at night. I had placed the bed against the left-hand canvas of the tent, the open space in the centre and on the right being occupied with my saddle and holsters and the whole of my kit, lying in a litter on the floor. The Gurkha guards were presumably posted outside the tent.

Soon after midnight I woke, not with a start, but with the consciousness of which I had often read, though I had never before experienced it, that I was not alone in the tent. The darkness was black as pitch and thick as velvet; and though I listened intently without moving a muscle, I heard no sound. Half unconsciously I put out my left hand and dropped it between the bed and the canvas wall of the tent which the bed all but touched. It fell plumb, as though my fingers had alighted upon a billiard ball, on the shaven head of a man. I could feel the prickle of the sprouting hair against my palm. But in the same moment the object slid out of my grasp and a rustle indicated the stealthy withdrawal of the intruder. By this time I was wide awake. Springing up, I struck a match, seized my revolver, and dashed in my pyjamas out of the tent, shouting to the Gurkhas as I emerged. Not a man was to be seen. I rushed up the short slope to the guard-tent and tore aside the flap. The eight guards were all lying fast asleep on the ground.

In a few moments the whole camp was astir, the guilty Gurkhas were flying in every direction in pursuit of the intruder, and the place resounded with shouts and yells. But neither then, nor on the next morning, nor at any time afterwards was any trace of him found. The polite Seyids were visibly disturbed at this reproach upon their hospitality and the good character of their village. But they protested that the evildoer could not possibly be a Khagan man; no Khagani could be guilty of so outrageous and criminal an act; he was a *budmash* from across the border who had fled back incontinently to his own people.

I do not suppose that the *budmash* in question had come to kill me, unless indeed he was a Ghazi who wished to reduce by one the number of unbelievers in the world. He was much more probably a local thief who expected to find in my tent money or some other valuables, or who was ready to steal anything upon which he could lay his hands.

But I have always been grateful for the chance that led him to crawl under the left rather than the right canvas of my tent, and that led me to drop my hand upon his unsuspecting cranium at the very moment when he was just lifting his head to find out where he was. Had he effected his entry on the other side of the tent, he might either have absconded with some of my belongings or, had I interrupted him in the act, have dealt with me in a manner which would have prevented this anecdote from ever being written.

IV

THE GREEK EXECUTIONER

With devotion's visage
And pious action we do sugar o'er
The devil himself.

SHAKSPEARE, *Hamlet*, Act III. Sc. I.

FORTY years ago the administration of justice in Greece left much to be desired. Visiting the military prison of Fort Palamedes above the town of Nauplia in 1882, I was shown a number of condemned criminals, brigands of the worst type, who were exposed to view behind bars—a horrible sight—awaiting execution. King George, however, who was at that time on the throne, had an invincible repugnance to signing a death-warrant. Accordingly the condemned men were fairly safe as long as His Majesty was in the country. But as soon as he departed on tour, and the Government was put into commission, a death-warrant was at once made out and a few of the more desperate ruffians were disposed of. It may well be imagined that among the criminal classes the continental journeys of the Sovereign were awaited with much apprehension, and excited but little enthusiasm.

Still more anomalous was the case of the Public Executioner. He was himself a criminal, under sentence of death, who had only escaped that fate by volunteering to inflict it upon others. His term of office was ten years, and he was eligible for re-appointment if he gave satisfaction. In such general detestation, however, was this functionary held, that he was obliged to live specially guarded on a little island in the harbour. He would have been murdered at once had he shown himself without protection on the mainland.

A difficulty, however, presented itself when the Executioner, having completed his term of office, wished to retire. His life was still in danger, not from the unexecuted sentence of the law, which he had escaped by his own decade of faithful service, but from the vengeance of those whose friends he had been instrumental in despatching to another world. The last incumbent of the office had solved the difficulty in a manner that did credit to his ingenuity, even if it did not conclusively demonstrate his penitence. He had turned monk and sought the security of a devotional life.

V

BY THE WATERS OF BABYLON

> The sun's rim dips, the stars rush out,
> At one stride comes the dark.
>
> S. T. Coleridge, " The Ancient Mariner."

ONCE more I am camped on the banks of the Euphrates. The river rolls its dirty volume by. It is the late afternoon. There occurs that wonderful interlude before sundown—a time half of mystery, half of sadness—when the day passes through its death-throes and prepares for dissolution. In the tranquil radiance the river-side villages are redeemed from the filth and squalor of the day, and assume a fleeting beauty that has in it something of the divine. A bluish vapour rises from the broad river-bosom and swathes the banks with filmy kerchief. The pitchy hulls of the big one-masted boats, moored along the shore, tremble inverted in the glassy current. A rosy pink strikes redly on mud wall and mouldering rampart, and high above the flat house-tops the columnar stems and quivering plumes of a hundred palms are pencilled against the sky. Bands of saffron fringed with green, and of turquoise blending into pink, are stretched like scarves round the horizon, except where in the west the sinking orb turns half the heaven into a forge of fire. In the distance is heard the creaking of the pulleys as the oxen draw the last skins of water from the muddy wells. Nearer, the mingled sounds of human and animal life, the barking of dogs and braying of donkeys, the shrill clamour of children, the raucous ejaculations of the Asiatic mule-driver, and the eternal hubbub of the bazaar, ring out a strange but not unmusical chorus. From the village mosque tower a brazen-lunged Seyid, with fingers pressed against his ears, intones the evening prayer. And so, as the suave pomp of the Eastern sunset wanes, river and village and people and the glowing sun itself sink slowly to rest; the enchantment seems coldly to fade out and expire; an undulating vapour curls upward from the river-bed; and presently the same grey misty monochrome has enveloped all alike with its fleecy mantle. The day is dead.

VI

THE HAVILDAR OF SARHAD

> The poet, wandering on
> Over the aerial mountains which pour down
> Indus and Oxus from their icy caves,
> In joy and exultation held his way.
>
> SHELLEY, " Alastor."

IN the course of my visit to the Pamirs in the early autumn of 1894 in order to determine the true source of the Amu-Daria or Oxus

> In her high mountain cradle of Pamere,

I descended from the lofty passes where the Hindu Kush and Mustagh ranges join and are merged, into the valley of Wakhan. This narrow valley, down which the Oxus flows, had just been assigned by the Pamir Boundary Commission to the Amir of Afghanistan, as a buffer state between British and Russian territories and ambitions, and it was believed to be sparsely occupied by Afghan troops. I camped for one night at Bozai Gumbaz, the place where Sir Francis (then Captain) Younghusband had been arrested by Colonel Yonoff in August 1891—a bleak and cheerless spot—and from there my companion and I made our way down stream, over *paris* or cliff tracks of appalling steepness, to a spot where the river, released from its long mountain imprisonment, spread itself out in countless fibres over a wide watery plain, closed on either hand by magnificent snow peaks. Below us lay the terraced fields of Wakhan. Oxen, goats, and sheep were being driven in at the sunset hour, and thin curls of smoke arose from the settled habitations of men. My companion and I were a good deal in advance of our caravan, which we had left struggling on the mountain tracks, and we arrived alone at a group of Wakhi villages in the valley bottom, to all of which the Afghans apply the collective title of Sarhad. This spot is 10,400 feet above the sea. It was a place of somewhat evil reputation for English travellers: for there in 1890 Mr. and Mrs. St. G. Littledale, the well-known explorers, had been stopped for twelve days by the officiousness or discourtesy of the Afghan captain from Kila Panja, 50 miles farther down the river.

To guard against any such contretemps, I had written in advance to the Amir of Afghanistan, whose guest I was going later to be at Kabul, asking him to send word to his officials in Wakhan of my intended arrival. This he had done, and the petty officer at Sarhad was well aware of my identity. Nevertheless, the opportunity of swaggering a little at the expense of a Great Power before the inhabitants of this remote spot was too good to be lost, and, the local officer having presently been joined by his superior officer, a *havildar* from the little Afghan fort of Chehilkand, lower down the valley, these worthies, who wore a nondescript combination of uniform and ordinary dress, informed my companion and me that we were Russian spies and must consider ourselves under arrest until their commanding officer could arrive from Kila Panja. In the course of my travels I have, on different occasions, been mistaken for a good many things and persons, but it was a happy novelty to be suspected of being a Russian spy!

Retaining our equanimity as best we could, we watched with anxious eyes the mountain defile from which our camp and escort must presently emerge, the while we palavered with the intractable and insolent Afghans. Presently, as the welcome caravan debouched upon the plain, the relative strengths of the two parties were reversed; we found ourselves in a very decided numerical majority, and, promptly turning the tables, I informed the two Afghans that if they and their seedy sepoys took the smallest step to impede our progress, they should themselves be placed under immediate arrest. This was sufficient; and after a warning of my sincere intention to inform the Amir at Kabul of the hospitable reception accorded at Sarhad to his impending guest, we packed our loads and marched away.

Two months later at Kabul the Amir himself

raised the matter in my first audience with him, having received my letter of complaint and made inquiries. The reply of the *havildar*, however, had been of such a character as to excite my reluctant admiration. " He was still awaiting," he said, " the arrival of the great English Lord *sahib*, who would no doubt presently appear in uniform with an escort of 1000 men. In the meantime two of the Lord *sahib's* servants (*i.e.* my companion and myself) had already passed through with an insignificant following. He himself would continue diligently to await the great Lord."

I heard later that this estimable intention on the part of the polite *havildar* had been frustrated by an imperative summons to Kabul. What happened there I do not know, though from my knowledge of the Amir I should fear the worst. For my own part, I could not help feeling a sneaking admiration for the ingenuity of my two inhospitable friends of Sarhad in Wakhan.

VII

IN THE BULL RING

NOTICIAS TAURINAS

La Corrida de Cadiz fue buena. Los toros de Nuñez de Prado resultaron bravos y de empieje despachando 15 caballos. Frascuelo estuevo disgraciado y Angel Pistor bien. La Corrida de Malaga fue mala. El publico silbo a Lagartijo y Cara-Ancha. Los toros de Benjumea saluron muy malos — Uno de ellos fu fogueado.

El Liberal, April 29, 1884.

I SAW the usual sights of the Spanish Bull Ring. I saw Lagartijo and Mazzantini kill eight bulls in eight strokes at the great Easter festival at Seville. I witnessed the revolting spectacle of the half-disembowelled horses forced upon the horns of the artificially infuriated animals, the agility of the *banderilleros*, the cruelty of the inflammable darts, the amazing skill, agility, and courage of the *espada* or *torero* in the final encounter. The entire performance filled me, as it has filled so many others, with alternate admiration and disgust. Far more than the bull-fight itself was I interested in the scene on the eve before the fight, when the bulls were driven into the town at night, thundering along the closed streets amid clouds of dust to the waving of lanterns and the cries of the horsemen urging them on, until they were penned in their stalls in the great amphitheatre, where they were to be shut up foodless till their ordeal of the morrow.

But the feature of the Spanish crowd that struck me most was its personal attitude, sometimes of frenzied admiration, sometimes of passionate ridicule and fury, directed at the principal actors, whether human or animal, in the drama. If one of the fighters showed skill and address, he would be frantically applauded; if he missed a series of strokes or offended against any of the rules of the game, still more if he appeared to be lacking in personal courage, he would be as unmercifully hissed, and oranges, empty bottles, old shoes and hats would be hurled at him from the crowd. Similarly, if the bull put up a good fight, he was loudly cheered. If he funked or declined to fight, he was overwhelmed with derision and contempt—poor brute—as though he had been guilty of some culpable misdemeanour. Indeed, not only was he personally abused, but his family and ancestry were held up to equal execration.

All this seemed very foreign to British ideas of sport. English crowds occasionally indulge in a little " barracking " if a particularly " stonewall " bat defends his wicket without adding to the score. But I have never heard a football player hissed for missing a goal; still less a racehorse calumniated for coming in last in a race.

But the Spanish temperament in its ardour for the national sport identifies itself with the triumphs or the *lâches* of man and beast alike, and, if it applauds their exploits, is equally indifferent to their failure or suffering. I can never forget one such scene of which I was a witness in the great Bull Ring of Malaga.

Just as the *espada* lunged with the sword, at the very instant that he sprang aside, the bull with a rapid twist of its lowered head was upon him. He was caught and tossed like a feather bolster into the air; he fell; in a second again he was aloft, transfixed on that terrible point. There was a vision of glittering silver spangles, violet silk breeches, and white stockings, as they were twirled round in mid-air, and then a heavy thud as the body was dashed again to the ground.

A cry of momentary horror broke even from that callous assembly. Thousands sprang excitedly from their seats; many dashed down to the arena to get a nearer view of what was happening; the personal friends of the bullfighter leaped the barricade to offer their services. The unhappy man, staggering for a moment to his feet, and striving ineffectually to combine with the physical courage that never deserted him the strength that was fast ebbing away, fell into the arms of the surrounding *matadors*. He had two gaping wounds, one in the back of the right thigh, the other in the groin—the two places where the cruel point had been driven home.

One of the doors in the barrier was opened; the procession carrying the wounded man disappeared down the gangway beyond. The excitement subsided as quickly as it had arisen; the crowd resumed their seats, and the entertainment proceeded exactly as though nothing had occurred. That evening the victim died.

Few perhaps who see the sport and applaud the skill realise the prodigious risks incurred in the final stage. The death roll of famous *toreros*, though perhaps not great in proportion to the numbers engaged, is the most eloquent comment. Of those whom I saw nearly forty years ago the most celebrated happily survived their experience of the arena. Mazzantini, who had been both a station-master and an operatic singer, ended his public career as Civil Governor of Cadiz! Lagartijo and Frascuelo became small landed proprietors, and remained popular heroes on their farms. But others, in addition to the Malaga victim, whose name I forget, were less fortunate, and lost their lives on the field of action. The most recent champion of the ring, Joselito, was killed at Talavera in 1920. The year 1922 claimed the lives of Varelito and Granero.

VIII

THE MAHARAJA'S ADJURATION

And the driving is like the driving of Jehu, the son of Nimshi; for he driveth furiously.

2 Kings ix. 20

It was a wonderful spectacle. Here Nature had spent upon the land her richest bounties; the sun failed not by day, the rain fell in due season, drought was practically unknown; an eternal summer appeared to gild the scene. In a fairy setting of jungle and backwater and lagoon, prosperous cities had been founded; and a race of indigenous princes flattered the pride and upheld the traditions of a tranquil and contented people.

The morning from the earliest hour—for it was very hot—was spent in ceremonial duties. State visits had to be paid, formal compliments exchanged, institutions to be inspected or opened, speeches to be made—all this under a cloudless sky and a tropical sun. Even in their white duck uniforms the staff felt and looked hot; even the Maharaja, in all his panoply of silks and jewels, although inured to the climate, was perceptibly warm. The native crowds, however, who lined the streets and packed the public places, in their scantier attire were visibly happy, while not disdaining the use of sunshades of local manufacture. The massed school children did the requisite amount of shrill cheering at selected sites. The Prince's Body-guard galloped about on quite inferior mounts and attempted a display with which they were evidently unfamiliar. The State landau had been pulled out for the occasion by the Maharaja for the use of the Viceroy and his wife; but neither the horses nor the native coachman on the box appeared to have any clear appreciation of their task or any particular aptitude for performing it.

The procession was about to start from one ceremonial scene to another; "God save the King" was being performed in a somewhat precarious and spasmodic fashion by a native band; the crowds began to cheer, the cavalry escort fell into place; but the carriage and horses seemed reluctant to start, while the native coachman appeared to be so overcome with his responsibilities as to be incapable of anything but futile gesticulation.

Then it was that the Maharaja, whose knowledge of English was limited, but who realised that his reputation as a prince and a host was at stake, rose in his place and ejaculated in tones of thunder two words and two alone:

"D-r-iver! D-r-ive!"

It was felt by every one that the command was adequate to the occasion. The Maharaja sank back into his seat exhausted, but with the air of a great duty solemnly performed; the native coachman ceased gesticulating and with recovered confidence handled the reins; the steeds sprang forward with an unexpected *élan*; the procession fell into line; and the next stage in the morning's performance was securely and triumphantly achieved. The two words of the Maharaja, like the " Open Sesame " of Ali Baba, had successfully solved the problem.

IX

THE YOUNG JUDGE

O wise young judge, how I do honour thee.
SHAKSPEARE, *Merchant of Venice*, Act IV. Sc. I.

THE death of King Victor Emmanuel in January 1878 produced an immense sensation throughout Italy, where he was not merely regarded as the national hero who had re-established the national unity, and placed Italy once more in the front rank of states, but had endeared himself to the people by his sporting instincts, his indomitable gallantries, and his interest in the life of all classes of the population. The title "Il Re Galantuomo" fitly represented the national conception both of his character and his service. The demonstrations of sorrow were universal and sincere, and all Italy yearned to testify its sense of the irreparable loss which the nation had sustained. Inasmuch as the whole of the country could not participate in the obsequies at Rome, where the King had been buried, it was decided to hold a great ceremony for Northern Italy at Milan, where a service was announced to be held in the Duomo, and a Requiem Mass performed. Tens of thousands of persons poured into Milan from all parts of the country, and the city was as packed as though, instead of conducting a service over a man already interred elsewhere, the body of the King himself was to be carried by his mourning people to the actual grave.

I happened to be in Milan with my old and trusted friend Oscar Browning; and we considered in what way we could, without any special credentials, see the spectacle and take part in the celebration. We decided in any case to put on black evening clothes, top hats, and white ties, as likely to be in harmony with the sentiment of the hour. Thus attired we sallied out in the morning and made our way through the crowded streets to the Prefecture to see if we could obtain permission to enter the Cathedral. There was a great crowd round the official building, where processions of provincial mayors and district judges were being organised, and were in some cases already starting on their way. Observing that some of these gentlemen were garbed in raiment almost identical with our own, we insinuated ourselves in their midst, and walked with admirable composure in their company through the long covered gallery or arcade that leads into the Piazza before the Duomo. O. B.'s fluent command of Italian enabled him to cope easily with the situation. But I was a little embarrassed when my neighbour in the procession addressed me with the remark that I appeared to be an exceptionally youthful Judge, and wanted to know whence I came. I acknowledged the precocity, but refrained from otherwise adding to his information.

At length we emerged into the great Piazza, which was filled with an enormous crowd, and, crossing this, marched up the main steps of the Duomo and entered by the central door. At the head of the nave stood a gigantic catafalque on which rested the empty coffin, draped in purple and black, that represented the absent body of the King. Whether the illusion that we were Judges did or did not continue to prevail, at any rate no one obstructed our passage to the foot of the catafalque, where the bishops assisting in the ceremony took their seats at our feet. From this vantage ground we witnessed without interruption the entire ceremony.

It was not free from tragedy. For after the processions had entered and the service had already advanced far on its way, the crowd in the Piazza, who had not been permitted to enter the Cathedral, burst through the great door that closed the northern side aisle and flocked into the building. Like a flood they poured up the aisle, climbing the monuments, overturning the occupants of the seats, and crushing and trampling each other under foot. A part of the Mass was being chanted by a tenor with a divine voice, whose name was Tommaso or Tommasino (or some such name); but loud above his glorious notes rang through the marble colonnades the agonising shrieks of the tortured men and women. The next day we read in the papers that not a few persons had been crushed to death in that desperate and almost demoniacal struggle.

HUMOURS OF TRAVEL

I

THE "PIG AND WHISTLE" AT BUNJI

I will fetch you a toothpicker now from the furthest inch of Asia.

SHAKSPEARE, *Much Ado about Nothing*, Act II. Scene I.

NOTHING is more remarkable than the character and spirit of the young men, British Subalterns as a rule, who on the outskirts of our Indian Dominions are upholding the fabric and sustaining the prestige of the British Raj.

In remote mountain fastnesses, amid wild tribes, far from civilisation, in a climate sometimes savagely hot, at others piercingly cold, with no comforts or luxuries, often amid cruel hardships, they face their task with unflinching and patriotic ardour, dispensing justice among alien populations, training and disciplining native forces, and setting a model of manly and un complaining devotion to duty, which reflects undying credit on the British name.

Scattered as they may be over wide areas, it will be rarely that they can meet together to enjoy society or to exchange experiences. When they do, warm is the hospitality and high are the spirits that prevail. On my march from Kashmir to the Pamirs, in the autumn of 1894, I came across such a place, and I was lucky in joining such a gathering at a spot known as Bunji, not far from the Indus on the mountain road to Gilgit. It is a forlorn and melancholy spot, destitute either of amenities or attraction. Here, however, stood a humble single-storied bungalow, consisting, as far as I remember, of three small rooms, one of which was used as a mess-room, where the young officers from time to time foregathered as they went up and down the road. With a somewhat forced jocularity, seeking to invest this dingy meeting-place with the simulacrum of a tavern, its frequenters had christened it the " Pig and Whistle."

On this occasion, hearing of my visit, they had collected from far and near. I was accorded the sleeping-place of honour in a flea-haunted bedroom, where I spent a night of horror. But the real entertainment was in the so-called mess-room, where was dispensed whatever of hospitality the limited local resources might permit.

As we sat down to dinner, however, I noticed that on the bespattered walls of this primitive hostelry were pinned a series of portraits of famous English beauties, cut from the pages of illustrated newspapers. There I saw the likenesses of a number of great ladies whom I knew well in England—Georgina Countess of Dudley, Millicent Duchess of Sutherland, Lady Warwick, and others whose names I cannot now recall. Each visitor, as he journeyed to and fro and enjoyed the modest hospitality of the "Pig and Whistle," had written his name in pencil against the portrait which he thought the most beautiful, thus offering his humble and innocuous tribute at the shrine of Venus. Such was the solitary recreation of these gallant but futile lovers.

When I arrived, the result was a tie between the three principal competitors; and upon my revealing that I knew the subjects of all the portraits, I was invited with uproarious enthusiasm to append my name to the most lovely, and so to award the apple. I did so, but to whom I gave the prize I have never revealed, nor would wild horses now induce me to disclose. It remains a secret buried for ever in the unwritten records of the "Pig and Whistle" at Bunji in the Himalayan Mountains.

II

THE TOP HAT AT TEHERAN

The hat is the *ultimum moriens* of respectability.

O. Wendell Holmes,
The Autocrat of the Breakfast Table, viii.

When I was at Teheran in the autumn of 1889, as the guest of the British Minister, Sir H. Drummond Wolff, the latter procured for me an audience with H.M. Nasr-ed-Din Shah. But for this purpose I was informed that a black silk top hat such as we wear in the streets of London was indispensable. Now, though I should never think of travelling either to Timbuctoo or even the North Pole without a dress suit—for in anxious circumstances this is a recognised hall-mark of respectability throughout the world, and will procure an audience of almost any living potentate—I had not encumbered myself in my Persian journeys, where all my effects had to be strapped on to the back of a horse, galloping sixty or seventy miles in the day, with anything so perishable as a top hat. Nor was such an object to be found for love or money in the shops of Teheran.

The British and other foreign Legations were ransacked for what they might be able to produce in the shape of the obligatory headpiece; but, although a few somewhat battered specimens were forthcoming, the diplomatic cranium generally appeared to be of so ill-developed a character, at any rate as represented at that time in the Persian capital, that not one of them could I persuade to rest upon my head, which happens to be unduly large and round. I amused myself by repeating the famous remark of Jowett in his funeral sermon upon Dean Stanley, which I had heard when an undergraduate at Balliol some years before, when the Master had said that though mitres rained upon Stanley as thick as hailstones from heaven, his head was so curiously shaped that none of them would precisely fit it.

The British Minister himself had a head of creditable dimensions; and I found by experiment that his hat, which was decent though tarnished, could be comfortably fitted on my brow. But alas! when I suggested that he should surrender it to me and go to the audience —for he was to present me—in his cocked hat and diplomatic uniform, he absolutely declined to do anything so subversive of the official etiquette at a private audience. His top hat was his own, and upon no other head should it repose.

Amid this sequence of cruel disappointments the time sped rapidly by until the eve of the day of audience arrived.

No top hat had yet been procured, and I contemplated the probability of having to go bareheaded through the streets, a not too enviable experience under a midday Asiatic sun.

On the very last evening, however, a young Persian Minister had invited me to dinner at his house in the Persian style, to which a few other Europeans had also been bidden. We passed a very pleasant evening, and tasted rather than consumed an immense number of succulent Persian dishes; among the company being a French *savant* of world-wide reputation, who had arrived at Teheran in the pursuit of certain anthropological researches. As we left the house at a late hour—the party to which I belonged being the first to go—and passed through the vestibule, I started with an exclamation of almost rapturous surprise when I beheld standing upon the table, prominent and inviting, a black silk hat, glossy, capacious and new. With a presence of mind on which I have never ceased to congratulate myself, I clapped it on to my head, over which it came down nearly to the ears, ran out of the house, jumped on to my horse, and returned at full gallop to the British Legation.

On the next afternoon I was duly presented to His Majesty the Shah, my top hat being the admiration of all observers, and in the evening the headpiece was returned, with profuse apologies for the slight mistake, to the learned *savant*. He is doubtless unaware to this hour that but for his head and his hat I should never have had the honour of an audience with H.M. Nasr-ed-Din Shah.

III

THE ENTRY INTO KABUL

Fortes Fortuna iuvat.
PLINY.

Blesses his stars and thinks it luxury.
ADDISON, *Cato*, Act I. Scene IV.

WHEN in the autumn of 1894 I received an invitation from Amir Abdur Rahman Khan to visit him in his country, and was making the preparations for my journey, I had to consider the dress in which I should present myself at the Afghan capital. As I was the first private visitor for many years to Kabul, and as the Amir had paid me an exceptional compliment in the invitation, knowing that I was a Member of Parliament and had been Under-Secretary for India, it was desirable that my appearance should be adequate to the occasion. So many incorrect versions of my visit have appeared in print that I will here set down the facts. If I practised a slight measure of deception I trust that it was as innocent as it was successful.

The only official uniform that I possessed, apart from the pseudo-military outfit of a Deputy-Lieutenant, was that which is worn by an English

Under-Secretary of State (I was not at that time a Privy Councillor); and I remembered the mediocre impression which this exceedingly plain and unattractive garb had produced at the Court of Korea. Moreover, I was not the owner of a star or cross or medal of any description. I also remembered that in conversation with Mr. Ney Elias, the famous explorer and member of the Indian Political Department, a few years before, he had told me that the main reason for the excellent impression he had produced when engaged upon a Boundary Commission in Afghan Turkestan, was the extreme width of the gold stripe which he had taken the precaution to have sewn upon his trousers, and the size of the sword with which he had girt his thigh. Acting upon this prudent hint I decided that, if I were to produce the desired effect at the Afghan capital, I must not be too strict in my observance of the rules laid down by the Lord Chamberlain at the Court of St. James. After all, while in Afghanistan as the guest of the Amir, I should be regarded not merely as an ex-Minister of Great Britain, but also for the time being as a representative of my own nation: and it behoved me therefore to represent this double personality with becoming dignity.

Accordingly I devised a costume which, made up as it was, partly in London, partly at Bombay, and partly in the Punjab, was certainly composite, but would, I thought, be appropriate to the occasion. In London, before starting, I called upon Messrs. Nathan, the well-known theatrical costumiers, and there I found a number of stars of foreign orders, which had no doubt once adorned the bosoms of foreign diplomats, and been purchased by Messrs. Nathan for the purpose of their business. I negotiated the hire of three of the most gorgeous of these for the space of six months, for a very moderate sum. What they were exactly, I do not remember; but I think that they belonged to some of the smaller states of Eastern Europe, and I fancy from its splendour that one was Russian. I also discovered and hired by far the biggest pair of gold epaulettes that I have ever seen. They must have decorated the shoulders of some eighteenth-century Admiral of vast proportions, about the time of the French wars; and they reposed in a beautiful tin case, which was almost the size of a hat-box.

This was the English contribution to my equipment. Then, while I was in India, it struck me that, for the purpose of an entry on horseback, the blue trousers and the boots of the ordinary levee dress were hardly sufficiently business-like or imposing. I accordingly ordered from a well-known Bombay bootmaker a gorgeous pair of patent leather Wellington top-boots, which I still possess, and which certainly lent a much needed elegance to the lower extremities of my person. Finally, while staying at Abbottabad with my friend Sir William Lockhart, then Commander-in-Chief in India, before I entered Afghanistan, I consulted him as to procuring a cavalry sword of suitable dimensions and splendour, in preference to the miserable skewer that is an appendage of the English Court dress. He replied that he had the very thing, and forthwith produced a gigantic curved weapon with an ivory hilt and a magnificent chased and engraved scabbard, which had been presented to him in honour of some successful campaign, and the blade of which was covered with a lordly inscription. The clatter made by this weapon when hung loosely from the belt was of the most approved and awe-inspiring description. Such was the get-up with which I approached my fateful journey.

Well do I recall the anxiety with which, when I drew near to Kabul, I extracted these objects from their resting-place and proceeded to don my variegated apparel! A special tent had been pitched for me, by order of the Amir, a mile or more from the city walls, in order that I might halt and exchange my travel-stained riding dress for something more becoming to the occasion. I was very near to a fiasco, for I had completely forgotten that epaulettes (which I had never worn) require a special attachment to the shoulders of the particular uniform of which they form a part. Still more was this the case with appendages of the titanic proportions of my purchase. At the last moment it was only possible to correct this unfortunate oversight by a liberal use of needle and thread, and I had over an hour's hard work with both in the endeavour to sew the epaulettes into a position of becoming stability on my shoulders. Even so, at any sudden jolt or movement of the body they were liable to jump forward with a leap that sent my heart into my mouth and nearly tore asunder their frail attachments. However, all was at length adjusted. The patent leather boots with a pair of handsome spurs shone upon my legs; Sir W. Lockhart's presentation sword rattled at my side; my breast was ablaze with the insignia of unknown diplomats of the past; and a cocked hat nodded on my head.

Thus attired I entered the town, and was escorted to the Palace. I flattered myself, as I was conducted into the Durbar Hall of the Amir, that I created the desired impression, though I was a little perplexed when His Highness betrayed an admiring interest in my trophies, and wished to know exactly what services or exploits they commemorated, or the favour of what monarch they testified. To these inconvenient queries I could only return the most general and deprecatory replies. But for the gilded epaulettes, with their ample bullion, hanging in rich festoons, there was reserved the greatest triumph. For the Amir, sending for the Court tailor, pointedly called his attention to these glittering appendages as of a character necessitating serious notice and even reproduction at the Court of Afghanistan; and for all I know, they may have left a permanent mark upon the sartorial equipment of the God-granted Government.

Little more than four years later I had as many genuine orders on my bosom (though not drawn from quite so wide a range) as it could conveniently hold; and I was corresponding with my friend the Amir as the authorised representative of my Sovereign. But I still cherish the fond belief that my improvised entry into the Afghan capital was not altogether without *éclat* and even distinction.

Somewhat later, in the course of my reading, I came across a passage which showed that I was by no means the first English traveller to find it desirable to pay special deference in respect of costume to the ideas or etiquette of an Asiatic Court. When W. Hawkins went out in command of the newly-founded East India Company to India in 1607, to proceed to the Court of the Great Mogul (Jehangir), "in order that he might appear with becoming splendour, he was furnished with scarlet apparel, his cloak being lined with taffeta, and embroidered with silver lace."[1]

Hawkins, it is clear, easily beat me in point of raiment, but I flatter myself that he had not my unique collection of stars.

[1] W. Foster, *Early Travels in India*, p. 62.

IV

THE ANNAMITE GIRL

I am black but comely.
Song of Solomon, i. 5.

WHEN I came back from one of my long journeys in the East, in the course of which I had visited the French possessions of Tongking, Annam and Cochin-China, I delivered a lecture at the Royal Geographical Society on the subject of my travels. The meeting was held in the Theatre of the University of London in Burlington Gardens, and was honoured by the presence of King Edward VII., then Prince of Wales, who occupied a seat upon the platform. Every bench from floor to roof was filled, and many people were turned away. At the end of my paper the illustrations which I had selected from a large number of photographs, either taken by myself or collected during my tour, were thrown from a lantern on to the screen, each slide being preceded by a brief explanatory description from myself. All went well until, after exhibiting slides of the scenery and buildings of Tongking, I said, "I will now show you the picture of an Annamite girl, in order to prove that the native population, though possessing marked Mongolian features, are far from destitute of personal charm. Indeed," I added, "I thought some of them quite pretty."

All eyes were turned upon the screen, upon which there forthwith appeared, magnified to far more than life size, the figure of a seated Annamite girl, destitute of any but the smallest shred of clothing.

The audience, after a slight pause of bewildered surprise, burst into roars of laughter, again and again renewed, in which His Royal Highness heartily joined; nor did he ever cease to chaff me afterwards about my Annamite lady friend. No explanation availed anything. It was useless for me to declare—though it was the strict truth—that the photograph was one of a packet which had been presented to me by the Governor-General of French Indo-China, in order to illustrate the people and habits of that country, and that I had incautiously handed the entire packet, with marks upon those which were to be put upon the slides, to the lantern operator, who in a spirit, as I imagine, of mischief, had ignored my instructions and selected this unmarked photograph for reproduction.

No one believed me. But from the moment that the figure of the young girl was thrown upon the screen the success of the lecture was assured, in the same hour that the character of the lecturer was irreparably destroyed.

V

THE STATE ENTRY INTO DATIA

> Fallen, fallen, fallen, fallen,
> Fallen from his high estate.
>
> DRYDEN, "Alexander's Feast."

IT is customary, when the Viceroy of India visits the capital of a Native State, for the Prince whose guest he is to receive him at the railway station—should he arrive by rail—and to conduct him personally to the Palace or camp prepared for his reception.

The Chief on this occasion brings out his State equipages, and ordinarily ushers the Viceroy into a State landau, drawn by four horses with postilions, in which he takes his seat at the side of his guest, the remaining two places, with their backs to the horses, being taken by the Military Secretary and the A.D.C. in waiting.

On the occasion of my visit to the Central Indian State of Datia in 1902—the native Chief of which was a fine old fellow with henna-dyed beard, a great elephant rider in his day—I observed on arriving at the station that the Prince had paid me the unusual compliment of harnessing no fewer than six horses with three postilions to the State landau. Into this stately equipage we clambered, and proceeded at a smart pace towards the walls of the ancient town of Datia, situated at a slight distance on the crest of a hill, and crowned by the massive and sombre castle of Bir Singh Deo. The State troops lined the road: some were on foot, some on richly caparisoned horses; others were on camels, or in *palkis*, and held obsolete weapons in their hands.

All went well until we approached the city gates, when I realised that the fortifications of the town, which were mediaeval in origin and design, included, not a single barbican or outer gate, often placed for defensive purposes at right angles to the main entrance, but a double barrier of this description, so that any one entering the town had to turn a corner, almost at right angles, not once but twice before penetrating the main entrance in the walls. I realised the full peril of the situation when I saw the leaders with their postilion disappear altogether from sight, as they turned the first angle—to be followed presently by the middle pair. What was happening or might happen out of sight in the distance it was impossible to conjecture. It was bad enough that the landau itself was lurching heavily and with difficulty escaped impinging upon the sides of the great brick archways. By some unheard-of skill or good fortune the two corners were negotiated without disaster, but as the team pulled itself together and entered the inner gateway of the town, they seemed of one accord to realise that the strain was more than they ought to have been called upon to bear, and they broke into a sharp gallop which the postilions were powerless to restrain. The street was very narrow, was paved with stone and consequently slippery, and had no pavement—only a sort of gutter or ditch at the side. Moreover, the road presently descended by a rather sharp incline. The welcoming shouts of the good people of Datia, who crowded the galleries and roofs of the houses, added to the fright of the horses, the big landau began to sway dangerously from side to side, and the end was manifestly near.

Suddenly one or other, I daresay more, of the horses slipped up and came with a crash to the ground, the vehicle turned over, and my next sensation was that of finding myself sitting on the top of the old Maharaja, in all his finery of silks and jewels, in the stone gutter. No harm was done: an intelligent A.D.C. sat on the head of the plunging horses; the traces were cut; the carriage was with difficulty dragged on one side; and, changing into a later vehicle in the procession, we resumed our State entry unhindered and unhurt. The old Maharaja was very crestfallen; but, being a sportsman, he took the matter in good part, and soon recovered his equanimity.

An amusing sequel occurred when I passed on from Datia to pay my next visit to the neighbouring State of Orcha. In the course of my ceremonial visit to the Maharaja of Orcha, who had heard of the contretemps and was inspired by feelings of amiable rivalry towards his princely colleague, I explained to him what had happened. "At this stage," I said, "I found myself in the melancholy position of sitting upon the head of His Highness the Maharaja of Datia in the ditch." "And a very proper position for Your Excellency to occupy," was the immediate and courtly rejoinder of the old Chief, who, it was suspected, viewed the mishap that had attended his neighbour with some subdued satisfaction.

VI

THE CURIOSITY OF LI HUNG CHANG

There are some things which men confess with ease, and others with difficulty.

EPICTETUS, " On Inconsistency," cap. xxi.

TRAVELLERS in the East will be very familiar with one aspect of Oriental mentality, which is always amusing and often of value, if at times a little disconcerting. I allude to the idiosyncrasy which prompts the Eastern, even of the highest rank, to put and to answer, with equal good manners, and with a total lack of impertinence, the most searching and intimate questions as to age, profession, family history and income.

As a rule in the West you do not, on the first occasion that you meet a stranger, ask him how old he is, whether he is married, and if so how long he has borne the yoke, what is the size of his family, and what are the emoluments of his profession. There is a certain reserve about such matters, the discussion or disclosure of which is supposed to be the reward of intimacy and to mark the later rather than the opening stages of acquaintance. But the Eastern thinks and acts quite otherwise. He wants to know what manner of person he is encountering, and to place him fairly and squarely in his normal environment. For this purpose it is important to learn the details of his domestic existence, when he entered the world, what he has done since, what are his present circumstances, and so forth.

The Oriental is much more concerned to ascertain these elemental conditions than he is to exchange opinions or to analyse character. He is not bad at the latter operation either, but it must come in its proper place. Thus in all my travels, whether I was the guest of an Asiatic monarch, or a Kurdish chieftain, or a Persian satrap (though in the latter case the curiosity was apt to be veiled by an almost Gallic polish of manner), I was always prepared to be put through my paces in this respect, and to reveal the fullest details of my age and circumstances. I have related elsewhere how much I fell in the estimation of the Foreign Minister of Korea, when he learned that, though an ex-Minister, I was not married to a member of the British royal family!

Salary I found to be a perennial source of interest. The Eastern Governor—who lives as a rule by successful spoliation of his subjects or subordinates, and who regards office not as the gratification of an honourable ambition, but as the opportunity of replenishing a depleted exchequer—always wanted to know what an English Minister or ruler received or did in analogous conditions. What was his actual stipend ? What were his perquisites ? Was office a convenient and agreeable source of wealth ? What powers did it enable the occupant to exercise ? And did he wield them, as was fit and proper, for his own personal advantage ?

Furthermore, family details never failed to interest and enthuse. Exactly how old was the visitor ? How had he spent his life ? How had he fared in the marriage lottery ? How many children had he ? What was he doing with them or they with him ? I ended by feeling not the smallest resentment, but on the contrary a good deal of mild pleasure, in communicating these details—which seemed to place one on a footing of easy familiarity with the interlocutor—and I developed a laudable aptitude in putting the most penetrating questions in reply. Nor can I recall an occasion on which any of these questions either on one side or the other excited the smallest resentment, while they frequently resulted in the exchange of useful and diverting information.

I think, however, that among my hardiest interrogators I must give the palm to the famous Chinese statesman, Li Hung Chang. When I visited Tientsin in 1892, he was Viceroy of Chihli, and was already in somewhat advanced years, being over seventy-one years of age. Nevertheless at our interviews in his official *yamen* he interrogated me with a pertinacity which excited my warmest admiration ; and I recall his long lean figure (he was over six feet high) clad in a grey silken robe with black silk cape, his little beady eyes, his quizzical look, and the imperturbable gravity with which he put to me the most searching questions.

A few years later he came to England, when I was Under-Secretary in the Foreign Office to Lord Salisbury, and it became my duty to conduct him to the House of Commons, which provided ample material for his rather mordant curiosity, and also to Hatfield for a garden-party. It was on the latter occasion that he achieved what I regarded as the greatest triumph in the particular line of inquiry of which I am here writing.

While we were being photographed on the terrace, he suddenly asked me once again how old I was; and upon my replying that I was thirty-six—" Dear me," he said, " you are exactly the same age as the German Emperor." I acknowledged the impeachment, whereupon he continued as follows:

Li Hung Chang: " The German Emperor, however, has six sons. How many have you?"

Curzon: " I have only recently been married, and I regret that so far I have none."

Li Hung Chang: " Then what have you been doing all this time?"

To this question I admit that I could not find, nor even now can I suggest, an appropriate answer.

VII

THE STATE ENTRY INTO KOWEIT

> They have their exits and their entrances.
>
> SHAKSPEARE, *As You Like It*, Act II. Scene VII.

MY official entry into Koweit, at the head of the Persian Gulf, in November 1903, was of a character somewhat different from the less orthodox entry into Kabul, which I have before described. But it was not without its vicissitudes.

I was the first Viceroy of India to visit Koweit, and the Sheikh Mubarrak, with whom I had recently concluded a secret treaty of friendly alliance on behalf of His Majesty's Government, and who was himself a striking and powerful type of Arab chieftain, was anxious to treat me with becoming honour.

This desire on his part demanded a ceremonial entry into the capital of his State; and in order that this might be accomplished with becoming display, it was necessary that, instead of landing at the town itself, which is built on the shore of the Gulf, our party should be taken in boats to a point about three miles away, where we could land on a shelving spit of sand and be escorted from thence to the town. As we neared the landing-place I observed that the Sheikh with his principal retainers and a great crowd of mounted Arabs were assembled on the shore to greet me, and that in front of the crowd was a small open vehicle or Victoria, drawn by a pair of Arab horses and evidently intended for the accommodation of the Sheikh and myself. I was informed that this was the first time that such a vehicle had ever been seen at Koweit, and that it had been specially ordered by the Sheikh from Bombay to do honour to his visitor.

Accordingly, after exchanging the customary *salaams*, the Sheikh and I entered the equipage, which set off at a brisk trot for the town, escorted by the camel corps of twelve to twenty men, and by some two hundred to two hundred and fifty horsemen. Some of these wore helmets and coats of chain mail. The Sheikh's flag, with the timely inscription "Trust in God" sewn in white on a scarlet background, was carried in front.

Meanwhile the whole of my staff, including the British Minister at Teheran, who accompanied me, were provided with Arab mounts, the tall peaked saddles of which, with the shovel stirrups, are not always conducive to the comfort or even to the security of riders unused to them.

However, every one climbed up in due course, and the procession moved off in a cloud of dust. At this stage it apparently became necessary for the cavalry escort to express their rejoicing not merely by war-cries of the most blood-curdling description, but by firing ball cartridge promiscuously either in the air or into the ground at the feet of their prancing steeds. Others hurled their spears frantically into the air. The result was the wildest confusion. The air resounded with the fusillade, and the ground was a whirlwind of careering horses and yelling cavaliers and spurting sand. Some of the horsemen were bareheaded, and their plaited hair streamed in the wind as they dashed along; others wore flowing garments of orange and red and golden brown. The chief was clad in a broad-striped robe.

In the midst of the scene I saw the form of the British Minister shot clean over the head of his steed and deposited with no small violence upon the ground. Nothing daunted, he courageously resumed his seat and, amid a hail of bullets, continued the uneven tenor of his way.

As we approached the town, we passed through the entire population (the bazaars having been closed for the day), who were ranged in two rows on either side of our route. The prevailing colour of their men's dress was dark brown, but all wore the white Arab *keffieh* with the twisted camel hair band round the head. Behind them stood the women, closely veiled and with their figures concealed in dark indigo cloaks of an almost funereal appearance, below which were skirts of gaudy cotton prints. As the cortege passed they indulged in a shrill wail or series of ululations, which might have been mistaken for a dirge of exceptional poignancy, were it not that, as I learned, the sounds were intended to express the extremity of rapture and joy.

Thus escorted, we presently reached the so-called palace of the Sheikh, a modest edifice, built for the most part of sun-dried bricks and situated in a very narrow street or lane of the town. We climbed to the first floor of this building for the exchange of the customary courtesies, accompanied by coffee and cigarettes, of Arab etiquette.

As I sat there, bandying civilities with my host, a sound of violent rending and tearing, accompanied by loud shouts and plunging of horse-hoofs, broke the solemn hush of our palaver. Not a word was said on the subject. But when the interview was over and I descended to the street, only the fragments of the Bombay Victoria, reduced to matchwood, littered the ground, and the steeds had vanished! It appeared that these animals, who had never before been harnessed to a vehicle, had made up for their orderly behaviour, while conducting the Sheikh and myself from the landing-place to the town, by kicking the somewhat flimsy construction to pieces as soon as they were left alone. I doubt if a Victoria has been seen in Koweit since.

We had to feel our way very gingerly on foot over heaps of ordure and amid indescribable filth to a nearer point of embarkation for our vessel, which was lying at anchor at a considerable distance in the shallow waters of the Gulf. Thus began and thus ignobly ended my Viceregal entry into Koweit.

VIII

THE CAPTURED COLONEL

> But that I am forbid
> To tell the secrets of my prison-house,
> I could a tale unfold.
>
> SHAKSPEARE, *Hamlet*, Act I. Scene IV.

WHEN I was at Cairo in the winter of 1882 I encountered an English Colonel who was for a brief period the hero or the victim of a diplomatic incident that earned him no small notoriety, and involved Her Majesty's Government in a pecuniary sacrifice which they were very loth to accept. The Colonel, who was the owner of a small property near L—— in Turkish territory, was seized and carried off at night by a party of Greek brigands under a famous desperado, and was held in captivity, as he told me, for a period of thirty-two days. The bandits declined to surrender their prize for any less sum than £12,000, with a number of gold watches and chains thrown in; and this ransom, which the Colonel was alone in not regarding as excessive, had to be paid by Her Majesty's Government. Indeed the chief of the band sent a message to the British Consul, who was conducting the negotiations for the release, which contained the conventional but still formidable threat: "If the ransom is not paid to the last farthing, I shall send in six days his nose, in seven days his ears, and on the eighth day his head." In these circumstances Her Majesty's Government had no alternative but to surrender. With commendable astuteness, however, they reimbursed themselves by deducting the sum from the revenues of Cyprus, which were at that time paid over to the Turkish Government.

As such, the transaction was one that gave a certain degree of satisfaction to all parties. The Colonel regained his freedom, and was, so to speak, weighed, as certain Eastern potentates are in the habit of being, against his weight in gold. The British Government extricated their representative without being really out of pocket. The Turks, although penalised, nevertheless escaped the indignity of having to make a cash payment. The brigands got the loot and the watches which they desired.

But one thing rankled in the breast of the Colonel. The latter, who was an unmarried man, professed the greatest indignation that the announcement in the Press, circulated to the four corners of Europe, had been couched in the following terms:

> Le Colonel et sa femme ont été pris par les brigands.

This aspersion upon his moral character and upon the austerity of his domestic existence at

L—— would, he thought, greatly damage him in the eyes of the Government whom he served. He spent a good deal of time, therefore, in assuring me, as I have no doubt he had done to his official superiors, that the phrase in question was a misprint, and that what had really been sent out was the following:

Le Colonel *en sa ferme* a été pris par les brigands.

I believe that the Colonel was innocent. On the other hand, there was a strong party, indeed the majority, who persisted in holding, in spite of his asseverations, that the printer had been maligned, and that the revised version rendered insufficient homage to the traditions and the practices of the East.

IX

HOW I WON A VOTE

Cast thy bread upon the waters: for thou shalt find it after many days. **Ecclesiastes xi. 1.**

When I was standing for Parliament in South Derbyshire in the General Election of 1885—a contest in which I was handsomely beaten, but in which every vote might have been of value—my agent at Derby received a telegram from an unknown person a few days before the poll, which contained these mysterious words :

"Is the Mr. Curzon who is standing for South Derbyshire the gentleman who travelled in a first-class railway carriage from Catania to Girgenti on May 1, 1885? If so I will come and vote for him."

My agent, who had never heard either of Catania or Girgenti, brought me this cryptic message, as to the significance of which I was myself a little uncertain. It was true that in the spring of that year, after climbing Etna, I had proceeded from Catania to Girgenti by train. But I could not for the moment recall any more precise memory of the journey. Nor had I my diary with me to refresh my recollection of what might have passed.

The telegram was answered in the affirmative, and I forgot all about it, until on the polling day, happening to go into the agent's office, I found a gentleman there who acknowledged the authorship of the message and revealed his identity. Then and there I remembered an English traveller who with his wife had journeyed with me in the same compartment, and with whom I had entered into conversation. He had apparently seen my name on a label on my hat-box, and reading in the papers that a Conservative candidate of the same name was standing for South Derbyshire, for which he happened to possess a vote, and being a sound Conservative himself, he had, on receiving my agent's reply to his first inquiry, decided to come down and give me his support.

Gladly did we exchange salutations and revive the memories of that half-forgotten day. And then it was that I learned what had won the favour of my unknown friend.

"Do you not remember," he said, "that as the train wound in and out of the parched Sicilian valleys, the young man with the hat-box kept pointing to the sister heights of Castro Giovanni and Calascibetta, rearing their magnificent natural bastions, crowned with the ruins of feudal towers, high into the air; how he told us that Castro Giovanni, the nobler of the two elevations, 2600 feet above the sea, was the Enna of the Ancients, where Proserpine had been carried off by Pluto; how the young man quoted Cicero, who had thus described it:

> Enna est loco perexcelso atque edito, quo in summo est aequata agro planities, et aquae perennes; tota vero ab omni aditu circumcisa atque dirempta est; quam circa lacus lucique sunt plurimi et laetissimi flores omni tempore anni;

how he said that Newman in *Callista* had referred to its castled splendour; and how it reminded him somewhat of Acrocorinthos lifting its battlemented crest above the waters of the Gulf of Corinth; and also of the fortress Peak of Banias or Cesarea Philippi in Palestine; and how in those now desolate surroundings—the result of surface mining—Proserpine would hardly have been tempted to stray in search of flowers, and the hunting hounds could scarcely have lost their scent (as the legend goes) for the exceeding fragrance of the surroundings? Do you not further remember," he said, "as the train twisted in and out, now showing the great summit on one side now on the other, how the young man with the hat-box kept jumping up and insisting that his fellow-passengers should share his enthusiasm, and exchange seats with him, and enjoy the spectacle?"

Later on I looked up my diary, and there indeed was the reference, and there lay the explanation of the vote so easily and gaily won; and therefrom sprang a friendship with my companion of the Sicilian railway carriage, whose vote was ever at the disposal of the Conservative candidate for South Derbyshire, doomed in the great majority of cases, I regret to say, to be not more fortunate in his electoral fortunes than the young man with the hat-box was in November 1885.

THE SINGING SANDS

THE SINGING SANDS

And even things without life giving sound, whether pipe or harp, except they give a distinction in the sounds, how shall it be known what is piped or harped ?—1 Cor. xiv. 7.

Felix qui potuit rerum cognoscere causas.

VIRGIL, *Georgic* ii. 490.

IN "The Voice of Memnon" I alluded to the phenomenon known in different places and parts of the world as the Singing Sands, Sounding Sands, Rumbling Sands, Musical Sands, Barking Sands, Moving Sands, *i.e.* cases in which certain sands, either when set in motion, or even in some cases when apparently quiescent, give forth sounds as of music which are sometimes audible at a great distance. In former days these tales, when they appeared in the pages of mediaeval travellers, were attributed to local superstition or to an excited imagination, and were not supposed to have any scientific basis. In the course of my travels I have made a study of these cases, about which I have found a good deal not only of literary inexactitude, but of scientific uncertainty, to prevail; and as the records of the phenomena in question are widely scattered and accessible to but few, and as no attempt, so far as I know, has ever been made to collect and correlate them all, or to arrive at a definite classification, it may be worth while to set down the results of my own researches. The subject is one which, while severely scientific in one aspect, is in another full of a strange romance, since the voice of the desert, speaking in notes now as of harp strings, anon as of trumpets and drums, and echoing down the ages, is invested with a mystic fascination to which none can turn a deaf ear.

There has been a general inclination to confuse with each other all cases of Musical Sands, and to assume that they are produced by similar causes or can be covered by a single definition. The very reverse is the fact; for although a certain acoustic property is common to all these cases, it is of so varying a character, is created in circumstances so widely different, and is attributable to such divergent causes, that no one generalisation admits of being applied. I shall distinguish quite definitely between the Singing Sand-hills or slopes or dunes, and the Sand Beaches that also produce musical sounds. The former are mainly to be found in Asia, though examples have been reported in Africa and America also. The latter are much more widely diffused. It is about the Singing Hills of Asia that the atmosphere of mystery principally clings, and here I shall let each of the few travellers who have heard the music speak in his own words, so that we may compare their evidence before we attempt to form a conclusion.

I. Musical Sand-hills

The Sounding Sands of Tunyang

If the sands of the desert speak, it were strange indeed were their voice not heard in the illimitable solitudes of Central Asia, where pilgrims for centuries have wended their patient way across the wastes, amid every variety of formation that sand, under the influence of wind or climate, could assume. It is with no surprise, therefore, that we find the doyen of mediaeval travellers, Marco Polo—who saw so much and heard so much more, and who recorded both—when he crossed the Great Gobi Desert, thus narrating his experience:

> Sometimes you shall hear the sound of musical instruments and still more commonly the sound of drums.[1]

He does not actually say whether he heard the desert music. But the inference is reasonable; and if, as also seems probable, he is referring to a particular spot, then it can hardly be other than the celebrated Sounding Sand-hill near the Caves of the Thousand Buddhas in Tunyang.

This phenomenon is the subject of frequent mention in the works of early Chinese writers, where it is commonly called Ming-sha-shan, or the Rumbling Sand-hill. For instance, in the Tun Huang Lu, one of the Chinese MSS. brought back by Sir Aurel Stein from Tunyang, and

[1] Yule's *Marco Polo*, vol. ii. p. 203. London, 1874.

dating from the ninth century A.D., we find the following passage :

The Hill of Sounding Sand is 10 *li* away from the city. It stretches 80 *li* east and west, and 40 *li* north and south, and it reaches a height of 500 feet in places. The whole mass is made up entirely of pure sand. This hill has strange supernatural qualities. Its peaks taper up to a point, and between them there is a mysterious hole which the sand has not been able to cover up. In the height of summer the sand gives out sounds of itself, and if trodden by men or horses the noise is heard many tens of *li* away. It is customary on the *tuan-wu* day (the Dragon festival on the fifth of the fifth moon) for men and women from the city to clamber up to some of the highest points and rush down again in a body, which causes the sand to give forth a loud rumbling sound like thunder. Yet when you come to look at it the next morning the hill is found to be just as steep as before. The ancients called this hill the Sounding Sand ; they deified the sand and worshipped it there.[1]

Similar references are to be found in the Wu Tai Shih, where the hill is described as "emitting, summer and winter, a rumbling noise like thunder," and in another Chinese record, which says that "when the weather is bright and sunny the sand emits sounds which are heard in the city."

When Sir Aurel Stein himself visited this locality in 1907 he thus described the phenomenon, situated on the shores of the Crescent Lake, quite close to the caves :

---

[1] *Journal of the Royal Asiatic Society*, pp. 43-44, January 1915. *Vide* also Bretschneider's *Mediaeval Researches*, vol. ii. p. 216 ; Rémusat, *Ville de Khotan*, p. 77 ; and Palladius, *Journal of the North China Branch of the Royal Asiatic Society*, N.S., vol. x. p. 5 (1875).

The southern shore of the lake was occupied by a number of picturesque Moslem temples rising on terraces from the water's edge and decorated with a queer medley of Buddhist and Taoist statues and frescoes. Just in front of them and across the lake rose the famous Resounding Sand-hill, often mentioned in old Chinese records. . . . I had ridden out to this secluded spot to enjoy undisturbed work. . . . But Chiang, my only companion, though he had brought out work too, could not forego the temptation of climbing to the top of the huge dune in his dainty velvet boots, just to make the sand slide down from there and hear the "miraculous rumbling" it produced. . . . We all duly heard the faint sound like that of distant carts rumbling, and Chiang felt elated and put it down in his journal.[1]

The sound, it will be noted, is here likened not so much to that of any musical instrument as to a distant rumbling noise, arising clearly from the displacement of the particles or grains of sand.

Reg-i-Ruwan, or the Moving Sands of Kabul

In the generation immediately succeeding Marco Polo, *i.e.* in the early fourteenth century, another European traveller, the inimitable Friar Odoric, of Pordenone in Italy, also made his way across the Asiatic Continent and also heard the Singing Sands. His description is more precise :

Another great and terrible thing I saw ; for as I went through a certain valley which lieth by the River of Delights, I saw therein many dead corpses lying. And I heard also therein sundry kinds of music but chiefly

[1] *Ruins of Desert Cathay*, by M. Aurel Stein, vol. ii. p. 161. London, 1912.

nakers,[1] which were marvellously played upon. And so great was the noise thereof that very great fear came upon me. Now this valley is seven or eight miles long; and if any unbeliever enter therein he quitteth it never again, but perisheth incontinently. Yet I hesitated not to go in that I might see once for all what the matter was. And when I had gone in I saw, as I have said, such numbers of corpses as no one without seeing it could deem credible. And at one side of the valley, in the very rock, I beheld as it were the face of a man, very great and terrible, so very terrible indeed that for my exceeding great fear my spirit seemed to die in me. . . . And so I came at length to the other end of the valley, and there I ascended a hill of sand and looked around me. But nothing could I descry, only I still heard those *nakers* to play, which were played so marvellously."[2]

Making every allowance for the superstitious inaccuracies of the Friar, there can, I think, be no doubt that the great image by which he was so terrified was one of the colossal rock idols of Bamian, hewn in the walls of a gorge in the main Hindu Kush range, to the north-west of Kabul—they are images of Buddha—and that the hill of sand which gave forth the music of drums was the Reg-i-Ruwan or Moving Sand, some forty miles to the north of that city, on the slope of the Paghman range. The corpses which he saw were doubtless those of the hapless travellers who had been robbed and slain by the bandits who infested that region. This is the first definite reference by a European traveller to the Afghan Singing Sands. It is true that the Reg-i-Ruwan

[1] *i.e. naqaras* or drums.

[2] *Cathay and the Way Thither* (Hakluyt Society), vol. ii. pp. 262-5.

is not so near to the Bamian Gorge as the words would seem to imply; but in the case of a traveller coming to Kabul from the North or from Afghan Turkestan, the direction and order are correctly given.

The Emperor Baber, who rode, and drank, and hunted in the neighbourhood of his capital, Kabul, and who had an eye for every wonder or beauty of nature, was not likely to be unaware of so strange a scene. He was more than once at Reg-i-Ruwan, where indeed he spent Christmas Day, 1519. He apparently did not hear the music, perhaps because he was not there at the right season of the year, but he repeated the popular belief:

> Between these plains is a small hill in which there is a line of sandy ground, reaching from the top to the bottom of the hill. They called it Khwajeh-reg-rewan. They say that in the summer season the sound of drums and *nagarets* issues from this sand.[1]

Then ensues a long gap in our records until, in the second quarter of the nineteenth century, the political and commercial interests of the Government of India were responsible for the appearance at Kabul of a number of British officers or travellers, who were allowed by Dost Mohammed a freedom of movement about his country which nearly a century later is still denied to the foreigner. The most famous of

[1] *Memoirs of Baber*, p. 146, translated by J. Leyden and W. Erskine. London, 1887. The original Turki has *duhul*, *i.e.* drum, and *naqara*, *i.e.* kettledrum.

these men was Captain, afterwards Sir Alexander Burnes, destined to be murdered at Kabul only a few years later. Among the others who were there at the same time were G. T. Vigne, the traveller, Charles Masson, the correspondent of the East India Company, Lieutenant John Wood, the explorer of the sources of the Oxus, and Dr. P. B. Lord, the companion of the latter in his journey.

The first of these in point of time to refer to the Reg-i-Ruwan was G. T. Vigne, who with Masson was in the neighbourhood of the spot in August 1836, though I think it is quite clear from their joint descriptions that they did not actually visit the sand-hill or test the sound, much less hear the music.

Vigne wrote as follows :

> On a detached and comparatively low hill a whitish streak is observed, extending from the summit to the foot of it. This is the Reg-Ruwan, or Running Sand, mentioned by Baber. The natives say that it runs up again, and that it is never diminished ; and that there is a cave at its foot, where noises are heard, and into which the sand falls and disappears. It may be partly owing to the decomposition of granite or other rocks, or to the peculiar shape or situation of the hill, which collects there the particles of sand, taken up by the mountain gusts, or perhaps to both these reasons, or neither.[1]

It will be observed that in the above passage Vigne is much more concerned with the pheno-

[1] *Personal Narrative of a Visit to Ghuzni, Kabul and Afghanistan*, p. 219. London, 1840.

menon of the perpetual re-creation of the sand-hill in this isolated spot than with the noise, which indeed he does not directly connect with the movement of the sand. His companion Masson similarly connects the sound with the cave and with the Mohammedan superstitions about the latter :

> At the hill of Regh Rawan, remarkable for the bed of sand lying upon its southern face, which gives it both its name and singular appearance, is a subterranean cave which has a descent by hewn and artificial stairs, and may therefore be supposed to mean something more than the ordinary rock cave. It has never been duly explored, and there might be danger in the attempt to descend into it. The Mahommedans have made it a *ziarat*, and have an idea that it is the spot where their expected Imam Medi will issue upon earth ; and they believe that on Roz Juma, or Sacred Friday, the sound of *nagaras* or drums may be heard in it.[1]

The local belief about the Mahdi would appear to have either started from or to have given rise to another incident which is thus reported by Vigne (p. 223) :

> Some years ago a fanatic from the Kohistan took up his abode in a cave near, I believe, the Reg-Ruwan, and said that he was Imaum Mihedi, who is expected by the Mussulmen to appear at the end of the world. He collected upwards of 20,000 men, many of whom dressed themselves as birds and beasts, and marched towards Kabul. They were met and defeated by the troops of the Vizier Futteh Khan.

[1] *Narrative of Journeys in Afghanistan, etc.*, vol. iii. p. 167. London, 1844.

Much more exact is the description given by Burnes himself, accompanied by a rough lithographic illustration, which depicts his native escort scrambling up the face of the sand-hill in order to evoke the music :

The description of Baber, though it appears marvellous, is accurate. Reg-Ruwan is about 40 miles north of Cabul towards Hindu Kosh, and near the base of the mountains. Two ridges of hills, detached from the rest, run in and meet each other ; at the apex of this a sheet of sand, as pure as that on the seashore, with a slope of about 40°, forms the face of a hill to its summit, which is about 400 feet high. When this sand is set in motion by a body of people, who slide down it, a sound is emitted. On the first trial we distinctly heard two loud, hollow sounds such as would be given by a large drum. On two subsequent attempts we heard nothing, so that perhaps the sand requires to be for a time settled before the curiosity is displayed. There is an echo in this place, and the inhabitants have a belief that the sounds are only heard on Friday, when the Saint of Reg-Ruwan, who is interred hard by, permits ! The locality of the sand is remarkable, there being none other in the neighbourhood. Reg-Ruwan faces the south, but the wind of Purwan (bad-i-Purwan) blows from the north for the greater part of the year, and has probably deposited it by an eddy. Such is the violence of this wind that all the trees in the neighbourhood bend to the south, and a field, after a few years, requires to be recleared of the pebbles and stones which the loss of soil lays bare. The mountains here are generally composed of granite or mica, but at Reg-Ruwan we had sandstone, lime, slate and quartz. . . . Reg-Ruwan is seen from a great distance, and the situation of the sand is so curious that it might almost be imagined the hill had been cut in two, and that it had gushed forth as from a sand-bag, though the wind could not have brought it together.[1]

Lieutenant John Wood's account closely follows that of Burnes, and he and his companion, Dr. P. B. Lord, appear to have visited the spot in the same month (October 1837), though not, it would seem, as members of the same party as Burnes. We read in Wood's book :

At the upper end of Koh Daman, on its eastern side, the face of the hills, at one particular spot, is covered with fine sand, called Reig-Rawan, or the Moving Sand. To this the natives of the valley ascribe the utterance of strange unearthly sounds, and by their marvellous relations induced us to visit the spot. The Moving Sand rests upon a base of 100 yards wide, and stretches up the face of the rock for 250 yards, with an acclivity of about 45°. At 3 P.M. the temperature of the sand on the surface was 103°, while at the depth of 10 inches it was only 75°. Looking down from the top of this sandy, inclined plain, it is seen to lie in a hollow of the rock fronting west-south-west. The formation of the adjoining rocks are limestone, and a loose, conglomerate sandstone. The first is both fractured and calcined, and the same appearance is observed at other places along the side of the valley, but is always local : that bordering the Moving Sand is strictly so. From Reig-Rawan there is no other sand deposit visible, though further south, and on the east side of the valley, there are one or two smaller strips, but which are not asserted to be vocal. The west side of Koh Daman is composed of granite, and the prevailing wind is from the north, but no sand is likely to come from either of these directions. From the known propensity of the ignorant to exaggerate everything connected with supposed supernatural agency, we did not

[1] *Journal of the Asiatic Society of Bengal*, April 1838, pp. 324-5.

come to the place very confident believers in the current tales of Reig-Rawan. However, we did as we were directed, and sent six men to the top of the sandy strip while we took up a position in the most favourable place to hear any noise that might be emitted. The party above came trampling down, and continued their march to the foot of the inclined plain; but without eliciting the slightest sound. This was repeated again and again, but only once with any success. The sound then heard was like that of a distant drum, mellowed by softer music. The secret of Reig-Rawan is, I should imagine, that of the Whispering Gallery. The slightest indentation in the sand is immediately filled up by the fall of the particles above. Moving waves are thus produced by the heavy tramp of a descending party; and the rustle of the dry sand is condensed and reverberated by the circular conformation of the rocks around.[1]

Wood's companion, the Doctor, was more brief:

On our way back through the plain of Koh-i-Daman we paid a visit to Reg-rowan (the Flowing Sand), which has long been an object of wonder and veneration to the natives. It is simply a bed of loose sand on the slope of the hill, which, if set in motion by any cause, as by the wind or a man rolling down from the top, produces lengthened sonorous vibrations not unlike those of the string of a bass viol.[2]

Wood, in the passage above quoted, referred also to the gardens of Istalif—the favourite holiday haunt of the Emperor Baber, who wrote of it: "A large river runs through it, and on

[1] Captain J. Wood, *A Journey to the Source of the River Oxus*, pp. 114-15. London, 1872.

[2] *J.A.S.B.*, June 1838, p. 537.

either side are gardens, green, gay and beautiful," and to the Panjshir River in the same neighbourhood; and I have little doubt that here or hereabouts we have the original of Odoric's "River of Delights"; for the mountain-sides and valleys at this spot have always admittedly been the beauty spots of Afghanistan.

But to return to the Sounding Sands. Wood's explanation, as we have seen, is that the sounds were produced by the movement of particles of sand, disturbed either by the trampling of feet or by some other artificial cause, and rustling as they fell. To this I shall revert later.

When I was at Kabul in 1894 I would have sought the Amir's permission to visit the Reg-i-Ruwan, had it been earlier in the year. As it was, I asked him about it. He was not in the least at a loss for a reply, which was of a severely rationalistic character, and was marked by his usual contempt for the beliefs or fears of his own people. I was the first person, he said, who had ever asked him a question about the Reg-i-Ruwan, and, having made a special study of the subject, he would therefore gladly explain it to me.

"The sand had nothing to do with the sound. The people in the neighbourhood and even at Kabul all believed that the sounds were of supernatural origin, and that within an adjoining cave in the mountains horsemen were shoeing their horses and beating their drums; and that from this recess a new prophet would presently come forth to restore the true faith throughout the world and annihilate the infidel.[1] But this was not at all the case, and the explanation of the sound, which he had heard himself, was quite different. There was a shelving face of rock, which was so covered with sand as to constitute a steep sand-slope. About half-way down this slope there was an orifice or cavern in the rock, running underground for a long distance. On the left side of the slope, at a little distance, were some more high rocks, in which there were similar cavities, at a place called Parwan.[2] It was only when the wind was blowing from the latter orifices, and impinged upon the mouth of the orifice in Reg-i-Ruwan, that then, being whirled round and round in the mouth and interior of the cave, it produced the humming sound which had been mistaken for drums and trumpets. When blowing from Parwan the wind made a whistling sound; but when it entered the hole in Reg-i-Ruwan, then it hummed. From a distance of ten miles he had first discovered this explanation with a telescope! Then he had been up to the place and had posted men to wait and see. They reported that only when the wind blew from that quarter was the sound heard, and the greater the wind the louder the sound. But if there was no wind there was no sound heard at all."

For his own part, the Amir added, so useful was the sand for building, and so useless for

[1] This is identical with Masson's story.

[2] Masson also mentions the caves at Purwan, vol. iii. p. 166.

musical purposes, that he was now bringing it down to Kabul to make bricks and mortar.

I have had a renewed investigation made of the Reg-i-Ruwan in the present summer (1923) by the good offices of the reigning Amir of Afghanistan and the British Resident at Kabul, for the special purposes of this volume, and I add the result of the investigations of the latter (Colonel Humphrys) in his own words. He spent the day of 24th June at Reg-i-Ruwan, and took the photograph which is reproduced here, and in which the little figures at the base of the sand-slope are men:

The range in which the moving sand is situated is semicircular in shape, with a concave face towards the south, and is an outcrop of the main Hindu Kush range, with which its greatest length—about half a mile—is parallel, running roughly east to west. It lies about 40 miles due north of Kabul, and three-quarters of a mile to the north-east of the village of Khwaja Muhammad. Height of base, according to the aneroid, 4950 feet above sea-level. Average height of the reef, 600 feet above the Panjshir plain. Formation of range, limestone, combined with some volcanic rock.

The Reg-i-Ruwan lies near the western extremity of the reef, faces due south, and is protected by the western wall of the semicircle from the direct impact of the Parwan wind, which blows with terrific force in the summer months from Parwan (or Jebel-us-Siraj), situated some ten miles away, as the crow flies, to the north-west. It may be conjectured that the western extremity of the reef, although it breaks the direct impact of this wind, gives rise to an eddy which the vacuum caused by the air rising from the extremely hot sheet of sand would draw upwards and might thus carry the sand from the bottom towards the top. This, according to local gossip, is the movement by which the bulk of the sand-slope is maintained. The angle of the sand-slope was measured to be 33½ degrees. Its shape is narrowest at the top, broadening towards the bottom, regularity being impaired on the eastern side of the sand-bank by an outcrop of rock which has been enlarged by an artificial platform used on the occasion of fairs. The sand does not run to the top of the reef but only about two-thirds of the height. The vertical height from the top of sand-slope to the bottom was shown by the aneroid to be 430 feet. The sand is formed of minute particles, apparently by decomposition from the surrounding rock. It is white at the top, yellow at the western side of the base, and streaked with black on the eastern side. A *ber* tree (*Zizyphus Jujuba*), plainly visible in the photograph, flourishes about half-way up the sand-slope close to the eastern edge, and another *ber* tree of massive proportions stands on the platform referred to above. There are some smaller sand deposits at the eastern extremity of the reef, facing north-west, and therefore meeting the full force of the wind, and on the northern face of the range to the south-east sand deposits of some considerable size could also be seen. None of these sands, however, possess the reputation of moving. There are no caves in the reef itself, but in the shrine of Muhammad Hanifi, some 500 yards from the foot of the sand-slope, is an artificial shaft which, about 15 feet below the surface, branches into two smaller tunnels, one reported by the custodian of the shrine to lead to the moving sand and the other to Ghazni! Both tunnels were obstructed by falls of earth. Access was gained to the tomb of Muhammad Hanifi by means of rough stairs cut in the clay. Length of sand-slope from top to bottom is about 800 feet, and greatest breadth 320 feet.

There was practically no wind on the 24th June when

the experiments were made. Men were sent to the top of the sand-slope and descended several times at varying speeds. As the sand became dislodged by their movements, it flowed down in parallel rectangular streams: the collapsing edge gradually worked upwards, and the downward flow continued for several minutes after the sand had been disturbed. These streams developed no lateral spread beyond three feet, and emitted a rustling sound which was faintly audible up to a distance of twenty yards.

The sand on the surface at midday was painfully hot to the feet, even through a boot, but about six inches below the surface it was saturated with moisture. The Afghan villagers stated that no rain had fallen in the locality for two months, and it seems possible that by the end of the summer, which is practically rainless, the sand grains would become incoherent to a considerable depth, and, according to the conjectures of former observers, would then be more likely to possess a sonorous quality.

All the local people asserted that the sand produced a sound like the beating of drums (*nagaras*) on certain occasions. Some said that these occasions were limited to Fridays, but the majority stated that the phenomenon occurred capriciously about ten or twelve times a year without regard to the season, and frequently without the assistance of wind or other extraneous agency. They insisted that, if the sand was carried by the wind or otherwise to a distance from the slope, it invariably found its way back to Reg-i-Ruwan during the night. This was due to a special sanctity which belonged to the place. I was informed by the Governor of Kohistan, who met me on my way back to Jebel-us-Siraj, that the late Amir Habibulla was very interested in the phenomenon, and had paid seven visits to Reg-i-Ruwan, but had not been fortunate enough to hear the music.

Colonel Humphrys, it will be observed, was unsuccessful in his experiment; but he intends to pay another visit to Reg-i-Ruwan later in the summer, when the sand may be drier and the chances of success improved. I am afraid that his description completely disposes of the too fanciful explanation of my friend the Amir, for the cave, so far from being in the reef, is more than a quarter of a mile away; and the telescope of the Amir must have been a very astonishing instrument if it did not enable him to discover this fact. No European would appear to have visited Reg-i-Ruwan since 1837, but it is evident not merely that the tradition survives but that the sands still speak.

Kalah-i-Kah, Seistan

Pursuing my way westwards, the next case that I take is that of the Moving and Musical Sand-hill at Kalah-i-Kah in Afghan Seistan, which is also called Reg-i-Ruwan. This place was well known to the Arab geographers from early times. Mukadessi, at the end of the tenth century, said of it :

> If water or any small object were thrown on the sand of this hillock, a great noise was heard like a humming sound, and very terrible to listen to.[1]

In the next century Biruni wrote :

> Further, there is a mountain between Herat and Sijistan, in a sandy country, somewhat distant from the road, where you hear a clear murmur and a deep sound as soon as it is defiled by human excrements or urine.[2]

[1] *Descriptio imperii Moslemici.*

[2] *Chronology of Ancient Nations*, p. 235. Translation by Sachaus. London, 1879.

These rather unsavoury details of course meant no more than that the music was heard if a movement were communicated to the sand-grains by any form of human agency.

By far the fullest account of this phenomenon is, however, that which appeared in the records of Sir Frederic Goldsmid's Mission to settle the boundary between Persian and Afghan Seistan in 1870–1872. It was in March 1872 that the Mission found itself at Kalah-i-Kah, five miles from which in the direction of the Harut Rud stands the famous *ziarat* or shrine of Imam Zaid. The account of this part of the Mission's work was written by Major (afterwards Sir C.) Euan Smith; but the member of the Mission who heard the music was neither the writer nor his chief, but Captain Beresford Lovett, R.E. The place and the sound are thus described:[1]

This *ziarat*, which is called the Rig-i-Rawan, or Moving Sand, is most remarkable and singular. At the extreme west of the range of hills which has been described as lying in a straight line due north of the Kala'h-i-Kah district, is a hill some 600 feet high and half a mile long. The southern face of this hill to the very summit is covered with a drift of fine and very deep sand—which has evidently been there for ages, as testified by the number of large plants growing on its surface. None of the adjacent hills have any trace whatever of sand-drift, and the surface of the surrounding desert is hard and pebbly. The westernmost portion of this elevated ground contains the *ziarat*, and the natives say, and with reason and truth, that at times the hill gives out a strange startling noise,

[1] *Eastern Persia*, edited by Sir F. Goldsmid, vol. i. p. 327. London, 2 vols., 1876.

which they compare to the rolling of drums. Captain Lovett, who was fortunate enough to hear it, describes its effect upon him as like the wailing of an Æolian harp, or the sound occasioned by the vibration of several telegraph wires—very fine at first, but increasing every moment in volume and intensity; and the secret strain is said sometimes to last as long as an hour at a time. The face of the hill is concave, its cavity is filled with the sand, and underneath there appears to be a hard limestone surface. It would be useless after a summary inspection to hazard an opinion as to the cause of the remarkable sounds that proceed from the hill—but it is noticeable that they may be produced by any large number of men, at the top, putting the sand in motion. It should be remarked at the same time that the noise is often heard in perfectly still weather, and when nobody is near the hill; and it is singular also that the limit of the sand at the bottom seems never to be encroached upon by falling sand from the summit, though the face of the hill and sand-drift is very steep. On watching the sand this morning at the time he heard the sound, Captain Lovett observed that its vibrations and the movements of the pilgrims who had gone to the summit of the drift, occurred at the same moment. The natives, of course, ascribe miraculous properties to the hill. It is believed to be the grave of the Imam Zaid, the grandson of Husain, the son of Ali. Tradition says that, being pursued by his enemies, he came to this hill for refuge, was covered one night by the miraculous sand-drift, and has never been seen again. They say that the sand, thus miraculously brought by heavenly aid, could be removed by no earthly power, and that were any one impious enough to try it, the sand would return of its own accord. They believe the hill, like the ancient oracles, to give out warning when anything important is going to happen in the district. Thus, in the time when the Turkmans used to make their forays as far south as this, the hill always gave warning the night before their arrival; and we are assured that the arrival of our Mission was heralded by the same sounds. The head of the district told us that the noise could be heard in still weather at a distance of ten miles ; and Sayid Nur Muhammad Shah declares he heard it distinctly last night at our camp five miles off. Shia'hs and Sunnis alike, unable to contend against the evidence of their ears, come to worship at this miraculous spot, and here find a common ground on which they can meet in amity. Obese Muhammadans do not generally subject themselves to so severe a trial of faith as that of visiting this particular *Ziarat-gah.* It is a very steep climb for them to the commencement of the band of sand, about 200 feet broad and nearly perpendicular ; and as they sink up to the thighs in this at every step, often must they regret that the Imam could not have hid himself in a more accessible spot. The tomb is situated at the top of the sand ridge, and it is in their descent that the faithful are generally rewarded for the trouble they have voluntarily undergone by hearing the miraculous noise. Sardar Ahmad Khan, all his attendants, and a great number of stalwart Afghans, went up the hill, and we observed that they were more than half-an-hour getting across the sand ; our more effeminate Tehran servants did not seem to care to make the attempt. The base of the hill is surrounded by graves of the faithful, who, it is to be hoped, are not disturbed in their last sleep by the unearthly warnings of the object of their devotion. It is probable, after all, that science could give a very simple explanation of the phenomena ; but he would be a bold man who tried to explain the same by natural causes within a hundred miles of its influence.

Dr. H. W. Bellew, who was a member of the party, also heard the music :

The sand fills a wide concavity on the southern slope of a bare rocky ridge detached from the Cala Koh range, and forms an isolated mass, as remarkable from its position as from the sounds it emits when set in motion. As we passed on, our late companions on the march toilfully plodded their way up the sandy slope and the summit of the hill. Their steps set the loose particles of sand in motion, and their friction by some mysterious acoustic arrangement produced a sound as of distant drums and music, which we heard distinctly at the distance of a mile. The sounds were not continuous, but were only now and again caught by the ear, and much resembled those produced by the Æolian harp or the wind playing on telegraph wires. These sounds are often emitted by the action of the wind on the surface of the sand, and at other times without any assignable cause.[1]

Jebel Nakus, Sinai

I now come to the particular phenomenon which, owing to its greater accessibility and to the fact that it has been visited and described by a number of European travellers, has won the widest reputation, and is commonly referred to by geographers as the classical case of a musical sand-hill. This is the Jebel Nakus [2] or Hill of the Bell or Gong, in the Peninsula of Sinai on the eastern shore of the Red Sea. The following is, to the best of my knowledge, a complete list of those who have left descriptions of it: Dr. U. J. Seetzen, November 1810; J. Gray (of Oxford), 1818; H. Ehrenberg, 1823; Dr. Edward Ruppell, 1827; Lieutenant J. R. Wellsted, January 1830;

[1] H. W. Bellew, *From the Indus to the Tigris*, p. 285. London, 1874.

[2] *Nakus* is not a "bell" in our sense of the word. It is the wooden board suspended horizontally which is struck by a hammer in Eastern monasteries to summon the monks to prayer. In the Greek monasteries, where it is still employed, it is called "semandron."

Lieutenant Newbold, C. Shute, June 1840; Capt. H. C. Butler, Rev. Pierce Butler, 18 ; Professor H. A. Ward, 1855; Professor E. H. Palmer, Rev. F. W. Holland, Captain Wilson, Captain Palmer, J. Wyatt, February 1869; Dr. H. C. Bolton, 1889.

Dr. Seetzen, the first European traveller to arrive upon the scene, said that he found the musical mountain composed of a white friable sandstone, presenting on two of its sides sandy declivities. He watched beside it for an hour and a quarter, and then heard for the first time a low undulating sound somewhat resembling that of a humming-top, which rose and fell, and ceased and began, and then ceased again; and in an hour and three-quarters after, when in the act of climbing along the declivity, he heard the sound get louder and more prolonged. It seemed as if issuing from under his knees, beneath which the sand, disturbed by his efforts, was sliding downwards along the surface of the rock. Concluding that the sliding sand was the cause of the sounds, not an effect of the vibrations which they occasioned, he climbed to the top of one of the declivities, and, sliding down, exerted himself with hands and feet to set the sand in motion. The effect produced far exceeded his expectations: the incoherent sand rolled under and around in a vast sheet; and so loud was the noise produced that the earth seemed to tremble beneath him to such an extent that he would certainly have been afraid if he had been ignorant of the cause.

Seetzen further compared the moving layer of

sand to a great violin bow thrown into tuneful vibrations.[1]

Our sole English visitor in the first quarter of the nineteenth century, J. Gray of University College, Oxford, described the noise of the Musical Sands, which he heard more than once, as "beginning with a low continuous murmuring sound, which seemed to rise beneath his feet, but gradually changed into pulsations as it became louder, so as to resemble the striking of a clock, and became so strong at the end of five minutes as to detach the sand. On returning to the spot next day, he heard the sound still louder than before. He could not observe any crevices by which the external air could penetrate; and as the sky was serene and the air calm, he was satisfied that the sound could not arise from this cause."[2]

Ehrenberg, in 1823, also climbed the mountain, and at every step heard a small strengthening of the tone, which swelled in volume with the increase of the amount of sand in motion, and at length became as strong as the distant thunder of cannon. He explained the vastness of the final effect as due to the piling up of small effects, as in the case of an avalanche:

The sand-bed, which is about 150 feet high and about equally broad at its base, rises at an angle of 50 degrees, and thus rests rather on itself than on the rock, which

[1] "Aus einen Schreiben des Dr. Seetzen," *Monatl. Corresp.* p. 396. Gotha, October 1812.

[2] *Edinburgh Journal of Science*, No. XI. p. 153, No. XIII. p. 51.

gives it but slight support. The sand is coarse-grained and composed of very clean, even-sized grains of quartz from one-sixth to one-half a line in diameter. The great heat dries the sand by day to a certain depth (whilst it is moistened throughout by dew each night) and makes it equally dry and resonant. If, then, an empty space is formed in the sand by the sinking of a man's foot into it, the whole layer situated above this point loses its support and begins slowly to move throughout its whole length. By the flowing in of the sand from the sides and the repeated tread [of the traveller] a large part of the whole sand-layer of the slope at last acquires motion, and by its friction against the motionless under-layer produces a noise, which from a humming becomes a murmur, and in the end passes into a roar, and is all the more surprising in that one sees but little of the trickling and general movement of the sand-layer. With the cessation of the disturbance the sliding also gradually subsides as soon as the gaps are again filled and the sand-columns gain a more stable basis and a state of equilibrium is reproduced.

Another German, Dr. Ruppell, who visited Jebel Nakus in 1827, and described it as a sandstone slope 200 feet high, heaped up when the north wind blows at an angle of 50 degrees, has left an account of his visit, but does not say that he heard the music, though he adds that it is when the west wind blows that it is audible.[1]

The first full description from an English source is, however, that of Lieutenant J. R. Wellsted, of the Indian Navy, who was despatched by the Bombay Government in 1829 in the ship *Palinurus* to conduct a survey of the Red Sea. He and his companions several times visited

[1] *Der Tonende Berg Nakus in Reisen nach Nubien.* Frankfurt, 1829.

Jebel Nakus, and he thus recorded his experience in January 1830,[1] together with a lithographic illustration, which a later American visitor regarded as somewhat deficient in accuracy :

Considerable attention has also of late years been directed towards the phenomenon connected with this remarkable spot, though the accounts hitherto furnished by travellers are neither so full nor so satisfactory as could be wished. It forms one of a ridge of low calcareous hills, at a distance of 3½ miles from the beach, to which a sandy plain, extending with a gentle rise to their base, connects them. Its height, about 400 feet, as well as the material of which it is composed—a light-coloured friable sandstone—is about the same as the rest of the chain ; but an inclined plane of almost impalpable sand rises at an angle of 40 degrees with the horizon, and is bounded by a semicircle of rocks presenting broken, abrupt and pinnacled forms, and extending to the base of this remarkable hill. Although their shape and arrangement in some respects may be said to resemble a whispering gallery, yet I determined by experiment that their irregular surface renders them but ill adapted for the production of an echo. Seated on a rock at the base of the sloping eminence, I directed one of the Bedowins to ascend, and it was not until he had reached some distance that I perceived the sand in motion, rolling down the hill to the depth of a foot. It did not, however, descend in one continued stream, but, as the Arab scrambled upwards, it spread out laterally and upwards until a considerable portion of the surface was in motion. At their commencement the sounds might be compared to the faint strains of an Æolian harp when its strings first catch the breeze : as the sand became more violently agitated, by the increased velocity of the descent, the noise more

[1] *Travels in Arabia*, vol. ii. pp. 23-27. London, 1838.

nearly resembled that produced by drawing the moistened fingers over glass. As it reached the base the reverberations attained the loudness of distant thunder, causing the rock on which we were seated to vibrate; and our camels, animals not easily frightened, became so alarmed, that it was with difficulty their drivers could retain them.

It is particularly worthy of remark that the noise did not issue from every part of the hill alike, the loudest being produced by disturbing the sand on the northern side about twenty feet from the base and about ten from the rocks which bound it in that direction. The sounds sometimes fell quicker on the ear, at other times were more prolonged; but this swelling or sinking appeared to depend upon the Arab's increasing or retarding the velocity of his descent. On a spot so desert and solitary they have an inconceivably melancholy effect, and the Bedowins trace them to several wild and fanciful causes: the tradition given by Burckhardt, that the bells belonging to the convent have been buried here, has often been repeated to me.

When I visited the Jebel Narkous on two other occasions the results were much less satisfactory. The first time the sounds were barely audible, and, rain having fallen a short time previous to my second visit, the surface of the sand was so consolidated by the moisture that they could not be produced at all. I therefore attribute the complete gratification of my curiosity in this instance to the sand being perfectly dry, and consequently larger quantities rolling down the hill. That the explanation of this phenomenon is intimately connected with the agitation thus produced can admit of no doubt; but the precise causes which lead to these results it seems difficult to explain. It may be broadly stated that the particles of sand, when in motion, roll over a harder bed, and meet in their progress the wind then blowing directly on the face of the hill at a certain angle. I should mention that the same sounds are produced when the wind is sufficiently high to set the sand in motion;

but I reject, without hesitation, the generally received opinion that the effects I have described are originated by this sand falling into cavities. Sounds thus produced would be dull and wholly deficient in the vibrations which I have noticed."

Ten years later, another British officer, Lieutenant Newbold, of the Madras Army, appeared upon the scene, and gave an even more ample account of his successful experience :[1]

Ten minutes' walk over sand and stones brought us to the base of Gebel Nakús. The apparent height is from 350 to 400 feet. On the western side, which faces towards the Red Sea, is a steep slope of a triangular form extending about 80 feet up the side of the hill, narrow at the top, but widening out as it approaches the bottom. This slope is bounded by low cliffs of sandstone on all sides except the base, and covered with a very fine quartzy sand of a light reddish-brown colour. The sand varies in depth from a few inches to five or six feet, according to the irregularity of the sandstone rocks which lie beneath it. It has evidently been conveyed to its present position, on the slope of the rock, by the strong prevailing westerly winds. Our Bedouin guide instantly pointed to this sandy slope as the spot whence issue forth those mysterious Memnonian sounds, to which the mountain owes its appellation, and which the superstitious Arabs, as noticed by Burckhardt, believe to be produced by the bells of a subterraneous convent.

We strained our ears to catch a sound, but in vain; a deep silence, hardly broken by the faint murmurings of the wind, reigned over the singularly dreary and arid wastes around. The Bedouin, having desired us to wait at a rock at the foot of the slope, commenced its ascent,

[1] " Visit to Gebel Nakús, or the Mountain of the Bell, in the Peninsula of Sinai, on June 10, 1840," *Journal of the Royal Asiatic Society of Great Britain and Ireland*, vol. vii. p. 79, 1843.

sinking knee-deep in the loose sand that covered it. Presently we heard a faint musical sound resembling the deeper chords of a violoncello at a distance, prolonged, and lightly touched. The Bedouin now descended ; and, on my expressing some disappointment at the result, remarked with much phlegm, that the day was not propitious ; but that, if we would come on the *Juma*, or Muhammedan Sabbath, we should hear the mountain strains to much greater advantage. My friend, Mr. Shute, of the Inniskillings, and myself, having now obtained some clue to the cause of the sounds, determined to put the guide's veracity to the test, and accordingly commenced the ascent, which we found fatiguing, from the depth and extreme fineness of the sand, and from the intense heat of the sun. Having reached the top, I seated myself at the base of the mural cliffs which crest the summit, and watched the course of the sand we had set in motion, as it passed downwards in undulating and gradually widening lines to the base. The particles of sand displaced in the lower part of the slope disturbed those immediately above and below them ; and, more slightly, those on their sides ; so that the disturbance of the upper layers of sand went on increasing on every side, somewhat resembling the effect produced on the surface of still water by dropping a stone into it.

About two minutes after the sand had been first set in motion, a faint rustling sound, as it rolled down, struck our ears : then the low, deep, distant, musical tone we had first heard, which generally became more and more distinct, and apparently nearer, in successive and fast repeated notes, whose sound partook of those of a deep mellow church or convent bell, and of the vibrations of a stringed instrument. On again disturbing the sand near the summit with my feet, the sounds took up a more treble and prolonged tone, resembling the wild strains of an Æolian harp, but gradually becoming deeper and louder, until at length they rivalled the continued rumbling of distant thunder, and fairly caused the sand on which I sat to tremble in distinct vibrations. This intensity of sound was produced a short interval after the whole surface of the sand had been set in motion from the summit to the base. The sensations imparted by the vibrations were most extraordinary; I can only compare them with those likely to be experienced by a person seated on the body of some enormous stringed instrument while a bow is slowly drawn over its chords. The greatest effect was produced by traversing the sand from right to left, and *vice versâ.*

I descended to the base during the greatest intensity of the sounds, and awaited in silence their cessation, which took place with that of the motion of the sand, at the expiration of about a quarter of an hour.

Travellers have frequently attempted the explanation of this curious phenomenon. Some are of opinion that the sounds are caused by the sand's motion over hollow rocks; others imagine them to proceed from the sand falling into cavities; some, again, suppose them to have their origin in subterranean volcanoes; and a few have thought that similar sounds may be produced by the action of the wind on the thin elastic plates of mica which abound in granite and gneiss. The notion of the Arabs, that the sounds are those of the bells of a subterraneous convent, has doubtless been derived from the idle tales of the monks of Mount Sinai, who declared to me that they had never been heard until after the destruction of one of their convents near Tor, and the death of the Forty Martyrs.

With regard to the first and third of these opinions, I can only observe that, on a careful examination of the rocks over which the sand rolled, they proved to be of a massive whitish sandstone or grit, of a granular texture, imbedding pebbles of quartz, and entirely free from caverns, or holes of any magnitude. No volcanic rocks, nor traces of extinct volcanoes, were found in the vicinity. Erratic fragments of porphyry, granite, greenstone and melaphyre, evidently transported from the lofty ranges of Sinai in the interior, occurred strewed on the surface of the desert not far distant. Were the sounds volcanic, they would be absolutely independent of the motion of the sand, which I shall have occasion to notice as an indispensable condition to their production. The idea of their being caused by sand falling into the cavities of the rocks appears to me to be nearly as satisfactory as the tale of the subterraneous bells. Sand in falling produces nothing beyond a dull, rustling noise, as may be readily proved by experiment. With regard to the hypothesis of wind acting on the thin and elastic plates of mica, I may remark that I could not detect a single plate of this mineral in the rocks of the locality, which were all of a sandy and calcareous character. I am not, however, prepared to deny the possibility of sounds being produced, under certain conditions, in the crevices of rocks of granite, gneiss, etc., which abound in mica.

My own ideas as to the cause of the phenomenon of the Mountain of the Bell coincide in a great measure with those of Lieutenant Wellsted, who has expressed his opinion that its explanation is intimately connected with the agitation of the sand. The inclination of the slope, down which the sand falls, is nearly that at which sand lies when poured down in a heap. It rolls down this slope, after having been disturbed, in a westerly direction; the surface of the subjacent sandstone rocks is uneven and step-like. In falling, the sand collects into waves, about an inch or two inches high, resembling those of a thick liquid flowing slowly down an inclined plane. These waves widen out as they approach the base of the slope, and acted upon by the wind, which was at the time of my visit blowing pretty strongly from the north-west, nearly at an angle of 45° with the course of the sand, form into festoon-like curves. The sounds produced on first disturbing the sand near the summit of the plane were, as before remarked, of a treble nature; but gradually deepened, and became graver and louder, as the undulations lengthened on their way downwards to the base ; apparently on the principle of the difference of sounds produced by the strings, of different lengths, of a musical instrument.

This effect was increased by the peculiar shape of the plane down which the sand glided, which, from circumstances of its being narrow at top and broad at the base, admitted of the gradual extension or widening of the waves of sand, or, if I may so express myself, the lengthening of the strings, and the consequent deepening of the strains, of this great natural Æolian harp.

That the sounds are caused principally by the motion of the sand is further proved by the perfect stillness of the locality so long as the sand remains undisturbed ; by the gradual increase, diminution and cessation of the sounds with those of the motion of the sand, and by their being inaudible in wet weather, when the surface is consolidated, as observed by Lieutenant Wellsted. That the action and direction of the wind is a favourable, if not a necessary, condition, is proved by the sounds being faint, according to the testimony of my Bedouin, in calm weather, and sometimes inaudible ; such was probably the case on the occasion of Lieutenant Wellsted's first unsuccessful visit. Further information, however, is desirable on these points ; and it would be interesting to visit the locality during the prevalence of an easterly wind. I hardly need remark that the north-west winds blow with so much violence occasionally as to disturb the sand, and thus produce the sounds without the aid of man. It would also be useful to take careful relative measurements of the locality, to ascertain the force and direction of the wind most favourable for producing the sounds, with a view of constructing a model on a small scale, from which similar effects might probably be produced artificially, and the curious question regarding the possibility of moving lines of loose sand producing, under any circumstances, musical sounds, decided beyond the shadow of a doubt. It is not a little singular that Gebel Nakús should be, as far as I am aware, the only known spot on the globe where the necessary conditions exist for producing those remarkable sounds,[1] although I have seen several localities in Arabia, Egypt and Spain where loose sand has been accumulated on the sides of rocks in an apparently similar manner. But it must be remarked at the same time that opportunity did not admit of a careful comparative examination of these localities.

I have not met with the account of the visit to Jebel Nakus of Professor H. A. Ward in 1855. But the well-known narrative of the expedition of Professor E. H. Palmer to determine the disputed sites of Exodus in the Desert of Sinai contains a full description of his visit to Jebel Nakus in February 1869.[2]

It is situated at about three-quarters of a mile from the sea-coast, and forms the north-western extremity of the range of hills which we had just crossed to our camp at Abu Suweirah. The mountain itself is composed of white friable sandstone, and filling a large gully in the side facing west-south-west, is a slope of fine drift sand about 380 feet in height, 80 yards wide at the base, and tapering towards the top, where it branches off into three or four narrow gullies. The sand lies at so high an angle to the horizon, nearly 30°, and is so fine and dry as to be easily set in motion from any point in the slope, or even by scraping away a portion from its base. When this is done the sand rolls down with a sluggish viscous motion, and it is then that the sound begins, at first a low vibratory moan, but gradually swelling out into a roar like thunder, and as gradually dying away again until the sand has ceased to roll. To me the sound seemed more like that caused by air entering the mouth of a large metal

[1] He was of course mistaken.

[2] *The Desert of the Exodus*, part I. pp. 217-221. Cambridge, 1871.

vessel, and I could produce an imitation of it on a small scale by turning my flask at a certain angle to the wind. We found that the heated surface was much more sensitive to sound than the cooler layers beneath, and that those parts of the slope which had lain long undisturbed, produced a much louder and more lasting sound than those which had recently been set in motion, thus showing that the phenomenon is purely local and superficial, and due in some manner to the combined effects of heat and friction. A faint sound could also be produced by sweeping portions of the sand rapidly forward with the arm; and this caused such a peculiar tingling sensation in the operator's arm as to suggest that some electrical influence was also at work. When a large quantity of the sand was set in motion and the sound was at its height a powerful vibration was felt, and straws stuck into the sand trembled visibly although there was not a breath of wind to disturb them. The sand on the upper part of the slope where it branches off into the gullies above mentioned is coarser and more adulterated with extraneous particles, *detritus* from the overhanging rocks, and pieces of seaweed blown up from the shore; it is consequently less easily set in motion, and we found it to be much less sensitive to sound. The inclination of the slope is the "angle of rest" of the sand in its normal state; but excessive heat or drought, wind, animals running over the slope, falling rocks, and many other accidents might act as disturbing causes; in any of these cases the sound would occur, and its spontaneous production, which has caused so much speculation, may be therefore easily accounted for. Besides the large slide there is a narrow slope to the north; and part of this, being in shade the whole day long during the winter months, afforded us an opportunity of determining the comparative sensitiveness of the heated and cool sand. We found that the sand on the cool, shaded portion, at a temperature of 62° produced but a very faint sound when set in motion; while that on the more exposed parts, at a temperature of 103° gave forth a loud and often even startling noise. Other sand-slopes in the vicinity were also experimented upon, but these, which were composed of coarser grains and inclined at a lower angle, produced no acoustic phenomena whatever. The Arabs declare that the sounds are only heard on Fridays and Sundays, and tell the following legend respecting their origin :

An Arab whose people were encamped by the palm-grove of Abu Suweirah, happened to stroll alone by the sea-shore, and coming to the spot in question, which he had hitherto believed to be barren and uninhabited, he was surprised to find a small monastery and a pleasant garden on the mountain side. The brethren received him courteously, and invited him to partake of their meal, to which, being hungry and fatigued, he gladly consented. Having shared their hospitality, he prepared to depart, but first, at the instance of his hosts, he took a solemn oath that he would never reveal to any living soul the secret of their retreat or of his own meeting with them. He was accompanied for a portion of his way home by two of the monks, who reiterated their injunctions of secrecy and took their leave. The Arab, however, prompted either by curiosity or baser motives, took the opportunity of dropping the stones of some dates which he had eaten, in order that he might have a clue by which to find the place again ; and on reaching the tents of his tribe he at once related his adventure, regardless alike of his oath and of the sacred laws of hospitality. His people refused to credit his account until he offered to conduct them himself to the place ; but, when he attempted to do this, he found that all the date-stones had been removed. He did, however, succeed in identifying the mountain, but the monastery, gardens, and monks had all disappeared, and nothing remained to show that they had ever existed save the sound of the *nágús* calling them to prayers within their mysterious retreat in the very heart of the mountain. The Arab who had thus disregarded the sacred obligations of bread and salt, not only forfeited the esteem of his own people, but misfortune after misfortune overtook him until he perished miserably, an outcast from his fellow-men.

I have quoted Professor Palmer's description of Jebel Nakus at length, because, if reference to it is desired, this will be easily accessible to any reader. But a nearly identical, though more purely scientific, account was given by Captain H. S. Palmer, R.E., in the official publication, entitled *Ordnance Survey of the Peninsula of Sinai*, which had been brought out by H.M. Government two years earlier, in 1869. The description of the sounds, as heard by the party, is even more precise (pp. 131-134):

> The sound is difficult to describe exactly; it is not metallic, nor like that of a bell, nor yet that of a *nágús*. Perhaps the very hoarsest note of an Æolian harp, or the sound produced by rubbing the finger round the wet rim of a deep-toned finger-glass, most closely resembles it, save that there is less music in the sound of this rolling sand. It may also be likened to the noise produced by air rushing into the mouth of an empty flask or bottle; sometimes it almost approaches the roar of very distant thunder, and sometimes it resembles the deeper notes of a violoncello, or the hum of a humming-top.

Captain Palmer went on to say:

> The motion may be produced by design in various ways—by scraping away a portion at the foot of the slope; by walking directly or slantwise up it; or, which is the most effectual method, by ascending the cliffs at its side, and then scrambling rapidly along the whole

face of the upper part of the slope, or slipping down and displacing the sand with one's hands and feet. The sand thus set in motion from any high point rolls slowly down over the surface in thin waves an inch or two deep, just as oil or any thick liquid might roll over an inclined sheet of glass, and in similar festoons or curves. In its passage, each wave slightly disturbs the sand below it and at its sides; then the waves gradually spread as they descend over the constantly widening surface of the slope, and the sound soon reaches its highest pitch; approaching the bottom the film gets thinner and thinner, at length all movement ceases, and with it the sound.

Of the various natural causes by which motion of the sand and consequent singing might be produced, Captain Palmer named the wind (the prevailing direction of which is from the north-west), intense heat, and drought. Among possible artificial causes he enumerated the movement of animals, such as gazelles, hyaenas, wolves, foxes, hares, or jerboas, crossing the slide; or rocks rolling down from the heights above; and, of course, the accidental or deliberate actions of man.

With the Ordnance Survey was published an engraving of the sand-slope of Jebel Nakus, which is reproduced here, and which may be compared with Lieutenant Wellsted's drawing engraved in his book.[1] The latter sketch represents the sand as apparently lying at a much steeper slope, and suggests exaggeration. Indeed the American, Dr. Bolton, said that it was quite inaccurate.

[1] *Travels in Arabia*, vol. ii. p. 24.

Such was the record of their experience and impressions left by a series of English travellers of knowledge and repute in the second and third quarters of the past century. It is remarkable to me that, Tor being a regular station for visitors to Sinai, so few, even among professional travellers who have touched or halted there, have seized the occasion to visit Jebel Nakus. Burton's ship was detained at Tor on his journey to Mecca, but he does not refer to the hill on that occasion. Nor does H. Brugsch, who spent three days in the town.[1] Élisée Reclus gives a clear local map showing the Nakus, but does not even refer to it in his text.[2] No modern addition, indeed, has been made to the rather scant compendium which I have compiled until, in the 'eighties, a number of American scientists, who had devoted themselves with great application to the study of the problem of Musical Sands, turned their attention to Jebel Nakus, one of their number, Dr. H. C. Bolton, eventually deciding to visit the spot. The narrative of his journey in 1889 contains our latest information. In May 1889 Dr. Bolton's Report appeared in the *Transactions of the New York Academy of Sciences.* It will be seen that he heard the music, but in no striking degree :

The name Jebel Nagous is given by the Bedouins to a mountain nearly three miles long and about 1200 feet high, composed of white sandstone bearing quartz

[1] *Wanderung*, p. 22 *et seq.* Leipzig, 1866.
[2] *Géographie Universelle*, vol. ix. p. 822.

pebbles and veins. On the west and north-west are several large banks of brown sand inclined at high angles. The sand on one of these slopes at the north-western end of the mountain has the property of yielding a deep resonance when it glides down the incline, either from the force of the wind or by the action of man. This bank of sand I distinguish from the others by calling it the Bell Slope. It is triangular in shape and measures 260 feet across the base, 5-8 feet across the top, and is 394 feet high. It has the inclination of 31° quite uniformly. It is bounded by vertical cliffs of sandstone and is broken towards the base by projecting rocks of the same material. The sand is yellowish in colour, very fine, and possesses at this inclination a curious mobility, which causes it to flow, when disturbed, like treacle or pitch, the depression formed being filled in from above and advancing upward at the same time. The sand has none of the characteristics of sonorous sand found on beaches. When pulled downward by the hand, or pushed by the feet, a strong vibration is felt and a low note is plainly heard, resembling the deep bass of an organ-pipe. The loudness and continuity of the note are related to the mass of sand moved, but I think that those who compare it to distant thunder exaggerate. The bordering rocky walls give a marked echo, which may have the effect of magnifying and prolonging the sounds, but which is not essential. There are no cavities for the sand to fall into, as erroneously reported. The peak of Jebel Nagous rises above the Bell Slope to the height of 955 feet above the sea-level.

In October 1889 Dr. Bolton made a further Report of the same visit, in which he described the sand of Jebel Nakus as very fine granules, yellowish white, and composed chiefly of quartz and calcareous sandstone, and added that " the sand of the slope is derived partly from disintegration of the rock itself and partly from the more distant plain below, from which violent winds blow it up on the mountain side."

Other Arabian Sands

The same thought, however, occurred to Dr. Bolton as must have presented itself to some of my readers, viz. whatever the cause or explanation of the sounds, how comes it that in countries and in regions where sand-dunes, sand-hills, and sand-drifts abound, apparently not differing widely from each other in shape or composition, the music is heard in so few places, and that Singing Sands, instead of being a normal, are so rare a phenomenon ? Accordingly he began to search in the neighbouring area for parallel sites, and without difficulty he discovered another sounding sand-hill 45 feet high, in the Wadi Werkan, five minutes off the regular caravan route to Egypt, and one and a half days by camel from Suez. The spot is called by the Bedawin Ramadan, and is thus described by Dr. Bolton. The sand, when blown by the north wind, is carried over a range of cliffs and is deposited on their south side, where it rests on the steep face at an angle of 31° at the top and 21° or less below. On being stirred by the hand, the sand yielded the bass note, already heard at Jebel Nakus, and audible 100 feet away.[1] Probably, if similar investigations were conducted, a good many

[1] *Transactions of the New York Academy of Sciences*, May 1889, p. 182.

sand-dunes, where the particular combination of conditions, essential to the production of the music, exists—what they are I will discuss later on—could be found; attention having been concentrated on a few sites where the phenomenon, whether in respect of the size of the sand-hill, or of the sounds produced, is on a larger scale, or has become associated either with the burial of a saint or some local superstition.

Burckhardt, when he was in the Sinai Peninsula in May 1816, heard of Jebel Nakus, and the Bedawin tales concerning it, but made no effort to test them by visiting the spot. On the other hand he heard even more precise stories about a similar phenomenon in another mountain of the Sinai group:

> Several Bedouins had acquainted me that a thundering noise, like repeated discharges of heavy artillery, is heard at times in these mountains; and they all affirmed that it came from Om Shomar. The monks (of the Convent of St. Catherine) corroborated the story, and even positively asserted that they had heard the sound about midday five years ago, describing it in the same manner as the Bedouins. The same noise had been heard in more remote times, and the Ikonomos, who had lived there forty years, told me that he remembered to have heard the noise at four or five separate periods. I inquired whether any shock of an earthquake had ever been felt on such occasions, but was answered in the negative.[1]

Burckhardt then made a special visit to Om Shomar, but without result.

[1] *Travels in Syria and the Holy Land*, pp. 587-591. London, 1822.

Niebuhr, who was in the same neighbourhood in the previous century and gave an illustration of Tor, makes no reference either to Jebel Nakus or to any other Sounding Sand in the vicinity.

Another German traveller who made the journey from Cairo to Medina and Mecca in April 1845, Dr. G. A. Wallin, also refers to a place, called by his guide Wadi Hamade, somewhere in Northern Arabia north of Medina. He did not apparently either visit it or hear the music. But the Arab informed him that sometimes very strange sounds, like those of kettledrums, are heard to rise from the earth, without any one being able to account for this extraordinary phenomenon.[1]

So great a traveller and so profound a scholar as C. M. Doughty could not be expected, in his classic of Arabian travel, to leave the phenomenon of the Sounding Sands unnoticed, and accordingly we read with no surprise the following passage :

In the Nefuz, towards El-Hyza, are certain booming sand-hills—Rowsa, Deffafiat, Subbia and Irzum, such as the sand drift of Jebel Nagus, by the sea village of Tor in Sinai ; the upper sand sliding down under the foot of the passenger, there arises, of the infinite fretting grains, such a giddy loud-swelling sound as when your wetted finger is drawn about the lip of a glass of water, and like that swooning din after the chime of a great bell or cup of metal. Nagûs is the name of the sounding-board in the belfry of the Greek monastery, whereupon, as the sacristan plays with his hammer, the timber yields a pleasant musical note which calls forth the formal *colieros*

[1] *Journal of the Royal Geographical Society*, vol. xxiv., 1854.

to their prayers; another such singing sand drift, El-Howayrîa, is in the cliffs (east of the Mizham) of Medain Salih.[1]

H. St. J. Philby, the most recent and adventurous of British travellers, in the *Heart of Arabia*, which title he has given to his excellent book (1922), tells me that he never heard the phenomenon himself, but that he was often told about it by the Arabs, more particularly in relation to the dead city of Jahura, never visited by a European, and hidden away in the Great Desert, somewhere about the 22nd parallel of latitude and the 51st of longitude, midway between the borders of Hejaz and Oman. There the sounds of drumming and moaning are regularly heard at night by passing travellers, by whom they are of course attributed to *jinns* or ghosts, persons of weak intellect having even been known to lose their reason. This, however, may be a case of merely imaginary haunting, the product of superstition.

Sir Richard Burton, though he does not appear anywhere to have heard the music, refers to examples in Midian. He also only quotes the evidence of others. A party from his expedition, headed by Lieutenant Amir Rushdi, were at a distance of about three hours, or eleven miles, from Sharma camp, when—

Some pyramids of sand were pointed out in the Wady Ratiyah. The Bedawin call one of them the Goz el-

[1] *Travels in Arabia Deserta* (*circ.* 1876), vol. i. p. 307. Cambridge, 1888.

Hannan (Moaning Sand-heap). They declare that when the Hajj-caravan passes, or rather used to pass, by that way, before the early sixteenth century, when Sultan Selim laid out his maritime high-road, a *naubah* (orchestra) was wont to sound within its bowel. This tale is told of two other places in Midian.[1]

It is true that some of these tales only repeat second-hand hearsay or even more remote tradition. But they testify to a widespread belief in the existence of a phenomenon which there is no reason to doubt, and the manifestations of which are much more calculated to surprise us by their rareness than by their frequency.

Jebel-ut-Tabul

In my studies I came across a passage in the travels of Ibn Batutah, the Moor of Tangier, who journeyed extensively in the East about A.D. 1330, and who thus described a place on the road between Medina and Mecca, which he called Jebel-ut-Tabul or the Hill of Drums.

At Bedr there is a spring the water of which forms a canal. The site of the well in which the idolaters—enemies of God—were thrown, is now a garden, and the burial place of the martyrs is behind it. The Mountain of Pity (Jebel-ur-Rahma), where the angels descended (Koran, iii. 119-121), is on the left hand of any one who enters upon this last spot in order to proceed towards Safra. In front is the Mount of Drums. It resembles a vast hill of sand, and the inhabitants of these countries declare that every night between Thursday and Friday they hear in this place a noise as of drums. The site of

[1] *Land of Midian*, vol. i. p. 65. London, 1879.

the hut of the Missionary of God, in which he spent the day at Bedr, in prayer to his Lord, is at the foot of the Mount of Drums. The place of combat is opposite to it.[1]

I sought for references to this spot in the published works of Burton, Burckhardt, and others who have made or described the journey from Medina to Mecca, but could not find any.

I then referred to King Hussein of the Hejaz, who replied that he knew the locality well, having built a small mosque at the foot of the hill to commemorate the famous victory of the Prophet, but that, though he was familiar with the rumour, he had never himself heard the drums. On the other hand, his son, Amit Abdullah of Transjordan, spoke of the phenomenon at Bedr as being of frequent and notorious occurrence.

He added the information, derived from his Bedawin followers, who claimed to have themselves heard the music, that sounds of thundering and groaning are also heard at night, and on most nights, in the sand-belt known as Arq-al-Subai in the neighbourhood of a locality known as Abraq-al-Manazil, on the way to Taif; and also in the sands near Khanug, which is described as lying ninety-five miles E.S.E. of Medina. These assertions, if true, are peculiar in ascribing the sound to night time, when the majority of the causes that are believed to produce the sound are unlikely to be in operation. In all these

[1] *Voyages d'Ibn Batoutah* (Defrémery), vol. i. p. 296. Paris, 1853. The allusion is of course to the famous battle of Bedr, in which Mohammed defeated the Meccans in A.D. 623.

cases it is difficult to distinguish experience from rumour and truth from superstition. But at least the testimony tends to corroborate the belief that the Arabian sands exhibit many instances of the phenomenon.

While I was writing this paper the representative of King Hussein, who happened to be in London and heard of my investigations, gave me the following note :

> There is a place at Beirut, called Es-Sadat, which is said to produce a musical sound. It is compared to a tambourine.
>
> The place is a cave dug out in a rocky hill situated in the extreme western point of the city of Beirut and faces the " Pigeon Rocks " or " Shubra." The hill on the north dominates a vast sandy beach, which stretches from the foot of the hill all along the coast to a point five miles to the north-west. The sandy beach rises in some places to form a sandy hill.
>
> The people of Beirut say that they hear the music on Friday nights, and it is attributed to the playing of the Sadat—the Masters. These apparitions gather on Friday nights in that cave and go through the *thikr* with tambourines in the manner of the *thikr* to-day, as practised in some places after prayers on Friday.
>
> There is a man from Beirut, now in London, who says that when he was a boy he himself heard the music. His son added that his grandmother used to sit on Friday nights till late to hear the tambourines of the Sadat. They said that there are some people in Beirut who pretend to have seen people in white clothes going into the cave at night.

I accordingly asked the British Consul at Beyrout to visit the place. He found that the ground in the neighbourhood of the cave is now in the occupation of the French naval authorities, who have erected a wireless station there, and that the cave itself, which is high enough to admit of a man standing upright in it, is used by the sailors as a petrol-store. The high ground on which it is situated dominates a large expanse of sand and sand-dunes, sometimes rising to a considerable height, but lying at some distance from the cave. The French have never heard any sounds; but native witnesses who have lived in the neighbourhood for many years have heard the music emanating from the cave (though not recently) and described it as resembling the sound of a beaten tambourine. They added the not unexpected detail that the music was always heard on Thursday evenings (*i.e.* on the eve of the Holy Day) and was accompanied by the voices of persons invoking the names of Allah and Mohammed! There I must leave it. It is quite possible that at an earlier date before the dunes were planted, as they have been in many places with pines, and built upon, some or other of the sand slopes may have been musical, and that the sounds so heard were connected by the superstitious natives with the mystery of the cave. The conditions which produced vocality, if it ever existed, may now have ceased to operate.

Before leaving the Continent of Asia, I should add that Sir H. Yule refers to a case in the hills between the Ulba and the Irtish, in the vicinity of the Altai, which he calls the Almanac Hills, because the sounds are supposed to prognosticate weather changes.[1] But the only reference to these mountains of which I am aware is in a German publication, where they are called the Kalendar Mountains, and are said to give out a sharp report before bad weather—a phenomenon not without parallel, but bearing no relation to the Singing Sands.[2]

The Libyan Desert

It would be strange if no similar tales were forthcoming from the immense sand deserts of Africa, where the necessary conditions could hardly fail in some places to exist. But in the meagre literature of the subject I have found no such reference, and I only owe the two following records to my own research.

In April 1909, W. J. Harding King, travelling in the Libyan Desert, to the west of the Nile Valley, heard the song of the sands amid the dunes, some sixty feet high, not far from the Dakhla Oasis. The plateau over which he was journeying consisted of sandstone, but the meteorological conditions were somewhat unusual. After a week of great heat, followed by a cool, almost a cold day, with slight showers, a downpour of rain occurred for a quarter of an hour before sunset. Then was heard the music.

The sound began at 7.30 P.M. and continued till about 8. It was very faint. There were two distinct sounds :

[1] *Marco Polo*, vol. i. p. 206.

[2] Statement by Meyer in Ledebour's *Reise*, vol. ii. p. 186. Berlin, 1830.

the one somewhat resembled the sighing of the wind in telegraph wires, and the other was a deep throbbing sound that strongly reminded me of the after-reverberation of Big Ben. . . . It was very difficult to determine the direction from which the sound came, but apparently it came from a place about a mile distant, where the sand poured over a low scarp. The sound was a distinctly musical one, as opposed to a mere noise.[1]

The Western Sahara

The German traveller, Dr. Oskar Lenz, who made long and adventurous explorations in the years 1874–80 in the Western Sahara, between Timbuctoo and Morocco, testifies to the same phenomenon at a spot in the Igidi region, near the well Bir-el-Abbas, a little north of 25° north latitude, longitude about 6½° west of Greenwich.

Here in this Igidi region I observed the interesting phenomenon of the Musical Sand. In the midst of the solitude one suddenly hears emerging from the interior of a sand-hill a long-drawn hollow tone, like that of a trumpet, which continues for a few seconds, then stops, only to sound again from another spot after a short interval. This makes a weird impression in the death-like stillness of the uninhabited waste. It should be remarked at once that there is absolutely no question of an acoustic illusion, comparable to the optical illusions to which one may be subject. Not only I, but all my people, heard these hollow tones, and the guide Mohammed already called our attention to this phenomenon the day before.

The long-extended sand-dunes of the Igidi, which form regular chains of hills with sharp corners and

[1] *Geographical Journal*, vol. xxxix., 1912, pp. 133-4.

summits, have, like all dunes, a gently rising surface directed towards the wind and in part at least a very steep fall on the opposite side. Here too they consist of a loose, very pure, light yellow quartz sand, which is heated as in a furnace by the sun. When these sand-hills are crossed by a caravan a movement is set up of the lightly-piled resonant quartz grains—which movement, at first limited to a small space, draws constantly larger circles into sympathy with itself, and, like an avalanche, spreads itself over the whole surface of such a sand-hill. The motion of the loose sand-grains causes them to collide feebly with each other, by which an ever so slight note is produced ; by reason of the great volume of the moving sand-grains and the summation of the, individually, extremely feeble tones, a noise results which may attain a quite extraordinary strength. As a rule the phenomenon occurs only when the sand is set in motion artificially, by men or camels, and when the disturbance of equilibrium penetrates somewhat deeply into the mass. Camels often sink knee-deep into the loose sand. A mere superficial movement, such as may be caused by the wind, will produce the phenomenon in a very much slighter degree.[1]

South Africa

I have found a single mention of a Singing Sand-dune in South Africa, on the west side of the Langberg Mountain in Western Griqualand, on dunes 500-600 feet in height. But the description of the musical sand is unfortunately omitted by the author, though apparently it had been recorded by him.[2]

[1] *Timbuktu : Reise durch Marokko, die Sahara und den Sudan*, vol. ii. p. 53. Leipzig, 1884.

[2] *Twenty-five Years in a Wagon in South Africa*, by A. A. Anderson, vol. i. p. 92. London, 1887.

North America

In North America I have come across a single record of a Singing Sand-dune, analogous to the Asian and African cases which we have been discussing, and differing from the Musical Sand-beaches, of which there are so many examples in the American Continent. This is in Churchill county, in Nevada, twenty miles south of Still-water. The dune is said to be 100-400 feet in height, and four miles long. When agitation of the sand starts it sliding a noise is produced like that from telegraph wires fanned by a breeze.[1]

South America

Tarapaca in Chile.—Here also we have the record of a Singing Sand-hill known locally as the Rumbling Mountain. It is described by a mining engineer, W. Bollaert, who in about 1830 was employed in the neighbourhood. He says :

> On the road from Tarapaca to Guantajaya, and six miles west of the Pozo (or well) de Ramírez, is the Cerrito de Huara, a *bramador*, or rumbling mountain, which is an object of curiosity to the traveller, but to the Indians one rather of fear. The sounds are generally heard about sunrise. This hill is situated in a desert plain. During the day the country around is exposed to great heat ; at night there is a considerable diminution of temperature, in consequence of the hot south wind having gone to the eastward, where it gets cooled by the Andes, forming during the night the land breeze. As the sun rises the air becomes heated, expansion takes place, rapid currents

[1] *Trans. New York Acad. Sci.* vol. iii., 1885, p. 97.

and even gusts of wind are formed, which, striking upon the sides of the mountains and setting the sand in motion, cause probably the roaring or rumbling sounds in question.[1]

Copiapo in Chile.—A few years later (in June 1835) Charles Darwin, travelling in Chile, records another El Bramador or Bellower. While staying in the town of Copiapo, he heard of, but did not himself visit, a neighbouring hill, covered by sand, where the sound was produced by people ascending the slope. "One person with whom I conversed had himself heard the noise; he described it as very surprising; and he distinctly stated that, although he could not understand how it was caused, yet it was necessary to set the sand rolling down the declivity."[2]

A full description of this place appeared in *Nature* in July 1909 from the pen of M. H. Gray, who visited it with the British Consul, and thus narrated his experience, although he made the mistake of supposing that the sound was caused or accentuated by the existence of old silver workings below the surface of the moving sand:

In a ravine a few miles to the west of Copiapo the sand has been carried by the sea breeze up the gully and lies at a slope equal to the flowing angle of dry sand. The place is locally known as *El Punto del Diabolo*, since, given conditions of time and weather, a low moaning sound, varying in intensity, can be heard for quite a quarter of a mile away. Amongst the superstitious natives the place is avoided. . . . On our arrival we

[1] *Journal of the Royal Geographical Society*, vol. xxi., 1851, p. 104.

[2] *Voyage of the "Beagle,"* p. 366. London, 1901.

found that the sands were quite silent, but on making a glissade down the slope a gradually increasing rumble was heard, which grew in volume as the sand slid away before us. As the sound increased we were subjected to an undulatory movement, so decided that it was difficult to keep one's balance.

Hawaii Islands

The Barking Sands of Kauai.—Lastly comes the remarkable case, said to have been discovered about the year 1850, of the so-called Barking Sands in one of the islands of the Hawaiian groups. Travellers in those strange and exotic scenes seem to have been largely unaware of or to have ignored the existence of this phenomenon. But they are mentioned in the works of Bates, Frink, Bird, Nordhoff, and some others. I take the following account from a newly published and official work on the Natural History of the Islands. The author writes as follows :

The Barking Sands of Mana (in Kauai) consist of a series of wind-blown sand-hills, a half-mile or more in length, along the shore at Nahili. The bank is nearly 60 feet high, and through the action of the wind the mound is constantly advancing on the land. The front wall is quite steep. The white sand, which is composed of coral, shells, and particles of lava, has the peculiar property, when very dry, of emitting a sound, when two handfuls are clapped together, that, to the imaginative mind, seems to resemble the barking of a dog. When a horse is rushed down the steep incline of the mound a curious sound as of subterranean thunder is produced. The sound varies with the degree of heat, the dryness of the sand, and the amount of friction employed; so that sounds varying from a faint rustle to a deep rumble may be produced. Attempts at explaining this rare natural phenomenon have left much of the mystery still unsolved. However, the dry sand doubtless has a resonant quality that is the basis of the peculiar manifestation, which disappears when the sand is wet. That the Barking Sands are found in only a couple of the driest localities in the group is also significant. Much of the shoreline of Kauai, for example, is lined with old coral reefs that have partly disintegrated into sand that forms the beaches.[1]

Dr. H. C. Bolton visited these sands in the spring of 1890 and thus described his experience :

At its steepest part, the angle being quite uniformly 31°, the sand has a notable mobility when perfectly dry, and, on disturbing its equilibrium, it rolls in wavelets down the incline, emitting at the same time a deep bass note of a tremulous character. My companion thought the sound resembled the hum of a buzz-saw in a planing mill. . . . The drier the sand the louder the sound.

Kaluakahua.—Pursuing his investigations, Dr. Bolton discovered another Sonorous Sand-dune at a place called Kaluakahua in the neighbouring islet of Niihau in the same group. Here the music is heard on the land side of a dune about 100 feet high, and at several points along the coast. " On the chief slope, 36 feet high, the sand has the same mobility, lies at the same angle, and gives when disturbed the same note as the sand of Kauai, but less strong, the slope being so much lower." [2]

[1] W. A. Bryan, *Natural History of Hawaii*, p. 108. Hawaii, 1915. *Vide* also J. Blake, *Proc. Calif. Acad. Sci.*, 1873-5, vol. v. pp. 357-8.

[2] *Trans. New York Acad. Sci.* vol. x., 1890, pp. 28-30.

Dr. Bolton added, as demonstrating that the acoustic property is independent of material, that, whereas admittedly the Sonorous Sands of all other known localities are siliceous, being either pure silex or a mixture of the same with silicates, such as feldspar, the Hawaiian sands are wholly carbonate of lime.

I have now completed my summary of the various localities in different and widely scattered parts of the world, where the phenomenon of the Singing Sands, either in steeply sloping sand-hills or in dunes, has been or still is heard; and I have shown that instead of there being only two or at the most three spots, as the majority of writers have alleged, where it exists, it is on the contrary widely diffused, and is to be found in both hemispheres and in every continent, except, as it seems, that of Europe, where the general paucity of sand, except in the neighbourhood of the sea, and the climatic conditions are presumably unfavourable to its reproduction.

I have also, I think, collected a body of evidence sufficient to allow of certain definite deductions to be drawn, both as to the cause of the phenomenon and the conditions under which it is most likely to be produced.

Firstly, let me deal with what I may describe as the predisposing, though not always indispensable, factors. These are to be found in a number of conditions—viz. geographical situation, orientation of sand-hill, slope of sand-hill, composition of sand, climatic or meteorological features. We can then proceed to an analysis of the sounds produced, and of the mechanical or other causes that produce them.

Although the music is heard from sand-slopes or dunes of varying height and dimensions, it undoubtedly appears that it is loudest and most renowned in the case of sand-hills piled up to a considerable height against a background of cliffs or rocks; these act in some cases as a sounding-board to the music, echoing and deepening the tones. We find this theatre of rocks existing in the case of the Chinese Rumbling Hill, the two Afghan Moving Sands, the Arabian hills of Jebel Nakus and Jebel-ut-Tabul, and probably in other cases. Against this background the sand, partly derived from disintegration of the rocks, partly swept up by the winds from the lower level, is deposited by the gales in a sloping bank, as a rule narrow at the summit and broadening as it descends. Sometimes the sand is blown over the top of the scarp by a wind from the opposite quarter. In certain of the localities there appears to be something either in the configuration of the ground or in the action of the wind that results in the concentration of the sand on the particular site where the sound is produced as distinct from any neighbouring spot. The principal sounding sand-hills in this category seem, as a rule, if not invariably, to face towards either the south or west-south-west. We hear sometimes of the sound as emanating from sand patches with another orientation, but in those cases the sound is much feebler. In other words, the action of the sun, beating continuously upon the surface of the sand, and causing dryness, is a material factor in the predisposing conditions.

Different authorities have given different figures—doubtless arrived at without measurement and as the result of a rough shot—for the angle of inclination of the musical slope. Some say 40°, others 50°. The more careful examination of Professor Palmer and Dr. Bolton showed that the angle of Jebel Nakus is 31°, which is the natural angle of rest of sand; and this is the figure, supported by other examples, which we may accept as the normal factor in the case.

In cases where the sand-slope rests against a wall of rock, from the decomposition of which the sand is partially formed, it is noticeable that these rocks are almost always, if not always, of a light-coloured friable sandstone, mingled sometimes with limestone. Similarly the sonorous sand itself is of the same or a similar composition, being yellow or whitish in colour and consisting of mainly quartz grains. The chemical composition of the sand probably does not differ materially in any of the Sonorous Sand-hills, whether in Asia or Africa. The Barking Sands of Kauai are in a rather different category, being, not quartz, but coral-sand and shell-sand, with 95 per cent calcite. In every case there is a complete absence of very fine particles of silt, and dunes where there is much shaly matter are not musical, although other conditions may be favourable.

Although the sound is heard at different times of the year, it is not surprising—viewing the large part that heat and dryness play in the production—that the dry season is regarded as the most favourable time, at least in those parts of the world where there are great variations of climate. Where there is a tolerably uniform degree of heat in the daytime, the precise season will be less material.

It is difficult to determine the exact part which the wind may or does play in evoking the acoustic property of the sand. There can be no doubt that, where the music is heard in circumstances which admit of no mechanical or artificial causation, the wind is capable by itself of playing upon the chords, and producing the vibration that is necessary for the manufacture of the sound. This is the explanation of the fortuitous occurrence of the phenomenon. Whether the music is louder when the wind blows from a certain quarter is not certain, although some of our observers appear to have thought that this was so. Lieutenant Newbold in particular, who was a man of scientific attainments, and whose account of Jebel Nakus is the best that we possess, was of opinion that the action and direction of the wind were important factors, and that experiment should be made to ascertain the wind conditions that were most propitious to sound production.

Differing from the case of the Singing Beaches, to which I shall come presently—where dryness after moisture appears to be the most favourable condition—it would seem that in the case of the Musical Sand-hills the drier the sand the more likely the phenomenon. Rain having fallen a short time before Lieutenant Wellsted's second visit to Jebel Nakus, and the sand being still consolidated by the moisture, he did not hear the music at all. Professor Palmer, at the same spot, found that the cool or shaded sand produced only the faintest noise, while the dry and exposed parts gave forth a loud reverberation. Only in the case of the Libyan sands do we hear of the music as following upon rain, and here the description is far from conclusive. It may, I think, therefore be generally accepted that the warmth of the air, and the consequent dryness of the sand, resulting in incoherency of the sand-grains, are elements of value in the case.

And now I come to the sound itself. A few writers have made fun of the varying reports and the conflicting similes of the writers who have heard the music. I, on the contrary, am impressed by their similarity and agreement. We all know how difficult in practice it is to identify a sound, for which no obvious or artificial cause is forthcoming, with the notes of this or that musical instrument. One man will find a likeness here, another there ; and this is all the more easy if the sound itself that is the subject of the comparison differs materially not only at different times, but at different moments of the same time. For nothing can, I think, be more clear in the case of the Singing Sand-hills than that they have different notes, dependent upon the degree of vibration set up in the sand-grains by the force of the external impulse communicated to them. The music seems to pass through at least three distinct phases or gradations. First there is the faintly murmurous or wailing or moaning sound, compared sometimes to the strain of an Æolian harp, at others to the humming of a top or the singing of a telegraph wire, or, when deeper, to the chords of a violoncello. Then as the vibration increases and the sound swells, we have the comparison sometimes to an organ, sometimes to the deep clangour of a bell, more frequently, in the case of the ancients, to the more resonant musical instruments with which they were familiar, namely, trumpets and kettle-drums. Finally, we have the rumble of distant thunder when the soil is in violent oscillation and the sand-grains are striking each other sharply as they glide into the vacant spaces. Because one auditor hears the fainter as compared with the louder music, there is no reason for accusing the witness to the latter of exaggeration.

The evidence also seems to be clear that the music can be heard at a great distance. Native witnesses testify to a distance of many miles. But trained and credible European observers have more than once spoken of a mile. The conditions under which the phenomenon has hitherto been investigated have not been favourable to the collection of scientific data of this supplementary type. Probably as time passes there will be a greater disposition, and perhaps fuller opportunities, to procure them.

Another interesting feature, about which it is at present impossible to dogmatise, is the length of time for which the music is heard. Few of our observers have been definite upon this point; and doubtless it is in large measure dependent upon the degree of vibration set up and the continuance or suspension of the determining cause. Captain Lovett reported of the Seistan phenomenon that "it was said sometimes to last as long as an hour at a time." Newbold spoke of the cessation of the sound, which was co-extensive with the movement of the sand, as having taken place after a quarter of an hour. Here again more scientific research will be of value.

Further, the vibratory motion of the sands is capable of being communicated to the observer. Professor Palmer, at Jebel Nakus, when he swept portions of the sand rapidly forward with his arm, felt a peculiar tingling sensation. Lieutenant Newbold spoke of the sensations produced by the vibrations as extraordinary. Lieutenant Wellsted described the rock as vibrating powerfully. Other observers, standing on the sands, while the music is sounding, have experienced similar vibrations. The Englishmen who visited El Bramador at Copiapo were so shaken by the oscillation of the sounding sand that they could scarcely stand. The American scientists record a tingling sensation in the feet or hands, when treading on or striking the Musical Sand Beaches, to which I shall presently turn.

Those who have followed me thus far will have no difficulty in arriving at an opinion as to how the sound is produced. We may roughly describe the causes of production as three in number. First, there are the occasions when the music is heard, without any visible or extraneous cause, *i.e.* when the sand vibrations are set up by extreme heat or drought. The Mohammedans of course attempt to connect these manifestations with their Sunday, which is our Friday ; but he would be an unwise investigator who confined his visits to those occasions. Secondly, comes the direct action of the wind, setting the sand particles in continuous but not violent motion and producing a murmuring or droning sound. Thirdly, is the direct intervention of artificial agents, taking the form as a rule of men or animals treading upon the surface, either when climbing the sand-slope or—which is easier—trampling down it, and producing the abrupt commotion which is the cause of the acute surface vibration noticed by some travellers, and of the long thunderous reverberations rolling and bellowing in the underground chambers. What the direct causes are, apart from wind, the casual passage of wild animals, or the accidental fall of rocks (where there are rocks), which produce the sound at night, if it is really heard then, it is more difficult to determine.

We can realise also how the actual sound is produced. As the surface is disturbed, the sand descends in gliding, sliding festoons, the music deepening as the undulations spread and the sand-grains rub and clash against each other in the course of their fall. The to-and-fro motion of the sand-grains sends out equally-spaced waves into the air with a frequency exceeding forty vibrations a second and probably very much greater. It may seem strange that the slight noise produced by the falling together of sand-grains should be able to swell to the note of a trumpet or the roar of thunder; but it is not inappropriate to refer to the analogous case of the avalanche, where causes the most minute can produce a final effect which is colossal.

It does not appear that the movement of the sand makes any material alteration in the extent or contour of the slope, for, as the vacuum is created and the sand descends, the empty spaces fill up again from below, equilibrium is re-established, and the shape of the sand-hill remains as before.

Why the resonance should be evoked at one attempt, and should refuse to respond at the next, must be due to some local and accidental variation in the condition of the sand or in the impulse communicated by the external agent, which it is impossible to determine with exactitude. For instance, if the sand has been trampled upon on one day, it may no longer lie at the angle of rest, and may not become musical again until, helped by wind and gravity, it has resumed the necessary conditions.

The restriction of the sound to so apparently limited a number of places (though I suspect that this is in the main the result of imperfect observation) and the silence of the sand in others (apart from the physical differences of site and surroundings and climate) must, I think, be attributable to some essential quality or conformation in the sand-grains themselves. As will be seen later on, experiments in the case of Singing Beaches have shown that their vocality is produced when the grains are of a certain size and uniformity and shape, so that they can strike against each other with the minimum of disturbance. And it may well be that some such distinctive properties are required of the sand-grains in the Singing Hills and dunes. Here again scientific researches might lead to more definite conclusions.

II. Musical Beaches

I now pass to the consideration of another branch of the problem, viz. that of the Musical Sands to be found in many places both in Europe and America, and I doubt not (were they searched for) elsewhere, on the beaches of lakes or the shores of the sea. I distinguish these sharply from the class which I have hitherto been examining, because (*a*) the physical conditions in which the sound is produced are quite different;

(*b*) the acoustic phenomena are on a far smaller and quite inconsiderable scale; (*c*) they are caused not by dislodgment of comparatively large masses of sand, striking against each other, and humming or booming as they collide and fall, but by properties inherent, either permanently or transiently, in the sand, and capable of excitement by a number of still obscure causes usually involving some form of impact or compression.

Island of Eigg

The first of these Musical Sands to be discovered and seriously noted upon in modern times was that in the Bay of Laig in the little island of Eigg in the Hebrides. Hugh Miller, the well-known geologist, discovered this Singing Beach in 1845, and described it, when struck by the foot, particularly obliquely, as emitting at each step "a shrill sonorous note, somewhat resembling that produced by a waxed thread when tightened between the teeth and the hand and tipped by the nail of the forefinger." He added: "As we marched over the drier tracts, an incessant woo, woo, woo rose from the surface, that might be heard in the calm some twenty or thirty yards away; and we found that where a damp semi-coherent stratum lay at the depth of three or four inches beneath, and all was dry and incoherent above, the tones were loudest and sharpest and most easily evoked by the foot."[1]

[1] *The Cruise of the "Betsey," or A Summer Ramble among the Hebrides*, p. 58. London, 1858.

The Eigg beach has since been visited by most of the experts who have been interested in the subject. They have reported the sand as white in colour, and as composed chiefly of quartz with grains of shell, magnetite, silicified wood, etc. When specimens have been taken away and experimented with, they have retained their musical character, though, after being wetted, they become immediately mute.

Studland Bay

C. Carus-Wilson, who has been the principal British student of the phenomenon of Sonorous Sands, has also reported upon a Musical Sand-patch at Studland Bay in Dorset. " The patch averaged 7½ yards in width and ran parallel with the trend of the shore for some hundreds of yards. The sand on the sea side of the patch was fine, and emitted notes of a high pitch ; that on the land side was coarse, and emitted notes of a lower pitch." This sand also retained its musical quality after being taken off the patch and experimented upon, *i.e.* struck at home.[1]

Other English Beaches

Patches of Musical Sand have been reported at other places along the English coast, *e.g.* at

[1] *Nature* (London), vol. xxxviii., 1888, pp. 415-540, vol. xlix., 1891, p. 322, and vol. lxxxvi., 1911, p. 518. The author had first mooted the subject in a paper entitled " Musical Sand," read before the Bournemouth Society of Natural Science on November 2, 1888, and published at Poole. *Vide* also *Discovery*, No. 5, 1920, pp. 156-8.

Tenby and near Barmouth,[1] and also at Lunan Bay, Forfar.[2] I do not doubt that they exist in many other localities and only await discovery.

Baltic Beaches

Other Singing Beaches in Europe are those on the Island of Bornholm, belonging to Denmark, and of Kolberg in Prussia on the Baltic. Here, as at Studland, only small tracts of the sand possess the acoustic property, and it is transient in its operation. Dr. Berendt, who investigated the phenomenon, attributed it to the saline crust on the beach. But this theory is discountenanced by the fact that precisely the same results are produced elsewhere, where there are no sea and no salt. Sands from both these places were procured by the American researchers, Dr. H. C. Bolton and Dr. A. A. Julien, and experimented upon in the course of their studies in 1884.[3]

American Beaches

By far the most famous of the Musical Beaches are those which have been found in great numbers —probably owing to the superior activity of the American inquirers—in the continent of America, and notably on the shores of Lake Michigan. The dune region extends along the eastern shore of the lake from Gary at the southern extremity to Mackinac at the northern, with few interrup-

[1] *Nature*, June 1911, p. 484.
[2] *Ibid.* vol. xxxviii., 1888, p. 515.
[3] *Trans. New York Acad. Sci.* vol. iii., 1885, pp. 97-9.

tions. Throughout the region the sands near the water's edge, in dry weather, emit a peculiar, but definite and unmistakable, sound, when the foot of the pedestrian pushes through them in an abrasive way. The sound is produced not only by the leather-shod foot, but is emitted also if the bare foot or hand is struck through the grains, or if a stick is trailed behind.[1]

The latest description of the Michigan Sands is contained in a paper by W. D. Richardson in 1919. He writes as follows :[2]

The sound has been compared to that produced by the pedestrian walking through soft snow ; to the crunching noise so frequently noticed when walking through snow after very cold weather or by the wheel of a vehicle on such snow ; also to the sound emitted by hard, granular snow when one walks through it ; but it is like none of these and has a distinctive character all its own.

The sound is produced only when the sand is dry, and apparently the dryer the sand is the louder the sound produced. In wet weather or when the sand is moderately moist, the sound is not produced. In summer and indeed in the hottest weather the sound seems to be loudest, other conditions being the same, but it can be clearly heard at all seasons of the year, including winter, whenever the sand is dry. As one walks away from the water's edge he may be astonished to find out that the sound-producing sand ceases rather abruptly about 50 to 100 feet from the shore line. These limits may vary at different locations, but on the whole they are substantially correct. Back and away from the shore line, in blow-outs and on the sides and tops of the dunes, the sound is never produced. There is no observable difference between

[1] W. D. Richardson in *Science*, vol. l., 1919, p. 493.
[2] *Science*, vol. l., 1919, p. 493.

the sand located near the shore and that located farther back or that forming the dunes, and indeed the sand which is washed up by the waves is that which, blown by the wind, goes to form the dunes.

The upper beach limit of the singing sands is practically identical with the upper wave limit, that is, the boundary reached by the waves during storms. This limit is marked roughly by the line of driftwood and the lower limit of vegetation. The singing sands are, therefore, all subjected to periodical contact with the water of the lake and are moistened and washed by that water.

These observations include, I think, all the obvious ones in connection with the singing sands. The most casual observer will remark with astonishment their very sharply defined upper limit. As one walks from the water's edge up the beach and crosses the upper wave limit he notices a sudden cessation of sound as he passes the upper line of driftwood and the commencement of vegetation. Beyond this point he may proceed into a blow-out of clear sand quite identical in appearance, macroscopic as well as microscopic, and of the same composition by ordinary methods of analysis, and yet this sand fails entirely to produce the sound of the beach sand. His first conclusion would be that the proximity of the water and waves of the lake must have some relationship to the sound-producing grains.

An equally famous beach is that of Manchester-by-Sea, Mass., which has been a good deal written about. Thoreau is the first writer whose record of the Manchester Beach I have encountered.[1] He visited it in September 1858.

One mile south-east of the village of Manchester we struck the beach of musical sand. . . . We found the

[1] "Autumn," from the *Journal* of H. D. Thoreau, p. 493. Boston, 1886.

same kind of sand on a similar but shorter beach on the east side of Eagle Head. We first perceived the sound when we scratched with an umbrella or the finger swiftly and forcibly through the sand ; also still louder when we struck forcibly with our heels, "scuffling" along. The wet or damp sand yielded no peculiar sound, nor did that which lay loose and deep next the bank, but only the more compact and dry. The sound was not at all musical, nor was it loud. . . . R., *who had not heard it*, was about right when he said it was like that made by rubbing wet glass with your finger. I thought it as much like the sound made in waxing a table as anything. It was a squeaking sound, as of one particle rubbing on another. I should say it was merely the result of the friction of peculiarly formed and constituted particles. The surf was high and made a great noise, yet I could hear the sound made by my companion's heels two or three rods distant, and if it had been still, probably could have heard it five or six rods.

Drs. Bolton and Julien, visiting the Manchester Beach in 1883, described it as a small crescent, three-quarters of a mile in length, and added :

When struck by the foot or stroked by the hand it yields a peculiar sound which may be likened to a subdued crushing. The sound is of low intensity and pitch, and is non-metallic, non-cracking. This phenomenon is confined to that part of the beach lying between waterline and the loose sand above the reach of ordinary high tide. Some parts of the beach emit a louder sound than others. The Sounding Sand is near the surface only. At the depth of 1 or 2 feet the acoustic properties disappear, probably owing to the moisture. Only the dry sand has this property. The sounds occur when walking over the beach, increase when the sand is struck obliquely by the foot, and can be intensified by dragging over it a wooden pole or board. A slight noise is perceptible upon mere stirring by the hand, or upon plunging one finger into the sand and suddenly withdrawing it.[1]

Yet another American Singing Beach is that of Far Rockaway, on Long Island, a sample of the sand of which, when removed from a bottle in which it had lain undisturbed for thirty-five years, poured into a stocking, and compressed, gave out its original high note, audible at a considerable distance. This, however, after the sand had been handled, it soon lost.[2]

So indefatigable were the American experts in their labours that, after a year of investigation, they had discovered, in 1884, in answer to their circulars of inquiry, no fewer than seventy-four places in the United States where the phenomenon of sonorous sand occurred. These were mostly on the Atlantic coast. In 1890, however, Dr. H. C. Bolton personally visited the Pacific coast and discovered Sounding Sands at a number of places in California. He also reported the existence of a sonorous sand-hill at the extreme southern end of the Peninsula of Lower California, where the sound produced by the sliding sand is like that of bells, and is explained by the Mexicans, like the music at Jebel Nakus, as proceeding from the bells of a monastery that once existed on this site, but was overwhelmed by the drifting sand.[3] I entertain little doubt that similar inquiries would produce similar results in other parts of the world.

[1] *Proceedings of the American Association for the Advancement of Science*, vol. xxxii., 1883, p. 251.

[2] *Science* (New York), vol. li., 1920, p. 64.

[3] *Trans. New York Acad. of Sci.* vol. x., 1890, pp. 31-5.

Costa Rica

At one of the meetings of the New York Academy of Sciences in March 1884, after an account by Dr. Julien of his visits to Eigg and to Manchester-by-Sea and other American sites, a visitor arose and described his experience on the shore of Costa Rica, on the Caribbean Sea, about seventeen miles south of Greytown, in 1864, where he had heard at 11 P.M. on successive nights sounds from the sea-beach that were "sometimes like a low roar or the barking of a dog, sometimes like the voices of men conversing, sometimes like hundreds of loud voices in the air, sometimes like singing, sometimes like the stringing of chords." He had attributed these sounds to the fact that the sand lay upon a coral reef, fissured by very deep clefts, and he had thought at first that it must be due to the movement of sea water in the hollows; but he now thought it must have been the sand.[1] It will be remembered that the Barking Sands of Kauai are mainly composed of disintegrated coral.

Other Musical Beaches

The continuous studies of the American experts have revealed the existence of the same phenomenon in such widely different parts of the world as Botany Bay, New South Wales; Brown's River Bay, Tasmania; Cape Ledo, and Liberia, West Africa. In fact, I do not doubt

[1] *Trans. New York Acad. of Sci.* vol. iii., 1885, p. 73.

that musical sand is frequent in both hemispheres, and only lacks the discoverer or the reporter to become much more widely known.

It will have been seen how widely different are these phenomena from that of the larger and more vocal group of sand-hills and sand-slopes before described. The former share with the latter the common feature of vocality arising from the vibration of sand-grains set in motion, but (*a*) they are found only on the shores of seas or lakes, and in a few recorded cases on the banks of rivers,[1] but not, so far as I know, on horizontal sand-patches in the interior; (*b*) the displacement of the sand-grains requires to be only of the slightest, in order to evoke the sound; (*c*) the nature of the sound, in respect of pitch and volume, is insignificant compared with the kettle-drums and trumpets, the thundering and rumbling, of the great sand-hills; (*d*) the acoustic property, given a certain degree of dryness and warmth, seems to be very consistent in its presence and action.

When we come to a scientific explanation of the exact causes which produce the vibration and therefore the sound, we are in an area of greater speculation, for I find that no two experts wholly agree. Among the theories which have been advanced, but which, though sufficient in some cases, seem to be inapplicable in others, are equality of size of sand-grains, resonance due to cellular structure, effervescence of air between

[1] *Trans. New York Acad. of Sci.* vol. x., 1890, pp. 33-5.

moistened surfaces, solarisation, reverberation within subterranean cavities, electrical phenomena.

The result of the experiments made by C. Carus-Wilson was to convince him that the phenomenon of Musical Sands is found (1) where the grains are rounded, polished, and free from fine fragments; (2) where they have a sufficient amount of "play" to enable them to slide or rub one against the other; (3) where the grains are perfectly clean; and (4) where they possess a certain degree of uniformity in size, and are within a certain range of size.[1] If these conditions are satisfied, and if the grains, rubbing against each other, produce a number of vibrations of equal length, then the musical note results. Elsewhere he says that the notes are due to "the rubbing together of millions of clean and incoherent grains of quartz, with no angularities, roughness, or adherent matter investing the grains; and that, though the vibrations emitted by the friction of any two grains might be inaudible, those issuing from millions approximately of the same size would give an audible note."[2]

On the other hand, the American researchers, Drs. Bolton and Julien, rejected all these hypotheses,[3] and, after years of study, arrived at the following conclusion:

[1] *Nature*, vol. lxiv., 1891, p. 322.

[2] *Discovery*, No. 5, 1920, p. 157.

[3] They said that Mr. Wilson's theory might fairly explain *squeaking* sand, but was insufficient to explain musical sand. They reported the

The true cause of the sonorous property is connected with thin pellicles or films of air or of gases thence derived, deposited, and condensed upon the surface of the sand-grains during gradual evaporation, after wetting by the sea, lakes, or rains. By virtue of these films the sand-grains become separated by elastic cushions of condensed gases, capable of considerable vibration. The extent of the vibration and the amount and tone of the sound thereby produced, after any quick disturbance of the sand, is largely dependent upon the forms, structures, and surfaces of the sand-grains, and especially upon their purity or freedom from fine silt or dust.[1]

The American experts would, I understand, apply this hypothesis to the explanation of all sonorous sands, whether on sea or lake shores or in the deserts. In other words, they postulate everywhere some degree of previous moisture, induced or exhausted by evaporation. This would indeed appear to be probable enough in the case of beach sands, and is supported by experiments showing that the singing quality of such sands is apt to become extinct after they have dried out.

How far this theory is applicable to the big sonorous sand-hills cannot be ascertained without meteorological data that are at present lacking. But I cannot help thinking that in the majority of the cases cited in the earlier part of this essay rainfall must be a very rare pheno-

former as existing in two places only, both in so-called boiling springs—one in Maine, the other in Kansas—where a shrill squeaking sound is produced by attrition when the sand is moist. This is, of course, quite a different phenomenon.

[1] *Trans. New York Acad. Sci.* vol. viii. p. 10. *Ibid.* vol. x., 1890, pp. 28-35.

menon, while in only one record of a successful visit is there any mention of previous shower or storm. That sonorousness anywhere is largely dependent upon meteorological conditions, *i.e.* the dryness or moisture of the atmosphere, is a less contestable proposition.

I should add that Drs. Bolton and Julien have never, to the best of my knowledge, published any experimental proof of the validity of their explanation, which is not generally accepted.

Another explanation is offered by Professor J. H. Poynting and Sir J. Thomson in their "Treatise on Sound,"[1] based on a paper by Professor Osborne Reynolds, "On the Dilatancy of Media composed of Rigid Particles in Contact."[2]

Reynolds showed that in granular media in which the grains are sensibly hard, so long as the grains are held in mutual equilibrium by stresses transmitted through the mass, every change of relative position of the grains is attended by a consequent change of volume. For such granular medium he assumed that the position of any internal particle becomes fixed when the positions of the surrounding particles are fixed: a condition which is very generally fulfilled unless there is considerable friction. It follows from this that no grain in the interior can change its position without disturbing the contiguous grains; hence in a medium in which the friction is sufficiently small the movement of any one grain in the

[1] *Text-Book of Physics.* London, 1913.
[2] *Phil. Mag.* Ser. 5, vol. xx., 1885, pp. 469-81.

medium involves the movement of every other grain in the medium.

The explanation offered by Poynting and Thomson is as follows: "There is an arrangement of minimum volume for a number of equal spheres in contact. We may suppose the sand to consist of equal spheres arranged, when undisturbed, so as to occupy minimum volume. When disturbed the mass may pass through many successive minima of volume before coming to rest, and if we can suppose the time occupied in passing from one minimum to the next is constant, a musical note should issue."

The condition that the grains are spherical is not an essential one, but such an assumption assists the imagination and facilitates calculations. The essential conditions will be that friction shall be low, and that the time occupied in passing from one minimum to another shall be constant—which implies uniformity of grain.

This explanation seems to be reasonable, but has not as yet been definitely proved by experiment. A slight adaptation of Carus-Wilson's idea that the sound is due to the rubbing together of millions of sand-grains of approximately the same size may lead us to a possible cause, or at least to a contributory cause, of the musical notes, and will give a note the pitch of which depends in the same way on grain-size and rate of displacement as does the frequency of the volume changes.

If the displacement of any one grain involves

the displacement of all the others in the mass, we have millions of grains undergoing similar displacements at the same instant. The displacement involves the repeated pushing of one grain over the next below it into the depression beyond. If we can imagine each grain falling over the edge of the grain below, striking the next grain with a little impact, and repeating this with perfect regularity every time it changes its position, we have a cause for a regular train of equally spaced sound-waves which, when of sufficiently high frequency, will give a musical note. The periods of the impacts will be identical with the periods between successive minima of volume in the Poynting and Thomson theory. The two effects may go on simultaneously, and will produce notes of the same pitch. The Poynting and Thomson volume-change is no doubt mainly responsible for the musical notes, but it is difficult to tell to what extent the actual contact of the grains is contributory to the sound.

And so, in this rather nebulous phase of speculative uncertainty, I leave the Sounding Sands to continue their mysterious song, confining their favours to the lucky few, and exciting the curiosity, but, I hope, no longer the incredulity, of the remainder. That they exist in their greater as well as in their lesser manifestations will not be contested. That their music covers a wide diapason of sound, from the twanging of a string or the humming of a wire to the rumbling of thunder and reverberation of drums, has been shown. That the phenomenon is to be explained in every case by natural causes is indisputable. And if I am conscious of not having found a common theory to account irrefutably for all examples, it is, in my belief, because no such theory can be made to apply ; while in the inability to formulate it with exactitude I am sustained by the reflection that I am in the company of all the learned professors, who, like most professors, disagree, but who may perhaps be grateful to me for having given a synthesis of the problem that may provoke their renewed examination.

INDEX

THE END

Books of Related Interest in Century Classics

Isle of Illusion
Asterisk
Introduction by Gavin Young
The identity of the author of these letters was preserved by their recipient who nicknamed his friend 'Asterisk'. The letters come from an Englishman of some education who, enchanted by Stevenson's accounts of the South Pacific, had run away from England before World War I to escape the boredom of schoolmastering.

The Golden Chersonese
Isabella Bird
Isabella Bird's courage during her travels in China and the Malay Peninsula in 1879 gives a new meaning to the apt word 'intrepid'; she even coped with the execution ground of a Canton gaol where a hundred heads a morning were lopped off. This remains an invaluable guide to the area.

The Island
A Journey to Sakhalin
Anton Chekhov
Introduction by Irina Ratushinskaya
Written by Chekhov at the turn of the century, *The Island* describes his gruelling journey to the unwelcoming island of Sakhalin which the Russian government had chosen as a place of exile for its most dangerous prisoners.

Raffles
Maurice Collis
Introduction by Jan Morris

Raffles was born aboard his father's ship on his return from America during the War of Independence. At 14, Raffles became a clerk in the East India Company's London headquarters where his intelligence and industry led to promotion and a posting to Penang. He married a widow 10 years his senior and became adviser to Lord Minto on the invasion of Java, where Raffles became the first Lieutenant-Governor. Raffles went on to found Singapore and, on his return to England, the London Zoological Gardens.

Chinese Women Speak
Dymphna Cusack

First published in 1958 this book was the first in-depth study of Chinese women. The author spent eighteen months travelling over 7,000 miles through China, and interviewing hundreds of Chinese women from peasant to Manchu princess.

At the Court of Korea
William Franklin Sands
Introduction by Christopher Hitchens

In the early 1890s Sands was sent by the US foreign service to Korea where he became the main adviser to the King until his dramatic ousting after two years. Written by someone who really knew and loved the country, it is a perspicacious and unique analysis of a country moving with difficulty into the modern world.

By Sledge and Horseback to Outcast Siberian Lepers
Kate Marsden
Introduction by Eric Newby

With recommendation from the Empress of Russia, Kate Marsden set out in 1890 for Yakutsk, in north-east Siberia, to help and comfort a colony of lepers, outcast from society.

Adventures of a Wanderer
S.W. Powell
Introduction by Colonel Geoffrey Powell

Covering the period between the Boer War and the end of the First World War, *Adventures of a Wanderer* is the enthralling memoir of a man with the desire to travel: from South Africa to the South Sea islands, from criticising Egyptian prostitutes in a Cairo brothel to drinking with the future Mahatma Gandhi in a Durban bar.

The Inland Sea
Donald Richie

Donald Richie's beautiful and poignant tribute to the people who live within the sea bounded by three of Japan's four major islands and their surroundings reflects and explores the glories of ancient Japan alongside the environment of the present.

Good Morning and Good Night
The Ranee Margaret of Sarawak

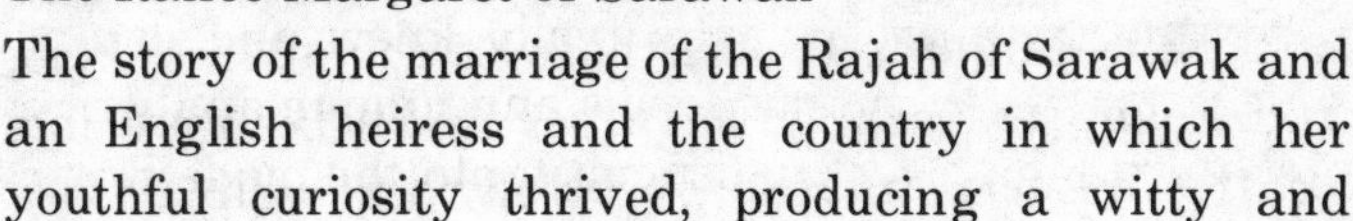

The story of the marriage of the Rajah of Sarawak and an English heiress and the country in which her youthful curiosity thrived, producing a witty and perceptive record of a colourful culture.

A Ride to Khiva
Fred Burnaby
Introduction by Eric Newby
A paragraph in a paper caused Fred Burnaby to beg leave from his cavalry regiment in December 1875 to set out on horseback to Khiva braving the depths of the Russian winter. The book is filled with memorable characters, Cossacks, sleigh-drivers and Tartar horsemen.

When Men and Mountains Meet
The Explorers of the Western Himalayas 1820–75
John Keay
The story of the quest for access to Central Asia and inland China through the formidable barrier of the Western Himalayas involved some characters as exceptional as the terrain through which they struggled.

A Person from England
And Other Travellers to Turkestan
Fitzroy Maclean
The dramatic stories and adventures of some of the agents and other travellers who, in the course of a hundred years, penetrated Khiva, Bokhara and Samarkand and the Khanates of Central Asia.

Forbidden Journey
Ella Maillart
Introduction by Dervla Murphy
Forbidden Journey is the story of a dream realized. In 1935, Ella Maillart set out in the footsteps of Marco Polo, from Peking to Kashmir, a journey said to be impossible for the Western traveller, certainly impossible for a woman. But Ella Maillart joined forces with Peter

Fleming and together they crossed the Takla Makan Desert, climbed incredible mountain paths beside gorges of breathtaking beauty, riding sometimes on camels, sometimes on horseback. Visiting the forbidden Chinese fortress of Kashgaria and Sinkiang, they crossed the high plains of northern Tibet, the 'roof of the world'. Her account of the journey is 'enough to place her among the great travellers of the world'. *Sunday Times*

Turkestan Solo
Ella Maillart
Introduction by Julia Keay
In the 1930s Ella Maillart spent six months travelling from Moscow to the Kizill Kun on a one-woman expedition, sometimes by camel. The legacy is a tale of far-off lands and their social history.

Full Tilt
Dervla Murphy
This highly individual account of Dervla Murphy's extraordinary bicycle journey from Dunkirk to India in 1963 is based on the daily diary she kept while riding through Persia, Afghanistan, over the Himalayas to Pakistan and into India. A woman traveller on her own with a bicycle (even with a revolver in her saddle-bag), in such hazardous countries still largely untouched by modernization, was an unusual focus of interest. Her resourcefulness matches up to her unexpected encounters, and the blind eye she turned on personal danger and her unselfconscious disregard of discomfort are remarkable.

On a Shoestring to Coorg
An Experience of Southern India
Dervla Murphy

This popular travel writer finds in the tranquil mountains of Coorg - once the smallest province in British India - the only place outside Ireland she could imagine being a permanent resident.

The Waiting Land
A Spell in Nepal
Dervla Murphy

In 1965 Dervla Murphy braved bureaucracy, danger and squalor to help Tibetan refugees in Nepal. As ever, her surroundings, the people who befriend her, and her Tibetan mongrel, Tashi, captivate her and inspire her writing.

Where the Indus is Young
A Winter in Baltistan
Dervla Murphy

The account of a journey with the author's daughter, Rachel, to Baltistan, also known as little Tibet. Undaunted by the onset of winter, they bought a pony for the six-year-old Rachel, and walked and rode through five valleys, including the perilous Indus Gorge. They met no other Westerners during their time there, and lived on the customary Baltistani diet of dried apricots. The adventures of this remarkable pair through a region containing the greatest concentration of high peaks in the world displays their ingenuity, fortitude and their sense of humour in the face of danger and discomfort.